SIR DAVID AMESS was born in the East a Member of Parliament for 38 years. Newham North West in 1979, before winning the Basildon seat — in 1983. When his seat was broken up in a boundary review, he was elected to Southend West in 1997.

He was Parliamentary Private Secretary to Edwina Currie, Lord Skelmersdale, and for nine years to Michael Portillo through most of his Ministerial career.

A lifelong animal lover he has campaigned on many animal welfare issues and introduced the Protection Against Cruel Tethering Act for horses, ponies and donkeys.

In 1999 he was successful with a Bill to create a programme of action for home heating and the reduction of fuel poverty, which became the Warm Homes Act 2000. He was a member of the Health Select Committee for ten years.

Sir David is a member of the Speaker's Panel of Chairs and is Chair of a number of All-Party Groups including Fire Safety and Rescue, Maternity, Liver Health, and Endometriosis.

David Amess's reflections on the deep and often disorientating changes in politics are essential reading, his insights into his fellow practitioners are filled with charm, and he lays out the triumphs and tribulations of his long life in politics with humour... David is a survivor, one of the most senior and honoured politicians in the land but he has never turned his back on his working-class roots.

MICHAEL DOBBS
author of the House of Cards trilogy

David is one of those MPS much loved by his constituents because they come first and foremost. His battle to make Southend a City has been a grand source of entertainment for many years – as this book will be – because he's contributed to public life for so many years.

JEFFREY ARCHER, author

David Amess rose to prominence with a grin: one of the largest ever shown on British television. When his victory in Basildon in the 1983 general election was announced, he abandoned the self-discipline that had kept his expression in check till the official proclamation, rocked back and beamed with joy. It was as emblematic of that great Tory landslide, as the loss of my seat in 1997 was symbolic of the Conservative rout that year.

Thereafter, David maintained his prominence by working into every one of his interventions in the House of Commons the name Basildon; delivered so loudly that the most senior Members whiling away the afternoon on the green benches were startled from their slumbers.

If David had squeaked in on a Tory avalanche, he was not going to be washed out on a Labour thaw. He dug into to his constituency and using his popularity and political acuity swerved constituency boundary changes to end up in a more secure seat.

While I trotted around various ministerial jobs, David followed me as my parliamentary private secretary. He knew the House of Commons intimately and loved it. He was therefore extremely useful to me, offering advice, mounting operations and watching my back against the plentiful Conservative daggers aimed against it.

We met up with a number of nervous Tories defending their seats during the 1997 election campaign. David was despondent, smelling the exit from parliamentary life. But it wasn't he who was on the way out, but I. That's 23 years ago and he is still there.

It's lucky that he entered young because his parliamentary service is now outstandingly long. Goodness knows how many Members have come and gone while he has continued so ably and loudly to represent his constituents.

I am not surprised that there's material for a book and it makes for very good reading.

MICHAEL PORTILLO,
journalist, broadcaster and former MP

Luath Press is an independently owned and managed book publishing company based in Scotland, and is not aligned to any political party or grouping.

All royalties generated from sales of this book will be shared equally between Endometriosis UK, the Music Man Project and Prost8 UK. More information about these charities and the work they do can be found at the back of this book.

Ayes & Ears

A Survivor's Guide to Westminster

DAVID AMESS

Luath Press Limited

EDINBURGH

www.luath.co.uk

I dedicate this book to my late parents, Maud and James Amess, who are entirely responsible for the journey I have been on. Also, to my wife Julia and my children: David, Katherine, Sarah, Alexandra and Florence.

First published 2020

ISBN: 978-1-913025-92-2

This book is made of materials from well-managed, FSC®-certified forests and other controlled sources.

Printed and bound by Ashford Colour Press, Gosport

Typeset in 11 point Sabon by Lapiz

Contents

Acknowledgments   6

Preface   7

Introduction – Humble Beginnings   9

Part 1 – Welcome to Westminster   27

Part 2 – Elections   86

Part 3 – Outside the House   127

Part 4 – The Future   181

Part 5 – Postscript   190

Glossary   245

Index   257

Acknowledgements

I WOULD LIKE to thank the following people who have helped in so many ways with the production of this book: my first secretary, the late Miss Marjory Shearmur, who spent many an hour on a golf ball typewriter, listening to me drone on about my life; the late Mr Lionel Altman, who was my rock and ran my office for many years; Paul Lennon, who has been my unpaid researcher throughout most of my time in Parliament; Paul Pambakian; Phil Campbell; Charlie Spellar; Luke Driscoll; Mark Woodrow; Edmund Chapman; and Gill Lee, my long-suffering secretary.

Preface

THE EVENING OF 9 June 1983 was without question the highlight of my political life. There I was, standing on stage being announced as the duly elected Member of Parliament for Basildon. It was a dream come true and something achieved against all the odds. It turned out to be the biggest political turnaround in that election, and yet not even one junior reporter was there to cover it!

Just four weeks earlier the local elections had taken place and the Conservatives had gained 28 per cent of the vote compared to Labour's 58 per cent. Elizabeth Dines, my one and only Conservative Councillor, had also lost her seat. I had never seen victory conducted in such a manner: the jubilance of the local Labour Party stays with me to this day. Arms interlinked, they sang as red flags were hoisted either side of the stage. It seemed a pretty insurmountable mountain to climb. Julia, my then fiancé, had certainly not been expecting to marry someone who was an MP. In time maybe, but she hadn't thought I would be elected when I was.

I will never forget the excitement, bewilderment and thrill of those heady times. When, a few days later, my supporters and I triumphantly boarded a coach to Westminster it was with trepidation as to how I might cope with my new role. I kept asking myself, how could someone like me, born into relative poverty and with no great political helping-hand, become a Conservative Member of Parliament. In hindsight, my upbringing was the making of me and I had everything to thank my family for. I was undoubtedly in awe of – and quite possibly overwhelmed by – the high esteem in which I held the Palace of Westminster and elected politicians. Decades later my feelings at being re-elected as an MP for the ninth time could not have been more different.

In 2017, most people assumed that I would be comfortably re-elected, and indeed I was. In 1983, I had to fight in a completely different way. I was totally inexperienced, without a doubt I was naive and I had nothing to lose. The leader of my party and the then Prime Minister, Margaret Thatcher, was most certainly responsible for my victory. Her dominant personality created opportunities and continued to do so in all the elections that she led.

The same cannot be said of 2017. My very new Prime Minister, Theresa May, came to lead the party under quite extraordinary circumstances. A referendum, which had given the wrong verdict from David Cameron's perspective, had catapulted the country into complete chaos.

While the 1983 election was a little early, it was more or less expected. The timing of the 2017 vote was a total shock and without precedent. When I stood on the podium at my count in Southend West, I had the opposite feelings to those of 34 years beforehand. I was not excited; I was not bewildered. When I returned to Parliament, I could not have been more underwhelmed by all that greeted me. The reality was that everything – the institution, the job, the people themselves – had all changed, and not universally for the better.

This book describes those changes and the events which made them happen. While it will be inevitably informed by my own experiences and shaped by my journey into politics, I believe it would be a little premature to write an autobiography. This book is far more concerned with the complete sea-change that has taken place in politics over the 37 years I have been an MP. The leaders, the procedures, the elections and the issues.

I hope this will be a testimony to historical events, interrelating the past, the present and the future in a way that is exercised far too little in our modernistic society. I hope to open up the world of Westminster and shine a light on issues in a way that readers have not seen before.

Introduction – Humble Beginnings

IT IS IMPOSSIBLE to begin writing a book of this magnitude and significance without introducing myself properly to the reader. It was a combination of my own humble beginnings and the force of nature that was Margaret Thatcher that informed my political perspective and resulted in my journey into the Conservative Party.

I was born on 26 March 1952 at Howards Road Hospital, Plaistow, the son of James Henry Valentine Amess and Maud Ethel Amess. Both of my parents came from relatively poor families. My mother, one of 11 children, was raised initially in Bow, within earshot of Bow Bells. In true cockney fashion her family then moved to a place in Studley Road in Forest Gate, where my grandfather had a sweet shop. It was the classic upbringing of three-or-four-in-a-bed, and my grandmother endeavoured to earn extra money by charging the window cleaner to keep his ladders in their side entrance.

My father left school at an early age and for most of his life worked as an electrician for the London Electricity Board. During the war he drove petrol tankers to various army camps, and it was during this time that he met my mother, who had volunteered for the Women's Land Army. 28 Leonard Road, Forest Gate would eventually become the family home. My father had purchased the property for his parents and when they died our small family moved in.

My children laugh in disbelief now, but I was born into a less well-off family. At the time it seemed perfectly normal, but we lacked many of the modern amenities that people today take for granted. We had no bathroom, no inside toilet, no refrigerator, no telephone and we certainly had no car. Instead, we had a tin bath hanging on the outside wall, an outside toilet and a larder. Despite this, my childhood memories are overwhelmingly happy ones. My mother more or less ran an open house and always seemed pleased to see people. She would walk me two miles to and from St Anthony's Catholic Primary School every day. We would always have wonderful Christmases, visiting grandparents on Christmas Day and my mother's brothers and sisters on Boxing Day.

One of my earliest memories from primary school was a tangle with authority. My first teacher, Miss Gray, believed I was a distraction to others in the classroom and asked to see my mother. She told her that I had severe learning difficulties and that despite having a lot to say for myself, I was unable to communicate it effectively. This was due to my speech impediment, meaning a slight stutter and severe difficulty pronouncing 'st' and 'th'. For the following two-and-a-half years, my mother would religiously take me to the speech therapist at the West Ham Clinic. The fact I can communicate today is entirely thanks to the teacher who originally brought the problem to my mother's attention and the speech therapist who treated me so effectively. I shudder to think of the difficulties I would have encountered in my chosen career path had this not been tackled so early.

In hindsight, my drive and hunger to succeed were the lasting effects of those early years. I was determined to achieve as much of myself as I possibly could, in spite of the fact that I came from a relatively humble background.

The hard work paid off in my final year of primary school. I sat the 11 Plus, which I passed, and was admitted into the grammar school St Bonaventure's. It was then, at the age of 11, that I decided to become a Member of Parliament. Terribly sad and unhealthy, I know. The chap who sat next to me in class wanted to become a meteorologist, and we both achieved our ultimate ambitions. During those secondary school years, I stood in the mock elections of 1964 and 1966. I had such big ideas and was so naive that I formed my own political party, The Revolutionist Party. From what I can remember my main policies were to abolish homework and set a national minimum pocket money allowance – as you can imagine I was terribly popular! My public meetings were packed but quite possibly for the wrong reasons, as the gatherings often gave other children the opportunity to behave appallingly and generally riot in the classroom – not too far removed from the House of Commons!

In no time at all, this had all gone to my head and as more and more students persuaded me to hold these meetings, practically every playtime, I got to a point where I found myself standing at the top of a fire escape in the playground addressing a large proportion of the school. Despite not quite being able to find the correct formula for victory, my fascination with politics had begun.

The schoolboy experience of jostling with opponents and changing things for the better meant that I was already learning important lessons. When I burst into tears upon finishing third in the 1964 mock elections, I promised myself to never again be unprepared for the worst, and to never show weakness to your opponent. This attitude resurfaced before the 1983 election count, when I gathered my loyal campaign team and advised them: 'Look, I think we have come a good second, but when we go to the count, we mustn't let our feelings show that we are disappointed. Let's keep big smiles on our faces and then when it's all done and dusted, we can come back, talk about the campaign and let off some steam.' Of course, I would go on to win in that election, but my attitude has always been to prepare myself for the worst.

While I understood very little about politics and had no natural inclination towards any of the parties in particular, I quickly realised that The Revolutionist Party was not going to be how I would become a Member of Parliament.

I was very much aware of the physical deterioration of the neighbourhood that I had grown up in. The route from 28 Leonard Road to St Bonaventura's was changing. The roads were being neglected, the housing was looking shabby and

I felt that the environment that I had come to know as a child was changing for the worse. So, I made it my business to find out who was responsible and, surprise, surprise, it was the Labour Party.

The local MP, who had been there for 40 years, did not live in the constituency nor did he hold any surgeries. His name was Arthur Lewis and he has long since passed away. The local council was 100 per cent Labour, as was the Greater London Council (GLC). At this point, it was simple: I had big ideas and I would oppose the current Labour regime.

It was during the spring of 1968 that a newsletter from the Forest Gate Ward Conservative Association Committee dropped through our letterbox. I was now 16 and I read the newsletter, which told of the ward having recently elected three Conservative Councillors for the first time in many years. As I read on, I noticed that the Treasurer of the Ward Committee was a Mr Catton, who actually lived in the house opposite. Although my mother knew the family well, I had taken little notice of him, other than regarding him as being an extremely smartly dressed man who looked a little like the French actor Maurice Chevalier. The newsletter was appealing for members and asked anyone interested in joining to contact Mr Catton. It did not take me long to come to my senses and I wrote to my neighbour expressing how impressed I was with the changes his organisation wanted to make. Everything that was said regarding the state of the borough had really resonated with me. It was clear that the propaganda had worked. I joined the party and have never looked back since nor regretted my decision.

Margaret and Me

So the deed was done and I had made my first move to enter the political domain. It was then that I would begin to encounter and revere my greatest political inspiration.

Without any question Margaret Thatcher, or as she later became known, Baroness Thatcher, was the greatest, most outstanding and most thought-provoking politician that I have ever known in my lifetime. It's difficult to think of anyone else who has changed our country and the world as much.

I believe that she was a force for good and made our country a better place in which to live. Most of my colleagues now reminisce about Margaret. They were not MPs when she was Prime Minister, they only knew her in later life when her incredible work had taken its toll on her health. I regard myself as being incredibly blessed to have been in Parliament for two of her terms, when she was at her peak, and to enjoy her dominance of Westminster. But how did it all start, the admiration I hold for this great leader?

My opinion of the governments that preceded her moulded my interactions with, and my views of, Margaret. At the time I joined the Conservatives, a Labour government (1964 to 1970) led by a brilliant politician, Harold Wilson, was in power. Sir Alec Douglas-Home, whom I was privileged to meet later in life, had become leader of the Conservative Party in extraordinary circumstances. Harold Macmillan was ill in hospital when he told the nation he could no longer carry on as Prime Minister. He advised the Queen that his successor should be Douglas-Home, which of course could never happen now. Douglas-Home was a lovely man, a real gentleman, but far too nice for the rough and tumble of politics. While he did nothing wrong, he was no match for the wily Wilson who won the 1964 election by five seats. Sir Alec immediately resigned, and the party elected a new leader, Edward Heath.

It is not within my nature to speak ill of the dead (may God forgive me) but I was never fond of Ted Heath. I found him a rather cold and remote figure, but much worse he was a Europhile and that I certainly wasn't – I was intensely patriotic. When, somewhat surprisingly, he won the 1970 general election, he told the nation that he was determined that we should join the European Economic Community. I was horrified. I felt, even as a post-war baby, somewhat aggrieved at the way Charles de Gaulle had treated Macmillan when we had first applied to join. We had sheltered, protected and rearmed France during World War II, treating him as a world leader long before anyone else did. But this had clearly not been enough for him, and the legendary rebuke of 'non, non, non' represented the fundamental difference between the United Kingdom and the rest of continental Europe.

Ted's premiership was a rather sad affair. He became known for his love of culture, as a conductor and connoisseur of fine arts. In a sporting capacity he also became famous for his love of yachting – sailing with a crew. This was all in stark contrast to the job he had been entrusted with, running the country. It took him no time at all to become embroiled with the unions. There was a pay freeze and an enormous U-turn. Strikes had become the order of the day when he crazily called a general election in 1974 with the battle cry: 'Who runs the country, the government or the unions?'

To my mind if you ask a silly question you get a silly answer. The British people decided that they didn't quite know who ran the country and they left Ted Heath's government short of an overall majority. He made overtures to the Liberal Party leader Jeremy Thorpe to go into coalition. Sound familiar? Thorpe was very close to becoming Home Secretary but unlike one of his successors, Nick Clegg, he was eventually dissuaded by his party's grassroots who outright refused to have anything to do with a Conservative-led coalition.

The result was that Wilson's Labour Party came back to power, albeit with a minority government which resulted in another general election being held in October of the same year. Labour were returned with 18 more seats and a majority of three. Ted, instead of resigning as leader as he should have, resolved to carry on.

Margaret Hilda Thatcher had been the only woman in Ted's cabinet and was Education Secretary. Well-known for her splendid hats but rather plain pinafore dresses, she had a tough time in her position, during which free school milk for primary school children was removed. Her enemies chanted that she was

'Margaret Thatcher, Milk Snatcher'. As politics so often is, it is just another example of a long career being shortened to one digestible newspaper headline. The reality is that, as cabinet papers have since revealed, she was forced into this concession by the Treasury. What's more is that it was simply a continuation of Labour's education policy which had abolished free milk for secondary school pupils in the 1960s.

So, while it was undoubtedly a difficult period for her, it was also an invaluable one. During her time in cabinet she formed bonds with right-leaning intellectuals such as Keith Joseph and Airey Neave and joined a group of politicians who felt that there should be a different leader of the Party. Ted was not only damaged goods but had been taking the country in the wrong direction. The most difficult decision to make was who would lead the challenge. Keith Joseph was felt to be the right candidate, but he declined, leaving a clear run for Margaret. From that moment onwards, Thatcherism as a political force was born.

While I didn't know a huge amount about her at the time, there was something about her that drew me to support her. The press of course were enthralled at the prospect, however remote it might be, that a woman would be elected for the first time as leader of the Conservative Party. She gained ample media attention, but it was still thought that the contest would be a formality for Ted. How wrong the pundits were. Margaret won 130 votes compared to Ted's 119 in the first round.

When Sir Edward du Cann, Chairman of the 1922 Committee, announced the result gasps of breath were drawn. Ted was furious and deeply hurt at what he saw as Margaret's betrayal. He resigned immediately and, in what became known as 'the longest sulk in history', he never forgave her. The reality was that she had the guts to take him on at a time when no one else had.

There had to be a second ballot and other candidates came forward. The momentum was with Margaret and so she triumphed. I happened to be at home at the time I heard the result and I could not have been more pleased. By this time, having become the Association Chairman in Newham North West, I was becoming more active in politics and had accrued a growing number of loyal supporters. A small group of us went to her home in Flood Street, Chelsea, and handed over a flower arrangement in congratulation on her election. A new era in Conservative Party politics had started and, although I didn't know it at the time, it was to shape the future of my political journey.

I stood as a candidate for the GLC elections in 1977 when Horace Cutler was the leader of the GLC. I greatly enjoyed the campaign and, as it turned out, came a very respectable second. I was then adopted as the prospective parliamentary candidate for Newham North West. The vote was close, but I was delighted to have been selected.

By this time the Labour Government had well and truly fallen apart. Harold Wilson had dramatically and unexpectedly resigned, with no one quite knowing why. There was intense speculation, as there invariably is over matters such as this. The conspiracy theorists would have us believe that a rogue department of the security services went after him, thinking that he was a Soviet Agent. They bugged his devices, broke into his friends' homes and pushed black propaganda to the media, forcing him into an early retirement. Personally, I find the most persuading case to be that Wilson knew his brain was fading and decided to quit while he was on top, before the Alzheimer's really kicked in. All very sad.

Jim Callaghan defeated Tony Benn in the ensuing Labour leadership contest. I imagine most of my readers will be aware of just how grim the 1970s had been. Commercial users of electricity were only allowed to work three days a week, strikes grew intensely, rubbish was piling up on the streets and we couldn't even bury our dead. The final humiliation was the then Chancellor, Denis Healey, having to get the IMF to bail the UK out. The irony of a union supported government not being able to prevent 'The Winter of Discontent' was not lost on the electorate. Our once proud nation was humbled and at the heart of it all seemed to be the overweening power of the unions. Her Majesty's Loyal Opposition would not let this go unnoticed.

The first time I met Margaret was when central office asked me to appear in a party-political broadcast with her. I was delighted, if not enthralled. Margaret's likes and dislikes were not always conventional or straight forward. She immediately clicked with a Conservative working-class activist in Thurrock, Ted Attewell. Well-known for his somewhat extreme political views, he was present on this occasion to make the broadcast, which would be filmed at Elstree Studios. Margaret appeared with an aide and we all climbed into something that resembled a campervan.

From the moment we set off, Attewell never stopped talking, jabbing his finger at Margaret and not allowing her to get a word in edgeways – something that would seem most foreign to her in later years. I remember thinking during the ride, my goodness, this woman is incredible. If it would have been me that Ted was ranting at I think I would have bluntly told him 'shut up for God's sake'. The extraordinary thing was that when we got to the film studio and it was Ted's turn to speak, he completely dried up and no matter how many retakes we filmed, he couldn't get a single word out!

The party-political broadcast itself was nonetheless completed, and even if I say so myself, I thought it got the point across extremely well. It illustrated the debt that Labour had accrued by a ball and chain wrapped tightly around a baby's foot (or at least a doll's foot). Under today's rules, you wouldn't be allowed to make such an 'emotive' film.

By 1979, Callaghan seemed to go from crisis to crisis, even if he refused to acknowledge so. 'Crisis, what crisis?' would be a phrase that he would never live down, with celebrities such as Twiggy and the Bee Gees condemning his remarks as those of a silly old man.

The criticism that came his way was damning and Margaret played it to perfection. On the 28 March 1979 at 10.19pm, a vote of no confidence was called in the House. I was excited by the prospect of an election and happened to be at the home of my agent, Joan Short, at the time. The vote hung by a thread, and two individuals in particular would play an integral part in the future of the government. First, it all seemed to depend on whether or not an Irish member would support the government and be dragged away from his pint of beer in one of the Commons bars. Second, Sir Alfred Broughton, who was mortally ill at the time and died a few days after the vote, had been desperate not to let his government down. All options to get him on site were explored, including driving him to Speaker's Court in an ambulance. A discussion regarding the complications that would have been caused should Sir Alfred have died on his way to Parliament resulted in Callaghan insisting that he did not risk his life.

As it turned out, these two votes would prove crucial as the Government lost 311 to 310. When the Speaker read out the results, Joan and I jumped up and down in joy and hugged one another. We were really excited by the prospect of an election; little did we know how important it would turn out to be.

When the campaigning got going it was a real inspiration. Margaret had assembled an excellent team around her, including the likes of Willie Whitelaw and Sir Geoffrey Howe. There were endless photo opportunities and a real focus on image. Sally Oppenheim-Barnes, the glamorous Consumer Minister, (she still looks glamorous today at the ripe old age of 92) was photographed in a supermarket holding two shopping baskets, one being full at the start of the Labour Government and one being nearly empty at today's prices, such was the effect of inflation. Maurice Saatchi also launched a brilliant visual campaign with posters of a long queue of people headlined: 'Labour isn't working'. This all added to the tide of anger at how the country had been governed and gave a real sense that outright victory was possible.

In my local campaign in Newham I was determined to make a similar impression. While the seat that I was fighting for had always been Labour and returned the first Labour Member of Parliament, Keir Hardie, I was absolutely determined to get a good vote. We had plenty of razzmatazz, posters and balloons, even a procession down the high street, including a float on which sat a beauty queen, Miss Bluebell.

The nation was gripped with election fever. The slogan 'time for a change' rang so true. I came a good second in Newham North West and Margaret swept into 10 Downing Street with a healthy majority of 43 seats. She stood on the famous steps of her new home and delivered a carefully choreographed speech, quoting the words of Saint Francis of Assisi:

> Where there is discord, may we bring harmony. Where there is error, may we bring truth. Where there is doubt, may we bring faith. And where there is despair, may we bring hope.

These words would be mockingly used against her towards the end of her period in office. The nation was electrified at the prospect of Britain's first female Prime Minister and again Newham North West Conservative Association sent a basket of flowers to Margaret's home.

Despite not being elected in 1979, I was privileged to be chosen to represent Basildon in 1983 and then again in 1987, so I was there for two of her three terms in office. It was probably during the first of those that her powers were at their peak. Seeing her in action was a huge influence and inspiration for me. She changed the Conservative Party, our country and the world for the better.

Seeing her at work, I would say that she undoubtedly understood the hopes and aspirations of ordinary people. She was quite different from her predecessors in that she did not come from a privileged background but from an ordinary family who ran a shop in Grantham. Her father was involved in local politics and had been the mayor of the town. Her family were also devout Methodists, but her upbringing was such that she understood the basic concepts which lay behind business – how to beat the competition, how to please customers and how to account for incomings and outgoings.

Margaret's fundamental principles soon set about changing the way we ran our country. She was horrified at the way the unions had moved away from their original purpose, which had been to secure rights for workers. Margaret felt deeply that the last Labour government had shown beyond any doubt that the union leadership had become far removed from the hopes and aspirations of their actual members. She had witnessed how they had brought down the Heath government and was determined to avoid the same mistakes. So, when she decided that the mining industry had to be reformed, she chose to pick a fight with one of the most vocal and vociferous union leaders, Arthur Scargill. He stood accused of undermining parliamentary democracy and economic performance through consistent strike action.

For many years the mining industry in the UK had been in decline. Mining communities were built and depended upon the work which the mines provided. However, as a result of foreign competition, UK coal mines quickly fell far behind their international competitors. Resulting closures of mines were met with fierce resistance and more strikes by Scargill. By preparing fuel stocks, appointing hard-liner Ian MacGregor to run the National Coal Board and ensuring that police were adequately trained and equipped with riot gear, Margaret had broken their resolve and gave a warning to others that she would never tolerate the country being held to ransom again.

But this was not all she ought to be known for. The electorate were enthusiastic about her policies, and those that she introduced were to be copied worldwide as her fame spread. She defined herself by a radical programme of privatisation. She felt it was an enormous drain upon the public finances to prop up inefficient industries. She combined this with a crusade to encourage ordinary people to own shares. One by one, industries which were formerly in public hands became privatised – electricity, water, gas, telecoms and the railway.

As the MP for the largest new town in the country, I had first-hand experience of the enthusiasm of council tenants, often of long standing, to secure their own homes at a heavy discount. Margaret was instrumental in allowing this to happen. You could always tell when a council property had been bought by the change in the doors and windows. They would be a different colour from the often-bland appearance of those still owned by the council. The windows themselves would also often be removed and replaced with something more modern. The front gardens would invariably be different. The bog-standard council bell or door knocker would be removed and the curtains which adorned the windows of bought properties would invariably be more lavish.

Today Canary Wharf is taken for granted, but for someone like me, coming from the area and recalling the deserted docks only too vividly, it is an inspiration to see what a centre for economic activity the docklands has become. Margaret's drive and vision made that happen. I recall visiting the old docks with parliamentary colleagues to see the area where London City Airport was planned. A truly amazing concept and one which has been of enormous benefit, not just to Londoners, but for people far and wide.

Among the many and various infrastructure projects which Margaret pioneered, the most remarkable was probably the Channel Tunnel. Who would have thought that Mrs Thatcher, with her sceptical views of the European Union, would have met with President François Mitterrand and agreed to join the UK to mainland Europe? All sorts of obstacles and objections were raised at the time, with some people believing that it was an unachievable project. How wrong they were. I remember only too well walking down the tunnel before its completion with Michael Portillo, the then Chief Secretary to the Treasury, and seeing first-hand the mastery of those who had successfully drilled the tunnel. However improbable it seemed at the time to build a tunnel between the UK and mainland Europe, that is what happened. So perhaps the incredulity with which Boris' idea of a bridge with Northern Ireland has been met with is a little premature!

There are so many stories that I could regale about Margaret and I will always regard it as an enormous privilege to have been part of the parliamentary party when she set about making Britain great again.

It was often said that she lacked humour and was a workaholic. The latter was certainly true, but the former was not. First of all, Margaret put her femininity to good use. She allowed her image makers to give her not only a make-over in style, but physically too. In time, the gap in her two front teeth disappeared and, although always a smart dresser, she developed her own style: Power Dressing. Well-cut suits, invariably electric blue, with padded shoulders. Her hair was boosted by whatever technique the hairdresser used, but she was always immaculately coiffured. Most importantly of all her voice was changed. She was coached by the very best to lower her tone by an octave or two, the point being that she should sound less shrill.

I believe Margaret relished operating in a man's world. This was particularly notable when she travelled abroad. In photographs with world leaders she clearly stood out as the only woman and her stylish dress was very distinctive.

Her femininity did not mean she was immune to men whom she perceived to be handsome. Two in particular took her favour: Cecil Parkinson and John Moore. Cecil at his peak looked somewhat like a matinée idol and he and Margaret had a great chemistry together. For that reason, she stood by him to reward his loyalty when he got into difficulties in his private life.

On the other hand, most women judged John Moore to be the one with movie star looks. He was often spoken of as a future party leader. Alas, this did not materialise. When he took over as Secretary of State for Health and Social Security, for some inexplicable reason he kept having problems with his voice. It later transpired that his voice had been ruined as a direct result of the failings of the air conditioning system in the department building at Elephant & Castle. As a Parliamentary Private Secretary (PPS) in the same department and often the same building, I do wonder whether it ever changed my own.

Back in the Chamber, and especially when Margaret voted in the lobbies, it was as if there was a glow around her. People were in awe of her physical presence. At Prime Minister's Questions, Margaret was absolutely dominant. She wiped the floor with the hapless, but very worthy, Michael Foot. Foot never recovered from the media drubbing he received when wearing a donkey jacket as he shuffled up to the Cenotaph to lay his wreath on Remembrance Day. It was generally agreed that his poor sartorial appearance was an insult to the fallen.

When Michael was succeeded by the Welsh Windbag, Neil Kinnock, Margaret had an absolute field day. While Neil's lauded oratory could be appreciated on some occasions, it was not well received in the House. His style could best be described as taking a paragraph to express one sentence. He also managed to mispronounce foreign sounding names or complicated words. Margaret developed a method of turning the tables on him over his party's policy inadequacies, no matter what he asked.

One myth that I would like to take this opportunity to try and dispel is that Margaret was a bad judge of character. She certainly appointed some very interesting PPSs – in itself an important job. The truth was that she possibly never found another PPS quite as able or outstanding as Ian Gow. Part of the job of a PPS was to ensure that one's minister was kept in touch with how ordinary members felt. The desired qualities in a PPS are someone who knows everyone, understands their ambitions, their reservations and deals with them before they've even had the chance to voice them. Gow would relay all messages to Margaret, no matter how unpalatable. The same cannot be said of all of his successors, the majority of whom were not best placed to relate with fellow colleagues.

The PM would, from time to time, meet groups of MPs and take soundings and suggestions from them about possible policy options. It was only towards the end of her time as premier that she was criticised for being out of touch, not only with the country but her own parliamentary colleagues. John Whittingdale, who had worked for her in Number 10, organised a meeting between her and about ten colleagues – one of whom was me. She sat there taking copious notes. When it got to my turn, I remarked that the government was being accused of running out of steam and suggested that she initiate some new big ideas such as those regarding council houses and shared ownership. She asked if I could think of any and I am afraid to say that my answer was in the negative.

Margaret's influence was not restricted to British shores. She also had an enormous influence in world affairs where she really became the dominant figure together with the US President Ronald Reagan and the young Russian President, Mikhail Gorbachev.

When Gorbachev became Soviet leader, Margaret enjoyed a new and quite different relationship with her opposite number. Previous leaders could best be remembered for standing on a platform in Moscow's Red Square, watching military vehicles drive past and soldiers march – rather like the situation in modern-day North Korea. They looked grim and austere figures. Gorbachev was young, vibrant and possessed the ability to smile – a rare feature at the time. As Margaret observed, he was a man that we could do business with.

There was something about this new Soviet leader that was impressive. It wasn't just his general demeanour. He was undoubtedly highly intelligent and felt a natural warmth towards the West that his predecessors had never possessed. I was invited to meet him early in my parliamentary career. The meeting was organised by the Inter-Parliamentary Union and I was chosen because, believe it or not, I represented the youth of parliament. Indeed, Gorbachev looked at me and said that I was very young to be an MP. I returned the favour by saying that he was very young to be the Soviet premier. It was only in much later years that I came to fully appreciate how incredible the opportunity was.

Margaret also enjoyed an excellent working and personal relationship with Ronald Reagan. They shared the same economic belief in an enterprise culture and the free market. While their characters could not have been more different, they had a great chemistry and undoubtedly cemented the Special Relationship between our two countries.

I'm often asked how she would view modern politics if she were alive today. In some senses, she would be in utter despair and disbelief. By her very force of personality, she would not tolerate some of the nonsense that Theresa May had to cope with. Furthermore, she would be in complete despair at the lack of quality of many of our world leaders today.

In so many countries the leaders appear to be inadequate for the posts that they have been elected to. Margaret would never have allowed the simpering Angela Merkel to dominate in the way that she has and would not have only stood up to Vladimir Putin and Donald Trump, but would have hand bagged them into submission.

On another level, she would have been delighted about the result of the EU referendum and while being a very different kind of PM to Theresa May, she would have been fully behind her in her efforts to get the best possible deal for the UK. She would be incredulous at the rise of Jeremy Corbyn to Labour Party leader and likewise would be astonished and appalled at the revival of the far left.

Finally, Margaret would find the House of Commons, as it is today, very odd. I have no doubt she would be saddened by the decline of parliament, with its reduced working hours, the imminent departure from the building itself and the rise of the unelected power of bureaucrats. After all, when she was Prime Minister, questions were held on Tuesdays and Thursdays for 15 minutes. We sat and worked very long hours and bills were not timetabled. Her concerns would be shared by me and I intend to talk about them throughout the rest of this book.

PART I

Welcome to Westminster

AT THE RISK of sounding like Victor Meldrew, parliament has changed and not always for the better. That said, I entirely understand that as the vast majority of MPs were elected in 2010, 2015, 2017 or 2019 – they have little to compare with the current state of affairs.

Age old traditions vanish with increasing regularity. I find it hard to compare any of the new recruits to those who defined the 20th century. Love them or hate them – Enoch Powell, Michael Portillo, Margaret Thatcher, Tony Benn, Michael Foot, Ian Paisley, Shirley Williams, Roy Jenkins, David Owen (and many, many others) – these politicians all had distinctive personalities. They could be unpredictable, yes, but they were fiery, impassioned and willing to put everything on the line for what they believed in and for the interests of those they represented. They also had the ability to make significant change. Too often I find myself telling constituents that I am unable to create change in the same way that I had done back in the 1980s. Being an MP is not what it used to be, mainly because unelected individuals increasingly pull the levers of power.

It might be that various high-profile scandals have forced this revolution. MPs are less trusted and are therefore scrutinised far more than ever before. Maybe it is just modern life, the increased transparency and accountability (which of course has many benefits) that social media inevitably brings. Every move is watched, every word recorded and silence means laziness rather than hard work. But I am not writing this book to explore why this has happened but rather to explain what has happened, to highlight the differences and peculiarities and to encourage others to reflect on when change is positive but also when it must be fought against.

Inside the House

Procedures and traditions have undoubtedly changed under the banner of modernisation. I suppose to some I could be seen as old-fashioned and living in the past. I would counter that by saying I like tradition. Often evolved over a very long period of time and with good reason, I think it's tragic to end our unique procedural practices. This is especially the case when the rationale is weak, and the main motivation is to sacrifice for the sake of it at the high altar of modernisation.

The current building, designed by Charles Barry and Augustus Pugin, looks much the same now as it did when it was completed in 1870. The debating chambers had been finished much before then, with the Lords sitting there from 1847 and the Commons since 1852. As a result, the place is awash with history. From Disraeli to Gladstone and Major to Johnson, all modern-day Prime Ministers have been answerable to parliament from the same despatch box. So, while parliament may look the same from the outside, what goes on within its walls would be unrecognisable to my predecessors.

At the risk of being controversial, I miss the camaraderie which was created as a result of the working practices of parliament. We used to sit five days a week. The working day, in parliamentary terms, always started at 2.30pm other than on Fridays. The argument for this was that Government Ministers were Members of Parliament too and it allowed them to get on with their constituency work in the mornings and to deal with departmental matters before the House sat. That may have been true, but there was also certainly an element which involved members having second jobs. For instance, a number of colleagues worked in the legal profession, which meant they would prepare their briefs in the morning, appear in court in the afternoon and still be ready for the votes at Westminster in the evening. Others were accountants or involved in finance. They again would work in the city throughout most of the day and spend their evenings voting. Those MPs who were journalists, writing columns for papers, had more freedom. In recent times, there has been much criticism of Members having second jobs. Despite having to declare their interests, that doesn't stop the media having an annual 'pop' at the outside earnings of parliamentarians. When George Osborne was relieved of his job as Chancellor and returned to being an ordinary Member, there was much fuss made of the fact that he had landed the fabulous job of Editor at The Evening Standard. The cry went up, 'how can he do both jobs?' An urgent question was asked on the matter. I was already sitting in the Chamber for a previous matter when George walked in for the start of the question and plonked himself next to me. In one sense it was awkward, in another it was nice to be there to hear at first-hand what was going on. Needless to say, he quickly realised that doing both would not be an option and he chose to leave Parliament which was a great loss.

As the word Parliament (Parli) indicates, the purpose is to talk, to debate and to scrutinise legislation. And so, our proceedings would often continue until 2.00am, 3.00am or even 4.00am. Members today would say this is crazy, what a way to run parliament! How could you have a family life? Well we did and we managed. Members and their families went into politics with their eyes wide open as to what the job entailed.

The first Committee Stage of a bill that I served on was the Rate Capping Bill. It was a very important issue to my then constituency of Basildon. Patrick Jenkin was the Secretary of State who led the Committee. Members who were serving on the bill were called into Patrick's Ministerial Office. I had no idea what it was all about, but he opened the session by saying, 'I want the bill!' I didn't really know what he meant. He told me to be alert during the debate as when the votes are called, they are done so in alphabetical order, so I would be first. When proceedings began, I soon realised what he meant. Government members were supposed to keep silent during the Committee Stage so the opposition would rabbit on endlessly but manage to keep in order. We literally had an all-night sitting during which, one by one, members began to fall asleep, including the Chairman of the Committee, Ted Leadbitter (then member for Hartlepool). When Harry Cowans eventually finished his speech – you always knew that he was going to speak for a long time when he used the expression 'opening Pandora's box' – Ted awoke startled and apologised with eloquence: 'the Committee has been on automatic pilot'. The division took place, my name was called out first and so I learnt the importance of staying awake. I was young of course and was used to staying up late so it wasn't as big an issue for me as it was for some of the others.

Working such long hours meant that you really got to know one another, whatever party you were affiliated with. Certain commentators would suggest all this led to alcoholism, with the Commons bars being kept open for as long as we sat. It is true that some members drank too much, but the reality was the tearoom was parliament's beating heart. All sorts of characters would frequent the tearoom. It was a wonderful source of gossip. At one end would sit the Labour members, at the other end the Conservative members and clerks to the House were allowed to sit behind a small screen. Members, and indeed ministers, would spend a lot of time chatting about all manner of things. Today, all that has been lost. It has become like a nine-to-five job. Rarely is there a late night, worse still we don't seem to vote very often, all of which means we have lost contact with each other and you only really get to know a colleague when you travel abroad with them.

There never used to be any timetabling of bills. Timetabling was introduced by Tony Blair, to curtail debate and meant that time slots were given to each bill. I always got the impression that Blair found Parliament to be a nuisance and didn't want to discuss much. This has contributed significantly to the death of filibustering. Two of my colleagues, Ivan Lawrence and Sir

Bernard Braine, both once made speeches lasting between three and five hours. One managed to speak for five hours about a Bill concerning the fluoridation of water! The power to filibuster was seen as an essential part of the democratic process, in terms of being able to delay and frustrate legislation. When timetabling was first introduced, scrutiny by the House was truncated and the art of filibustering well and truly lost. Although not a skilled filibusterer myself, in terms of being able to speak for hours, one occasion where I used Parliamentary procedure to its full effect has stuck long in my memory.

Dennis Skinner was one of those MPs who liked to 'give it' but quite frankly could not always 'take it'. He had wrecked Ann Widdecombe's Private Member's Motion to allow the House a vote on her Abortion (Amendment) Bill in the 1988–89 session. Skinner had moved the Richmond (Yorks) by-election after Lord Leon Brittan became an EU commissioner. Skinner's motion took priority and so most of the day was spent debating the by-election in Richmond rather than abortion law. Skinner himself spoke for three hours! He had similarly killed the Unborn Children (Protection) Bill's chances in 1985 when Andrew Bowden had tried to allow for its remaining stages to take place on 8 June (so this was not his first offence).

As luck would have it, Skinner was allocated an Adjournment Debate a few weeks later. Word got around and I and like-minded pro-life MPs, such as Ann Widdecombe and Ken Hargreaves, agreed to wreck it. We ensured that Strangers' Gallery wasn't empty by placing Ken's assistant, Anthony Court, and my assistant, Paul Lennon, to serve as the 'strangers'. As soon as the adjournment was moved, we let Skinner say a few words and then began numerous points of order. Having listened to a number of them, the Deputy Speaker, who must have been bitterly regretting being in the chair, finally refused to take any more. At this point in proceedings, Ken rose, pointed at Anthony and said 'I spy strangers' – a mechanism that requests the House sits in private. As procedure determined, a division was called. The motion was defeated 46 votes to one and

Skinner was left with five minutes for his debate. His face was complete poison. While I understand people's reservations regarding this tactic, on this occasion it was wholly justified as a deterrent to others. It shows that there are consequences if you simply disrupt bills that you disagree with from being heard and discussed.

I much regret the change from holding Prime Minister's Questions twice a week. They used to be held on a Tuesday and a Thursday for 15 minutes. In my view, the exchanges were of a far higher quality as a result. I was not in parliament myself to see how Margaret Thatcher, when she was Leader of the Opposition, dealt with the then PM. I only saw her against leaders of the opposition, the first being Michael Foot. He was a fine orator, but Margaret's style worked to her advantage at PMQ's. Major had a much tougher time against Blair who was sickeningly smooth during these weekly tussles. The reason the twice weekly sessions were better than what we have now, is that they were concise and given the pace of news, allowed Members two opportunities to raise current issues. Nowadays there is far too much triviality, just asking the PM to praise whatever it is the MP is doing in their constituency.

Underpinning all this was the televising of parliamentary proceedings. Up until 1989 parliament wasn't televised, instead it was broadcast on the radio. I and others, but not enough as it turned out, were opposed to this change. The reason for our view was that we felt that television would give an inaccurate impression of the work of an MP. To some extent, that has proved correct. We believed that the general public might not appreciate that, because they didn't see their MP stand up and say something, it meant that they weren't interested or were lazy. The concept of 'being called' is not widely understood. The general public have often thought that their Member can just go in and raise any issue, forgetting that the Speaker of the day has to actually call them to speak and that is why any colleague wishing that opportunity has to keep standing up and down. In the same manner, many MPs would be in their offices working away on behalf of their constituents or taking part in tedious, unglamorous Committee meetings. It seemed harsh that they faced being unfairly judged for being away from the chamber.

But I suppose our primary reservation was that once proceedings were televised and TV monitors were installed all over the Parliamentary Estate, the chambers would be empty. Why would anyone want to sit about waiting to be called to speak when they can just sit in the comfort of their office watching it all on their monitor? I fully appreciate that we can't put the clock back and there are some good things which have happened as a result of televising, but generally speaking it has killed the chamber. It is now very poorly attended and the dedicated parliamentary channel, which I applaud, is viewed by a relatively small proportion of the general population. The figures I attained at the time of writing show that BBC Parliament has a weekly audience share of around 0.25 per cent of television viewers.

Our move towards modernity and the televising of proceedings has without question hindered our ability to keep some of our most beloved traditions. The attendants in the chamber used to keep a top hat to be worn during a division which would allow a member to raise a point of order.

The doorkeepers are pretty wonderful people, as indeed are many of the remarkable individuals that keep the Palace running. The doorkeepers are not only part of the traditions of the place but are essential in ensuring that MPs are supported in the chamber. One of their more peculiar roles is to handle the snuffbox – a thing of legend. The box was first installed when smoking was banned in the chamber in the late 17th century. The box is fashioned from wood reclaimed from the bombed-out World War II chamber and decorated with a silver plaque. While I am not aware of any colleagues who currently do this, the Principal Doorkeeper is responsible for keeping alive the memories of a former Britain, if for no other reason but to remind us of how far we have come.

When I was first elected, I was bemused by the voting process. Bells would ring and you would have eight minutes to get to the division lobby, at which point you would be locked in. The journey can often be a bit of a hurry and the fantastic police officers that we have on site would regularly stop the traffic in order to allow MPs to get to the chamber – this occurs no more. I initially thought the whole process very bizarre. In this sense, I can empathise with the modern MP who believes a 16-minute vote to be a total irrelevance to modern Britain and a complete waste of time. They would much prefer electronic voting, as is often the case in European legislatures, but that would be a great shame.

Since holding office, I have learnt that divisions are a wonderful way of meeting your colleagues, having really useful conversations and lobbying ministers on particular issues. Pressing buttons is no substitute for the opportunity to physically express your vote and at the same time discuss the important issues of the day with other elected Members. As the mother of all Parliaments, copied and envied throughout the world, the style which we choose to vote I believe is of fundamental importance.

I feel equally strongly about the design of the Chamber itself. When I was first told about the white lines on either side of the Chamber floor, over which you could not make a speech, I initially thought that it was odd. I soon changed my mind when I had it explained that it symbolised the style of Parliamentary Debates. By this I mean that in past years, Members had come in wearing swords. So strong ran their passions that it was deemed necessary to separate both sides by more than two swords lengths, thus the tradition was born. This may sound awfully silly at first, but its meaning is far deeper. In a Parliamentary Democracy, arguments should be settled peacefully without recourse to violence. There is a name above every hanger in the Members Cloakroom. On every hanger is a pink tag and that is where you are supposed to hang your sword every day you come into work! Needless to say, I have a decorative sword hanging on my very own tag.

An institution that has held significant power over our democracy is the Whips' Office. It has always been a rather stern place, often led by richer colleagues of more mature years and with a military background. They really did know everything about Members' public and private lives. With this in mind, they could make or break careers. What is less spoken of is how supportive they can also be (although I suspect self-interest is at play here). They could fix anything. Unfortunately, as parliament has diminished so has the power of the Whips. They used to have tremendous patronage at their disposal. That power is no more.

One reason for getting along well with the Whips was to ensure that you could pair for certain votes. We Members are a very busy group of people and pairing occurs when one Member makes an arrangement with another (of the opposite persuasion) not to vote together and thus cancel one another out. This has huge benefits, especially when voting takes place at ludicrous hours and can severely interfere with other commitments. This could never be done during a three-line Whip, when under no circumstances can a vote be missed, but was permissible for a two-line whip. During my early years this was used to good effect but since the landslide of 1997 and elections since, pairing has very rarely been allowed. These days there seem to be an awful lot of one-line whips where you are not compelled to vote at all.

The slow death of customs such as pairing is one reason for the inferior influence of the Whips. Another is the choice of personnel. The PM would historically select Whips because of their focus on good service or an uncanny ability to deal with people. Nowadays, the role seems far less prestigious, with junior Members regularly appointed and moved on soon afterwards. The office is slowly becoming just another launch pad for a ministerial career. I am not sure whether this is a good thing or not.

An area in which Whips still play a pivotal role is the allocation of accommodation, and by that I mean office space.

When I first arrived, there was a fearsome woman called Mary Frampton, physically large, who everyone seemed to be afraid of. She was known by many as 'Bomber Command'. I had no hopes of what kind of office I might be given. I'm not sure I had even considered it, I was just happy to have been elected. So, when I was allocated a room in Abbey Gardens, along with three other people, I thought nothing of it. One of the desks was not occupied throughout the whole first year. I am not quite sure what the Member had been doing but I don't think he was in the library like Enoch Powell. It is safe to say that he was not re-elected. Much later, I was alerted to the opportunity to convert a broom cupboard in Abbey Gardens into my own office. It was a great decision and one for which I can thank Harry Greenway, former Member for Ealing North. He was a retired headteacher, a horseman and a real character.

Today's MP's are far more demanding than I ever was. They have their own office and quite often a separate one for their staff. There is extensive support available digitally and technologically. A major factor in this was the opening of Portcullis House in 2001. This has been built on what was, in hindsight, an absolute dump called Bridge Street, above Westminster tube station. There was a bit of a row about the money being spent, but it probably has been necessary thanks to the growing size of the estate. Having said that, I have always thought the building to be perfectly hideous, with its most unattractive architecture, rather silly planted areas and the expanse of individual tables and chairs at which people sit around drinking endless cups of tea talking absolute drivel, under the false apprehension that they are running the country.

It is also a magnet for journos, their previous hang-out, Annie's Bar, has long since ceased to exist. They seek out hapless colleagues who seem easy enough to rope in and then proceed to encourage them to share confidential information. I will never get over the naivety of any MP believing that they can have a personal or special friendship with someone in the media. What a joke!

Anyway, I digress. Ten years previously, 1 Parliament Street had been officially opened. While I did initially occupy the old broom cupboard, I have been afforded a far greater luxury as the years have gone by. My rather wonderful office, with its balcony overlooking Parliament Square, is entirely thanks to Ann Widdecombe and Mark Francois. Ann had occupied the room until her retirement and wanted me to have it once she had gone. Mark, the Accommodation Whip at the time, ensured that it was mine. I will be eternally grateful to them for ensuring I have the most perfect working environment and I would advise any young MP who is planning to stick around for a while to adopt a similar approach to my own.

One major development that has seen the importance of the Commons diminish considerably is the development of Select Committees. The late Norman St John-Stevas was responsible for setting up this system which we now enjoy. I am sure he never envisaged Select Committees becoming the apex of the scrutiny process and being the arena most feared by Ministers and officials. When Blair was PM, his huge majority meant that scrutiny became marginalised and legislation was steamrollered through. This became so regular that arrangements for the clerks in the lobbies were changed. The alphabet used to be divided into two, with letters hanging on the ceiling indicating where members should go to register their vote. Thanks to the huge majority, one lobby tended to be far fuller than the other and there was a large discrepancy in the time taken for Member's votes to be recorded. An extra Clerk was added to each lobby in order to help speed up the process. This was a good outcome from a sad situation, that being the inadequacy of parliament to hold the government to account. Select Committees helped bridge this issue, they had the powers to summon Ministers and they could not refuse to attend.

I was on the Health and Social Care Committee for ten years. It was an outstanding group, led ably by David Hinchliffe. We produced some ground-breaking reports which had significant impacts on public policy. More recently, we have witnessed a trend to call upon celebrities. Who can forget Rupert Murdoch appearing before the Culture, Media and Sport Select Committee? The drama of his then wife protecting her husband from an assailant was captured for posterity on TV. I myself had the opportunity to question Max Moseley and Bernie Ecclestone over the sponsorship of Formula 1 racing. The former continually interrupted the latter for fear he might put his foot in it. I also recall sitting behind Blair when he gave evidence to the Northern Ireland Committee about the Good Friday Agreement. You could feel the hostility of the public towards him.

Select Committees have clearly become an important part of the democratic process and I am glad that we have them. It is just a shame that the Commons is unable to fulfil this function as effectively as it once did.

Mister/Madam Speaker

One Member who has not become any less important is the Speaker. Perversely, they have regularly used their powers to exclude people from the Commons. I must confess that I rather enjoyed the spectacle of seeing the odd Member or two being removed from the Chamber. Quite how the sergeant-at-arms would have dealt with the situation if they had met any resistance, I do not know. Fortunately, it never happened. I almost jumped for joy when Ian Blackford, leader of the SNP, called for the House to sit in private – note the modernised call rather than the 'I spy strangers' described in the previous chapter – and was subsequently ejected by Speaker Bercow. My jubilation was not because I dislike the SNP so much that I wanted to see their leader banished, but that for the first time in God knows how long, there was real drama and a proper use of Erskine May to propel an issue into the limelight. There had been a time when such stunts were entirely commonplace.

Members who object to ministers' utterances in a debate have the right to stand in front of the table of the House, where the mace lies, to halt proceedings. Forty Members took up this right during one of Nigel Lawson's controversial budgets.

I vividly recall sitting behind Michael Portillo, the Minister replying to the end of day Adjournment Debate. The public gallery was empty except for two dozen Hasidic Jews. Without any warning, a Scottish Labour Member of Parliament called Ron Brown burst into the chamber, got hold of the mace and tossed it in the air, a little bit like tossing the Caber. The rather genial Deputy Speaker, Sir Paul Dean, initially ignored the event. The people in the public gallery must have thought that this was some sort of ancient tradition to end proceedings. Bells rang to call the end of the day. Sir Paul left the chair but was called back to it as the bells rang again to address Ron Brown. Ron was subsequently banished from the House for 20 days.

Talking about life inside the House without addressing the five Speakers – Bernard Weatherill, Betty Boothroyd, Michael Martin, John Bercow and now Sir Lindsay Hoyle – under whom I have served, would be a futile activity. While all being very different characters, they all had three traits in common: their love of Parliament, their determination to allow free speech and their desire to ensure that the humblest of backbench members voices should be heard.

George Thomas had just retired as Speaker when I entered the Palace. He had built up a fine reputation as a first-class parliamentarian who upheld the rights of parliament and it was his Welsh lyrical tones that were heard when proceedings were first broadcast on BBC Radio in 1975.

Thomas was succeeded by the late Bernard Weatherill who, as I understand it, was not Margaret's first choice. I would meet him upon my first visit to Westminster as the newly elected Member for Basildon in 1983. One of the first things I, and all other newly elected MPs, did was sign the register and swear an Oath of Allegiance. I stood in the long queue and waited my turn. When I eventually got to the table in the middle of the Chamber, a gift from Canada, I noted that Bernard looked like something out of Gilbert and Sullivan's *Trial by Jury*! This slightly odd-looking figure shook my hand and congratulated me warmly. My admiration for him grew steadily over the years and, in my opinion, he turned out to be one of the most outstanding speakers of the 20th century. He was supported faithfully by his wife Lynne. They really were a delightful couple, both kind and warm-hearted.

Although new Members might find it difficult to believe, the House used to be much more of a raucous place than it is today. Consequently, the Speaker needed to be far more authoritarian. So, on three or four occasions that I recall, Bernard had to temporarily suspend proceedings, as matters were becoming disorderly. I think his general presence represented parliament and all we stood for in the best possible light. He was personally very kind to me when I made my maiden speech, which I suspect wasn't half as memorable as he suggested. During the same debate, I was absolutely delighted to receive a congratulatory, handwritten note via a messenger. On a personal level, he very generously allowed me to have my children's christenings in the Speaker's state apartments, all of which was a great delight to those who attended.

Most Speakers serve between eight and nine years. So there was much speculation about who would succeed Bernard. I suppose even though the government had a majority, it was right that it was Labour's turn. Bernard is now dead, so I am unable to ask him the truth about what happened, but some people claimed that Betty Boothroyd, one of Bernard's deputies, decided that she wanted to be the Speaker. Accordingly, so it goes, she set up a little campaign team to gather support led by her friend Gwyneth Dunwoody on the Labour side and the former highly respected Leader of the House John Biffen. Whatever the truth of the matter was, when the election came Betty had it in the bag.

I did have a very minor part in the proceedings, which took place in 1992. I was asked to support my near neighbouring MP, Paul Channon, in his bid. Paul was the ultimate gentleman, someone of the highest integrity and a very generous spirit. He presided over a very tough time as Secretary of State for Transport. It was hardly his fault that national tragedies occurred over rail, sea and land on his watch. In 1987, 31 died in the King's Cross fire; in 1988, 35 were killed when three trains crashed near Clapham Junction rail station and later that year 270 died when Pan Am Flight 103 was brought down by a bomb over the Scottish town of Lockerbie; in 1989, 44 died when a British Midland plane crashed beside the M1 motorway in the Kegworth air disaster.

In terms of street fighting, he was no match for the brutish behaviour of John Prescott, who criticised him incessantly for underinvestment in the railways and a holiday he took shortly after Lockerbie in his villa on the island of Mustique. But he remained dignified, even while he and his wife Ingrid suffered the terrible loss of one of their daughters at university. His political luck was not about to change either and while most colleagues thought he was a lovely person, there was very little support for him becoming Speaker. This was in spite of my and Steve Norris's best efforts to get on the phone from Paul Channon's grand home to all potential supporters. As a result, he never became the third member of his family to become Speaker of the House of Commons.

The media seized on the candidacy of the only female contestant, Betty Boothroyd. I can't confess that I knew her terribly well, but in much the same way as Margaret Thatcher, many people liked the idea of a woman taking on a prominent position in public service. Her cross-party support grew not least because many people thought that following a Conservative Speaker in Bernard, it was only right that Labour should have a turn. The frontrunner on the Conservative side was Peter Brooke. When it came to the election, Paul was quickly eliminated and in the final vote Betty won comfortably. She soon became a dominant force in politics. Her head of luxurious snow-white hair meant it was unnecessary to wear the wig. Widely admired on all sides of the House for her determination for free and fair debate, she was a traditionalist and clearly became exasperated at Tony Blair's increasing attempts to side-line parliament. On the day she retired as Speaker in 2000, doorkeepers lined the route as she strode into the chamber for the last time.

The 1997 election had resulted in only 165 Conservative members being returned, so our ranks were greatly diminished. This was potentially problematic when trying to appoint a Conservative Speaker. One could have succeeded had the Party united around a single candidate, but we didn't. The vote was split, and the somewhat unlikely Michael Martin emerged as the frontrunner. I didn't know Michael at all. I had never had any dealings with him and because he always sported rosy cheeks, I had mistakenly assumed he was a heavy drinker. I would later discover that he was in fact teetotal and a devoted Catholic – that taught me to never judge a book by its cover.

He came from the union wing of the Labour Party, used to running things, but not naturally experienced in presiding over events. He was however seen as a champion of the working-class. I always found him very fair to deal with, but there were constant mutterings about his suitability for the role and the opportunity for a slightly early departure from his Speakership came when he was criticised in the Chamber by Douglas Carswell and others for his handling of the expenses crisis. In time, no doubt the truth of what happened will be reported on.

As far as Members, claims on allowances were concerned, for as long as I can remember, any attempt to increase the salary of Members was rejected on the grounds that it would be unpopular. So, the allowances were very much seen as a way of topping up one's income. I do not believe that Members as a whole made a concerted attempt to, as it was put, fiddle their earnings. Instead, the fees office, in their engagement with Members, was the driving force behind the way that claims were made. It is such a tragedy that the exposé did such huge damage to parliament's standing.

As it stands, Michael was portrayed as being complicit to a cover-up. History may well show however that he was an honest and straightforward man who only ever had the general standing of parliament itself as the main factor in the consideration of how to deal with the crises which he became engulfed in.

So an unexpected election took place. There had been little time for any individual to build a campaign team or nurture support and I was totally unaware that my colleague John Bercow had his eye on the job. I instead was involved with two friends in their own quests – Michael Lord and Ann Widdecombe.

Ann was a close personal friend who undoubtedly could have done the job extremely well. She had decided to retire at the next Parliament, so ran on the ticket of a short-term Speakership. Michael, one of the Deputy Speaker's whom I greatly liked, also ran and I initially backed his candidacy. Again, the vote was heavily split and through the middle of it all emerged John with what was described at the time as substantial support from the Labour Party.

Whatever the truth of the matter is, Parliament elected him as Speaker and while he attracted criticism for his style and manner from all quarters, his many qualities should not be overlooked. He fought tirelessly to protect the right of backbench Members of Parliament to be heard. He has been accused of being anti-Conservative, the party to which he has belonged to all of his life. It may be the case, of course, that when you are Speaker you overcompensate in terms of deference to members of the party to which you do not belong. That said, there can be no doubt at all that he is kind, honourable and compassionate. He has modernised parliament in a number of ways (not all of which I approve). Among his lasting legacies will be the magnificent education centre which has brought politics to future generations, and his programme of Speaker's Lectures.

He had a photographic memory and a level of eloquence which I do not possess. His critics cite that he entered the political fray too often, they point to various statements which a more traditional Speaker would not have become embroiled with. Nevertheless, he had a right to express a view on a potential visit to Westminster by President Trump given that he would be tasked with leading the welcoming party.

What can most certainly be said is that John Bercow was like none of his predecessors in style, manner and ambition. Only time will tell how he will be viewed in comparison to all the others. My hunch is that for the most part his legacy will be viewed in a positive light.

The next Speaker's greatest challenge will be presiding in another chamber. Sir Lindsay Hoyle must be above party politics, ensure that the ordinary backbencher's voice is heard on behalf of their electorate and that the Executive of the day is properly scrutinised. In terms of how long a Speaker can serve, I am not sure there has to be a set time period. John Bercow obviously did not expect an election to be called in 2017. This coupled together with the historic decision to leave the European Union would have been most challenging for an inexperienced Speaker to deal with. Sir Lindsay faces many different and unprecedented challenges, not least of which is the fallout from coronavirus. Creating a 'Virtual Parliament' is still very much a work in progress. I will be interested to see how he rises to the job.

As I have already said, the Speakers I have known have been quite different from one another in so many ways. This is quite naturally to be expected, given that there is no specification for their personalities. Speaker Weatherill had to deal with a very different House to that which Speaker Bercow addressed. For instance, the House was much livelier, noisier and more dramatic than now. From what I recall, Bernard was always on his feet calling for order and Members would be rejected and ejected on a pretty regular basis. I thought it was great fun. Today, he or she has to deal with Members who have been created to deal with the modern media. The language they use is very different and Erskine May – the rulebook which governs our proceedings – is hardly ever mentioned.

Colleagues

I suppose that when writing a book about Parliament, it would be slightly odd not to mention one's colleagues. The obvious difficulty being that total honesty about all of the current crop would require me to hire an armed guard to accompany me around the Parliamentary Estate! So rather than name people specifically, I shall describe the different categories of MP that I have had the good (or mis)fortune to work alongside. I pride myself on being a pretty good judge of character, but I have still made some catastrophic mistakes over the years. There are some colleagues that I have trusted that, had I been in my right mind, I shouldn't even have shared the same air with.

I should say that I am a keen observer of humanity and start from the premise that we are all sinners, some very big-time indeed! I haven't met many saints in my lifetime other than Mother Theresa, my own mother and my own dear wife, so let me analyse the different category of colleague I have known over the years.

Convictions/The Ideologues/The Believers

Many have pursued their ambition to be elected as a Member of Parliament for numerous years. Consequently, they have convictions. These may be aligned to a party or an issue but either way they will be very closely held and unwavering in the face of controversy. They believe strongly in their vision of society and want to convince everyone of it. They tend to pursue certain issues relentlessly, so much so that in the tearoom they are known as the Commons Bores. Those who report on these matters often take a rather cruel poke when an individual follows their beliefs. I am not saying that I would wish to be stuck on a desert island with any of these people (in fact from a number I would certainly try to escape) but many of them have had the last laugh. By this I mean what they originally suggested has actually come to pass. If they survive the tempers of the electorate then their relentless message is eventually received as they wear down the powers that be. I am rather fond of this type of colleague and regard them as characters.

The Careerist/Sans Conviction

This is the colleague who doesn't really have any convictions. If they did then they would jolly well soon jettison them in order to gain preferment. They may have hoodwinked their selection committees to adopt them as candidates, or they may have been chosen from one of these silly open primaries. Via this process you can end up with an individual who is not what you thought they were. A colleague without conviction may align themselves to whoever they perceive to be the up-and-coming leader. They do this in order to gain office, regardless of their abilities or true beliefs. They invariably sulk if they don't succeed in their ambitions and always pose the risk of going all the way and changing political parties in order to gain preferment.

The Whip's Nark

This colleague has no real backbone, never mind any convictions. They quickly realise that you need to do the Whip's bidding in order to get a job. I can well understand the naivety of colleagues falling into this trap initially, but I despair when they have been a Member for some time. They slavishly ask planted questions (no matter how stupid they might be); they agree to participate in debates, whether or not they know the first thing about the subject; they defend the indefensible; and can be guaranteed to become a cheerleader whenever someone of authority in their party speaks. They invariably spend a lot of their time up the back passage of the Chief Whip and can be spotted in the tearooms and on the terrace, licking the boots of whoever is perceived to be the 'Great One' of the day.

The Plain Stupid

When they get elected, we all squirm with embarrassment at what he or she might have to say. They may look odd, they may have a strange voice, but whatever they say is privately greeted with derision. The media absolutely loves these colleagues, so they are written about endlessly until it all ends in tears and they move on to the next one. This sort of colleague, even if they had ambition, does not have the intelligence to fulfil it. I do quite like these people and find them rather endearing.

The Media Tart

This colleague absolutely loves being in the limelight. They respond in a positive fashion to media bids even before they receive them; any newspaper, any TV company or any social media outlet. These people used to be known as rent-a-quote. They are often pompous and sanctimonious, but the media love them because when most are unavailable during the working day, not to mention weekends and late at night, these special few are constantly at the media's disposal. You see them sitting in Portcullis House with journalists, feeding them delicious titbits about some poor soul. They have convinced themselves that whoever it is they are talking to really likes them and is a friend. I have observed over the years how these so-called relationships invariably end badly.

The Sanctimonious Ones

They are terribly serious. They let it be known that they are well educated and come from a good background. They try not to show it, but they usually fail. They are superior to other forms of Parliamentary life. When they speak, they expect the House to be silent and to hang on their every word. They have inevitably perfected the art of delivering their pearls of wisdom, but you often hear them speaking with a catch or lump in their throat. They are sickeningly sincere and terribly boring. Their family lives are usually horrendous!

The 'Best Friends'

When I first became an MP, I was privately shocked by how colleagues behaved to one another. Sometimes they would smile at you and engage in conversation, the next minute they would walk right past you as if you had never met. This colleague, if there is no one better to talk to, will grab you in the division lobby and engage you in some sort of furtive conversation while looking over your head to see someone more important come past, in which case you will be dumped. Their peak season comes during election time. In recent years our procedures have changed, and we now have elections for all sorts of posts: Speaker, Deputy Speaker, Chairs of Select Committees, even membership of Select Committees. All of a sudden you will have a message or a phone call from them. Up until then, they hadn't given you the time of day but now you are that person's best friend and they want your vote. They are shallow and superficial but again I rather like them because you can always rely on them for a conversation.

The Good Guys/Girls

There are more of these to be found than you would think. These are the people who have broken out of all the previous categories. They are often discovered when you go on Parliamentary trips. It is when you are away with other Members, invariably abroad, that you find out what they are really like. Over the years I have been on many trips and formed a quite different impression of a colleague from that which I held beforehand. They have invariably led an interesting life, behaved well in both private and public and are well-mannered, kind, generous and thoughtful. They work on the maxim that the little things in life count – pleases, thank yous and handwritten notes. This is by far the largest category of colleagues.

The Crooks

The most sad and depressing category of all. As MPs are members of the human race there are bound to be colleagues who fall into this category. These people are not what they appear to be. You may think they are prosperous when they are riddled with debt. They may seem to be happy, but the reverse is true. They may give the impression of being truthful, where in fact they are inveterate liars. There are a number of colleagues, albeit not many, who over the years have fallen into this category. Their lives inevitably implode and it is terribly sad when that happens and the reality of their existence is revealed.

The Nasty Ones

Whether it be jealousy or genuine dislike, they have it in for others. They don't necessarily seize on the weak and powerless, but often target the strong and powerful. I am never quite sure what motivates them or what pleasure it gives them but whether it be through the Parliamentary Standards, the Whips' Office or the police, they go out of their way to make life hell for the colleague that they are targeting. They do all this regardless of the consequences for the families of the colleague that they wish to destroy. This sort sometimes gets their comeuppance, but they invariably remain discontent.

The Happy Colleague

This is someone who isn't entirely driven by ambition or, if they are, they manage to cover it up terribly well. They are a joy to know, good company and good support. Whatever problems they have at home, they do not bring to work. They are supportive of others when life gets tough for them, they judge the mood of the House well and are capable of sharing the odd quip when the ice needs to be broken in a tense situation. They are in that relatively rare group of colleagues who are fully aware of their own limitations and that is – not everyone can become Prime Minister!

As for which category I fall into, that is for my colleagues to decide. I would prefer not to know.

The Great Characters

The power of oratory is something to behold as far as I am concerned. It is not easy to maintain people's attention when making a speech, let alone to try and persuade them to your particular viewpoint. I do not mean this in any derogatory sense, but this power is greatly diminished from what it was when I arrived in the Commons.

In part it reflects the changing demands of the job. The way we communicate with each other has dramatically transformed. I only have to reflect on the way that I now deal with constituents' problems compared with the 1980s. In those days no one sent emails or text messages. My secretary sat at what would now be regarded as an old-fashioned golf ball typewriter, churning out responses to constituents' individual handwritten letters. The process of receiving and sending a reply through the post would, in itself, take at least a week.

Letter writing is a dying art though. I receive endless emails from various campaign groups which constituents are not always aware have been sent in their name. 38 Degrees is one organisation that consistently frustrates me. I find the vast majority of emails received from them to be ill thought through, knee-jerk reactions to the headlines of the day. They encourage the electorate to sign up and then attach their names to countless emails on certain policy areas. Trawling through these is not a constructive use of an MP's time. Social media continues to develop with such things as Twitter, Facebook, WhatsApp and the like continually shaping our interactions. The effect of this depersonalised communication is obviously different, and it is a trend which has greatly affected the quality of debate.

That is not to say it is without its benefits. My ability to communicate effectively and efficiently with constituents has increased three-fold. There is far greater transparency and accountability. My constituents know what I am doing at all hours of the day. I am sure this has helped kick any less motivated Members into gear. However, there are undoubtedly some downsides, some of which have affected the character of our elected politicians and have extensively intruded on what is left of our personal lives.

The days of politicians communicating with the electorate at a church hall meeting by way of a speech have long since gone. Any local politician holding a public meeting these days would get a very small attendance (or a very angry mob!) unless the meeting was regarding the closure of a local public service. Under the current circumstances, the job specification requires a different skill set to when I was first elected.

In the 20th century the public elected debaters, orators, people with the powers of persuasion, people with presence, who could fill a room and leave you with a sense of awe and amazement. What's more, the Chamber was invariably full and so anyone addressing the House had to be a master of their subject or risk being made to look like a fool pretty quickly by some clever or unexpected intervention. This produced some wonderfully colourful characters. Unfortunately (and it is a sign of the time in many professions) the same cannot be said of the current crop. Interactions are via third-party social media platforms and often debates are held with very few Members in the Chamber. The eccentrics have on the whole disappeared, but it is worth recounting some of the most notable individuals that I have had the pleasure to come across.

The old guard

ENOCH POWELL

Even if Enoch Powell had wanted to invite me for drinks, he had nowhere to invite me to. The remarkable maverick was still a Member of Parliament when I was first elected. However, he never had an office in Westminster, as he chose instead to work in the House of Commons Library, something that I would never be able to do.

I had known him before I was elected. He had come and spoken for me at the annual Ilford South Conservative Dinner. I found him and his wife Pamela delightful. Putting aside the Rivers of Blood Speech, and all that was suggested to lie behind his views on race, when his name came up on the annunciator, members would leave their desks to listen to what he had to say. He was a brilliant orator who had achieved a double first at Cambridge University in Classics. He did eventually lose his Wolverhampton seat but returned as an Ulster Unionist for South Down. He was never really the same again and rather demeaned himself by suggesting that the PM was either a traitor or guilty of treason at one PMQs. When he died, I attended his funeral at St Margaret's Church, where the Union Jack was draped over his coffin. It was a particularly poignant moment as he certainly was a great patriot.

TONY BENN

Tony Benn, Hilary's father, was another great orator who was also listened to more or less in silence when he addressed the House. I should confess that when I met him, I could not recognise the rabid socialist that he was portrayed to be. When he lost his seat in Bristol it was a great loss to Parliament. He was a first-class historian and it was entirely due to him that Emily Wilding Davidson and the broom cupboard were commemorated in terms of the Suffragette Movement and their contribution to women's votes. In those days you had to have Committee meetings for everything, not least to put a plaque on the door. He was taking a group of constituents on a tour and showed them the crypt – one of the most beautiful chapels you have ever seen which is hidden away under Westminster Hall. Unbeknown to the authorities he was armed with a screwdriver, screws, a picture and a plaque which reads:

> In Loving Memory of Emily Wilding Davison
>
> In this broom cupboard Emily Wilding Davison hid herself, illegally, during the night of the 1911 census. She was a brave suffragette campaigning for votes for women at a time when Parliament denied them that right. In this way she was able to record her address, on the night of that census, as being 'The House of Commons', thus making her claim to the same political rights as men.
>
> Emily Wilding Davison died on 8th June 1913 from injuries sustained when she threw herself under the King's Horse at the Epsom Derby to draw public attention to the injustice suffered by women. By such means was democracy won for the people of Britain.

Today, you can see the result of his efforts on the broom cupboard. Protests were made but the then Speaker Bernard Weatherill, a wonderful colleague, shrugged his shoulders at the protests as he thought it was a rather good thing. Many years later, Tony's body lay in state in the crypt the night before his funeral. A fitting tribute to a great parliamentarian.

MICHAEL FOOT

Another left winger whom I was fortunate enough to listen to was Michael Foot. He was an outstanding Parliamentarian and a fine orator, though he probably got the job of leading his Party rather too late in life. He never recovered from wearing a donkey jacket at the Cenotaph on Remembrance

Sunday. I am sure he meant no disrespect by his actions as he was a most courteous man, but the media had a field day. He was painted as redder than red and of course the manifesto that Labour fought the 1983 election on was described by Denis Healey as the 'longest suicide note in history'.

I entered Parliament at a time when his powers were starting to wane. Physically he was struggling but he remained a force to be reckoned with, very well educated and a master of how to deliver a speech. He was also a real gentleman. I do recall approaching him to sign a book on behalf of a constituent who was clearly enthralled by everything he stood for.

It's such a shame that some people will remember him for his unfortunate appearance at the Cenotaph. While it was a real faux pas, it did not reflect the true values of the man.

Some of my favourite blues

TED HEATH

I think it is clear by now that the most outstanding parliamentarian that I have known and worked with was undoubtedly Margaret Thatcher. The rivalry between herself and Heath was fascinating to be around – his bitterness really knew no bounds.

Upon our election, various 'select' members of the 1983 intake were invited to drinks at Ted Heath's home. He and his fellow dissidents were obviously trying to poison newly elected MPs against the PM. I was having absolutely none of it. When I made my maiden speech, I happened to follow on from Heath. The Chamber was absolutely packed, as it always was, and those present would have found it difficult to listen to two back-to-back speeches from Conservative members that were so totally far apart. Reading Hansard now, it is clear to see that Ted had castigated the concept of rate capping while I had lauded it. Taking the hint, Ted's acolytes decided that I was a hopeless cause and I was never invited for drinks again.

MICHAEL HESELTINE

I can recall many moments of drama, but one that sticks out is when the late Leon Brittan and Michael Heseltine were locked in an argument about the future of Westland Helicopters. Westland was Britain's last helicopter manufacturer and it was to be the subject of a rescue bid. Heseltine, then Defence Secretary, favoured a European solution, integrating Westland with a consortium of British, French and Italian companies. Brittan (and Thatcher) favoured a merger with an American company. Front page news ensued as Heseltine refused to accept Thatcher's choice and claimed that she had prevented ministerial discussion on the matter. He resigned and was followed out the door by Brittan when it was proved that he had leaked a confidential letter critical of Heseltine.

It was a shame that Michael left his post so prematurely, he was a formidable debater and commanded attention while at the despatch box. He was incredibly imposing – tall and stern with a sweeping mane of blonde locks. I got to know him a little bit during my time as PPS to Michael Portillo, when he was Secretary of State for the Environment. I found him to be engaging, interesting and highly intelligent. Against that he could be slightly aloof, and I was incandescent with rage about his role in Margaret's downfall. I recall going through a lobby close to him, a well of anger coming over me and Peter Bottomley saying, in a nice way, to calm down, but I did find it difficult at the time.

When I represented Basildon he kindly came to the area and addressed a gathering of business people. He had that indefinable quality of charisma. I will always remember being in one of the Commons' Dining Rooms with the Heseltines seated at another table. Margaret came into the room and given Michael's role in her downfall, I thought it was rather wonderful that she went up and spoke to him and enquired about his health. He had had a problem with his heart but had made a good recovery.

Michael is one of those extraordinary figures who remains active today and was used by David Cameron as a source of ideas to deliver the regeneration, in terms of infrastructure, of various parts of the United Kingdom.

GEOFFREY HOWE

The House was packed to the rafters, in my judgement for the wrong reasons, to hear Geoffrey Howe's resignation speech. As we all now know, he resigned from the government ostensibly because he disagreed with Margaret's appointment of an economic adviser.

Traditionally, he was not a great orator and I think Denis Healey got it just about right when he said being scolded by him was like being savaged by a sheep. Commentators however regard his resignation speech as his greatest ever. Margaret sat next to John Major and had to listen to Howe tell the House that working for Margaret in recent years had been like a captain of a cricket team sending out his opening batsman to the crease with a broken bat. You could hear a pin drop when he ended by saying that he had struggled with his conscience for too long and should have considered his position much sooner than he did. He even suggested that others should do likewise. This declaration was the signal to Michael Heseltine to lay down the gauntlet and challenge Margaret for the leadership.

The House was stunned, and it resulted in the removal from office of our greatest peace-time Prime Minister. That very day I wrote a letter to Geoffrey which to put it mildly was not terribly flattering about his good self. I was flabbergasted to receive, the very next day, the most courteous handwritten letter in which Geoffrey justified the action that he took. If I had been insulted in the way that I insulted Geoffrey, I would not have responded like he did. I think it says much for his integrity.

NICHOLAS FAIRBAIRN

I'd hardly ever been to Scotland, as I have never been that keen on travelling north of Watford Gap, so meeting Nicholas was quite the shock for me. His flamboyant Rupert Bear uniform in tartan and a working revolver on a chain attached to his belt, contributed to his larger than life image. Besides the woman-ising, the snuff box usage and the outbursts concerning issues like the performers at Nelson Mandela's birthday, I remember two particular asides which at the time made an impression on me.

The first was when going through the division lobby. I found myself next to him as John Major walked past: 'David, there goes the ventriloquist's dummy'. I must confess that I found it a little hard to keep a straight face whenever I saw John in subsequent years.

On another occasion when a debate was taking place on some mildly feminist motion, Nicholas was holding forth on the issue which he clearly was not too keen on. Edwina Cur-rie intervened on his speech to which Nicholas replied: 'The Hon lady should remember that she was once an egg: and very many members on both sides of the House may regret that it was ever fertilised.'

The House could not disguise its amusement.

EDWINA CURRY

Edwina and I were elected on the same day in June 1983. We did not know one another and in so many respects could not have been more different. She was the first to make her maiden speech, I was amongst the last. She appeared pushy, opinionated and arrogant, none of which I found appealing. In those days, a maiden speech was a very big occasion. A good piece of advice which I regularly pass on was when I was told 'David, take your time when choosing to make your maiden speech as it's the only time that the House will listen to you without interruption'.

One big issue was my battle with Labour controlled Basildon Council and what I and many of my supporters saw as its extravagance and blatant politicking. So, I waited until the Rate Capping Bill, which was a huge issue locally and in terms of the resources of the Council and could make a huge difference to the lives of constituents.

The second reading of the Rate Capping Bill gave me this precise opportunity. I could support the government while also demonstrating the exorbitant rates set by councils such as Basildon. My whip was John Major and he helped to prepare me for the event. Indeed, he assisted with the construction of my speech. The guidance was it should be brief, no more than ten minutes, should consist of a tribute to your predecessors and platitudes about how wonderful the constituency was and finish with reasons as to why I was supporting the Bill. So, when 17 January 1984 came around, I was well and truly psyched up.

Family members were in the public gallery and there was no space on the benches. Following Ted Heath's anti-government speech ensured a packed House. As I stood to make my delivery with some trepidation, I began with the words: Mr Speaker it is a great privilege to address the House for the first time. At which point, a female voice could clearly be heard saying: 'And about time too.' The voice belonged to Edwina – not good form for any colleague, let alone one on your own side. I was mortified but carried on regardless.

When I sat down I received a rousing reception to my speech, not because of its brilliance but because in those days, all colleagues were praised. Notes would regularly be passed around the Chamber because colleagues would spend so much longer in there. On this day, and I suspect maybe as a reaction to Edwina's remarks, I received a number of notes while in the Chamber. A particularly nice one was from Speaker Weatherill, and another from my then colleague Matthew Parris, who flattered me by saying he had never heard the House laugh so much.

So, going back to Edwina, if you had told me that years later I would become her PPS and a great admirer, I would never have believed you. She was undoubtedly an outstanding parliamentarian. She had no need of a spin doctor to get her message across. She possessed an uncanny ability to open her mouth and the headlines would inevitably follow.

The best-known example was when as Health Minister she told old people who were struggling to pay their bills to 'wrap up warm'. She was crucified for her attack on the elderly. An absolutely nonsensical press barrage followed, one that has been repeated since on others who dare to suggest that taking measures to increase your body temperature in the winter months is a good idea.

It was a privilege and pleasure to have worked with her as her PPS. Having had access to her diary, I always thought that the claims of a relationship with John Major must have been grossly exaggerated.

After one reshuffle we met in Central Lobby and she told me all about her new role. It was to be Prisons Minister and she said to me, 'David, I rejected it. I didn't want to do it and I wouldn't have been any good at it.' Honest as always. The job went to Angela Rumbold. The unfortunate experience she had with the salmonella crisis and her subsequent fall from grace happened after I had left her team, by which time I was sole PPS to Michael Portillo.

MICHAEL PORTILLO

I was just about to vote against a piece of government legislation when I took a call from the then Chief Whip, Richard Ryder, asking me if I would like to become a PPS. I was thrilled. While I hadn't a clue at the time, I would learn in later years that this a classic way of ensuring loyalty from a colleague.

Richard told me that the Department for Health was having a particularly tough time and an extra pair of hands was required. As such I would become PPS not to just one minister but three. Of the three, Michael would go the furthest in government and so it was that I would become his sole PPS.

I was delighted with my new responsibility. I didn't know Michael before I became an MP, but I grew to admire him, not least because he was a thoroughly decent human being, blessed with an abundance of intelligence, integrity and commitment to the Conservative cause.

I must have been the longest serving PPS – nine years to be precise. The powers that be must have decided in their infinite wisdom that I wasn't quite up to being a minister. On reflection, this is a little unflattering considering the quality and abilities of a number of people appointed as ministers over the years.

I was happy to chug along as Michael's PPS, particularly as in those days it was quite a different job to that which it has become now. I enjoyed, and was privileged to experience, many unique occasions. I will never forget the day when we were all sat in the Treasury. Ken Clarke was Chancellor and a lady came in with a trolley of tea. He turned to her and asked: 'What do you think we should do with interest rates?' Marvellous.

On another occasion, I was in the Ministry of Defence when Michael was the Secretary of State and the Chief of Defence (now Lord Guthrie) and James Arbuthnot were listening to me discuss boundary changes. This was of particular interest to me, as Basildon was being split into two. I was agonising about what to do. Should I contest part of the seat against the sitting member Teresa Gorman, tackle the other seat (which would not be won by the Conservatives) or seek a new seat? They encouraged me to do the latter. As it turned out, I was well advised.

They always say that to judge a minister, you need to ask his civil servants. There is no question that Michael was greatly admired within his department. A senior civil servant implied to me that when in social security, Michael was the first minister who didn't need his help, as he understood his portfolio. In some respects, it is very true that all political careers end in tears and Michael's was no exception. He quickly became the darling of the Conservative right. The media talked him up as a future PM and the true heir to Margaret. All of this was bound to be counter-productive and would encourage jealousy among colleagues.

Michael was devoted to Margaret and fought for her survival until the end. He did not enjoy the same relationship with John Major and soon they were at odds. John thought that Michael and others were undermining his authority. When, after endless turmoil surrounding Maastricht and other matters, John decided to resign as leader of the party and call a fresh election, challenging dissidents to 'put up or shut up', Michael's name was in the frame.

While I would be loyal to John as long as he remained leader, in an election I would support Michael. In the build-up to these events, a campaign room was set up in a property near to the House of Commons. The news of this leaked with disastrous consequences. Michael's candidacy was undermined and instead of him being the candidate, he stood aside for John Redwood.

John Redwood is an outstanding politician with a fine mind, which has been evident since the Brexit referendum in 2016. However, the media lampooned him at the time. He was likened to Dr Spock and ridiculed for a video clip which showed him mumbling his way through the Welsh national anthem while Welsh Secretary in 1993. This would come up again many years later with the BBC apologising for showing it again in 2007 when Redwood made an important intervention regarding red tape and British businesses. Anyhow, the Prime Minister's gamble was to pay off, for now at least, as he won 66.3 per cent of the Conservative members votes and remained in office. We will never know if Michael would have been able to close that gap any further, or indeed win.

Politicians, like many others in high level jobs, are only as good as the teams they have around them. Michael was no exception and would learn this the hard way through his agent, who had a habit of undermining him in his Southgate patch, or so it was alleged. A huge controversy broke out before the 1997 general election as the Enfield Southgate Conservative Association wanted to sell their building to the burger chain McDonald's. Local residents were shocked and appalled. This was the backdrop against which Michael would lose his seat. Some commentators say that I was the face of the 1992 election being returned victoriously for Basildon. The same people would say that he was the face of 1997 for the wrong reasons.

He was out of Westminster until November 1999, when he won re-election as the member for Chelsea and Kensington in a by-election. He was returned to the front bench as Shadow Chancellor, but was a shadow of his former self. He was not the same person. He had lost his fight and interest in politics and so when the leadership vacancy arose, he did not seem to have the appetite for the contest and lost by one vote.

GEOFFREY DICKENS

While not quite as large as Cyril Smith, Geoffrey Dickens' booming voice would fill the room as soon as he entered it. He had a round face with reddish cheeks which perhaps unfairly gave the impression that he was not averse to having a drink. Every time he stood to make a speech, it was somehow connected to evidence that he had about child abuse by those who held high positions. Most colleagues thought that he was either wrong or grossly exaggerating. Years later, and long after his death, it became clear that everything that he had said was absolutely and shockingly true. In hindsight the bravery and determination he showed to name those in the so-called Paedophile Information Exchange was quite remarkable. He risked a lot through challenging the wealthy and the powerful and even named former British High Commissioner to Canada, Sir Peter Hayman, as a paedophile in the House of Commons using parliamentary privilege to avoid being sued for slander.

Something that all of these characters (and indeed the vast majority of politicians) have in common is that all of their careers came to an unceremonious end. There's no such thing as a modest politician. We seek the office and so we all have a pretty high opinion of ourselves. Ambition is in almost every one of us. Once you reach the top, unless you retire, as Harold Wilson did, there's only one way that you are going to go. Often on the way up, we politicians surround ourselves with people who massage our egos and are not sufficiently critical of what we intend to do. It is very sad that this happens but is perhaps inevitable for most people. Power in its way does corrupt. With life expectancy increasing all the time, it is perhaps tragic that we lose leaders from politics at such a relatively young age. Two recent examples would be David Cameron and George Osborne – both of which had a huge influence on the shape of our country for a number of years. They both achieved high office at a very young age and accomplished a great deal. Yet both of them will be remembered, most unfairly, for being on the losing side of the argument over the UK's membership of the EU. It is the tragedy of elected office and one that will not go away any time soon.

Scandals

It would be improper of me to write about 37 years in Parliament without sharing my personal perspective on some of the most famous 'scandals' the building has seen. I hate the word. In all honesty, I no longer know what it means. What one person thinks of as scandalous is often quite mundane to another. During my time in politics however, there have been any number of things to have happened which people deplore and critique, usually involving sex and money.

I decided to include this section for a number of reasons. First, the human race, being what it is, always has an appetite for learning about something scandalous.

Second and more importantly, I thought it imperative to show that MPs are no different to any other person in terms of their human frailties. It is just their misfortune that anything remotely dramatic that happens in their work lives and private lives, is all played out in the public eye with all the embarrassment which that brings. Given that I myself was a victim of a stunt concerning 'Cake', you would have thought that Parliamentarians would have learnt by now, but we don't always learn the obvious lessons. I do hope that any new members will take notice of the warnings about entrapment.

Third, the scandals demonstrate the pressures which Parliamentarians come under. Like anyone else, these can be financial or personal. This hostile environment that has been created means that the general public show little or no sympathy for those MPs who may have simply made one poor error of judgement. I fully accept that if you stand for elected office and are successful, you must also expect the scrutiny which comes with it. What is grossly unfair however is when it impacts onto one's wider family and their daily lives.

In recent times, the most notable episode would be that surrounding the financial claims of Members of Parliament. You can go on many websites and read for yourself what occurred but only those who lived throughout the period can speak with knowledge of the events that unfolded.

Reputations and lives were destroyed and will never recover. The general public, by and large, have no sympathy for the plight of politicians. We are seen in the same light as any number of unpopular professions and activities. In 2017, the annual Ipsos MORI survey concerning professional reputations found that government ministers and politicians are the least trusted profession in the UK. 19 per cent trust the former and 17 per cent the latter. I do not find this shocking, but it certainly is very sad. This leads me to discuss a question that I do not believe is asked enough – what good has come from it all?

Parliament's reputation was destroyed. It will never be the same, at least not in my lifetime. Has the system which was brought in as a result of the events which unfolded saved money from the public purse? Absolutely not. Has democracy benefitted from the way that the issues were dealt with?

Absolutely not. Were old scores settled? Probably, yes. But history will prove that there were hidden consequences that have severely damaged our political reputation. Good women and men were put off becoming politicians, not only as a result of pay structures but because of their reluctance to subject their loved ones to the close scrutiny that inevitably followed. So, we will never know how Parliament would have evolved, or what characters we missed out on, but what we can be certain of is that it changed and not necessarily positively.

Much has been written about what went on during those years. How the information was originally obtained, what was done with it and what the repercussions were for various individuals. What I can categorically say is that as a result of what happened, those with an agenda to diminish the power of Parliamentarians seized upon their opportunity and Parliament's powers seeped away. No good came of the loss of so many excellent colleagues who resigned due to the press backlash.

Cash for questions

Another issue described as a scandal was that of 'Cash for Questions'. The news broke that certain MPs were being offered money to ask parliamentary questions. When I heard about this, I was completely taken aback. Who in their right mind would pay money for an MP to ask questions? I continually submit written questions or ask questions orally. No one has ever suggested that they would give me money for the privilege. It could be that I am regarded as a complete waste of space and so my asking a question would be of no interest to anyone. Through vanity, I just do not believe that. All I can imagine is that the colleagues who did ask for money misled those seeking answers to questions that they had some special power to elicit the answers they were looking for. Now this really is utter madness. Anyone with a modicum of common sense, which I think is in increasingly short supply these days, knows that to ask a question is one thing, but to get an answer is an entirely different matter. Half the time, you ask a question and you do not get an answer. Instead you are more likely to get a lot of old waffle. The civil servants see to that.

I knew most of the individuals who were accused of asking questions in return for cash reasonably well. As a result of their actions, their reputations were destroyed and their time in active politics essentially ended. The most well-known of these was Neil Hamilton. He fell out with Mohammed al-Fayed, a man of considerable means, who chose to tell Channel 4 about the transactions between himself and Neil. I really liked Neil and his formidable wife Christine. Neither of them took life seriously in the way that one or two of my more boring and sanctimonious colleagues did. They were both enthusiasts, very patriotic and great company. You have to hand it to them in terms of their resilience, that they have both managed to bounce back and not just survive but actually prosper, one as a kind of celebrity and the other in the Welsh Assembly. This is clearly the exception rather than the norm.

Not all those who fell prey to stings have flourished. You would think that being a politician would mean that your DNA make-up made you wary of any approaches from the media or the like. But vanity is in each and every one of us and we very much want to be loved and feel that out there is some sort of mystical army of people who will help us. That could not be further from the truth.

Entrapment by the media in its various forms has become common place. The nature of it has changed as a consequence of technological advances and social media. In my early years, I had many approaches from the media to do radio, television and the like. They are a savvy lot with a well-hidden ability to feed your ego and fill you with just enough self-importance before they strike you down. I now realise that many of the approaches made to me were done because I was young, but also naive and no doubt easy to poke fun at, which fitted the narrative of the day.

Unfortunately, you can never really distance yourself from these faux pas as they remain forever embedded on the internet. I am still regularly reminded of my mistakes on various social media platforms. To this day youngsters will rush up to me and say you're the bloke who said, 'Don't Eat Cake!' It is probably about time I put forward my own version of events.

Don't eat cake! and the media trap

I fell prey to Chris Morris and Brass Eye not just once, not even twice, but three times. How could I have been so stupid?

Well, a constituent of mine called Leah Betts had tragically died in a Basildon nightclub, a victim of Ecstasy. This is a trend that has become far too common in modern-day society. The latest Office for National Statistics figures showed 2016 to contain the most drug poisoning deaths since statistics began in 1993. I fear that when the figures for 2017 are released, it will once again be higher. When I was young, we took drugs for medicinal reasons but this is no longer true. Anyhow, I did what I could to support the family by joining with others to highlight the dangers of recreational drug use, to at least try and find something positive from such a dreadful situation.

My office took a call saying that a TV company was making a programme highlighting the potential dangers of drug abuse. They mentioned Leah Betts and asked whether I would like to take part. In light of the circumstances and rather understandably, my office said yes. This level of trust in 'lobbying' organisations is now non-existent and my team are expected to thoroughly research any potential organisations before bringing their requests to my attention. Weeks later, a camera crew arrived at 1 Parliament Street led by the interviewer, a tall chap with dark curly hair. What took place is preserved on YouTube for all future generations to see. The edited film shows me holding up a round object – representing this drug – and urging youngsters not to eat it. I had never heard of it before, and naively assumed that Cake had been a slang word. I submitted a Parliamentary Question on this:

> Mr. Amess: To ask the Secretary of State for the Home Department what action the Government propose in respect of the import of (a) khat, (b) gammahydroxybutyrate and (c) "cake" to the United Kingdom.

> Mr. Sackville: Neither the khat plant nor the substances gammahydroxybutyrate--GHB--or "cake", which we understand refers to 3,4-methylenedioxy-N-benzylamphetamine, are controlled under the international United Nations drug conventions or under the Misuse of Drugs Act 1971.

It was a long time afterwards that a TV programme was shown on Channel 4 in which this chap had duped not only me but many others into condemning 'cake'. The programme was billed as political satire. I and the other victims were not amused but of course many people were.

I found myself asking, how could you make a mockery of such a serious issue? I complained to the regulator and after a huge amount of effort received a grudging apology. Unsurprisingly, no one wanted to report it. The headlines had already been made – 'Stupid MP condemns fictitious drug'. The fact that the Civil Service had got the minister to reply to my questions indicated that there was indeed a slang drug called 'cake', but no one wanted to know.

On another occasion, my office took a call from another TV company who offered a filming opportunity for Conservative MPs to engage with younger people. You will have noticed a trend in how these things work and the importance of having staff that are both sceptical and tenacious in their attention to detail. Over the years, I have had a good few people work in my office. I have much to thank them for, but they were clearly not quite up to scratch on this occasion. Through stupidity I turned up for the 'shoot' in the West End and the media showed me playing noughts and crosses on a T-shirt worn over a young lady's chest.

Panorama is generally regarded as doing splendid investigative work but again I fell victim to a ridiculous and time-wasting agenda. This was not to be my only run in with the investigative BBC programme. As the MP for Basildon I had the highest number of single parents in the country together with high unemployment. The local authority loathed me so much that they produced a board and a huge arrow outside the Fodderwick Council offices indicating rising unemployment. *Panorama* made a programme about it.

I was asked to contribute in what I genuinely thought was going to be a constructive discussion. When I watched it air, I could not believe the travesty of what was shown. They had edited my contribution in such a way that it gave the impression that I thought unemployment was a good thing. The reverse of course is true and always has been. Absolutely farcical.

What they didn't show on the television is my arrival back at the office later that evening. My answer machine was full of abusive calls. In incidents such as the latter, the media are almost wholly responsible for inciting this kind of dangerous and vitriolic abuse. I could not comment on whether public figures were targeted like this before my time, but it seems that more and more consistently, some members of the press go after politicians personally rather than properly critiquing their policy and ideology. They have a lot to answer for and must share some responsibility for the anger directed towards MPs which can end in such tragic circumstances.

While it is easy to say that this is all part of the job, does it really have to be? The overwhelming majority of MPs do excellent work on behalf of their constituents, but often pay a terrible personal price. It is often forgotten that MPs are no different than anyone else and experience the joys and tragedies of life like any other person.

On this note, I have known colleagues lose family members in horrific circumstances and similarly many have taken their own lives in equally tragic ways.

The tragic consequences of a 'scandal'

There have been a number of suicides. How can one explain that Jocelyn Cadbury, a 36-year-old man, who was seemingly comfortable, enjoyed the fine things in life and agonised about constituency problems, would shoot himself? Iain Mills, not someone who I knew very well, but again seemingly without problems, was found two days after his death, face down on the bed thanks to alcohol poisoning.

A young Scottish Labour Member, Gordon McMaster, was found by his parents in the family garage slumped in his car. The suicide note indicated that he took his life because one of his fellow Scottish colleagues was blackmailing him about his sexuality. The appalling reality of this case is that Gordon seems to have been bullied by colleagues within his own party. Rumours were spread about his private life and leaked to the tabloids. These included the claim that he had HIV. Of course, this turned out to be absolute nonsense but would have undoubtedly been deeply upsetting for him and incredibly stressful to deal with.

One of the most shocking that I can recall was John Heddle's. He looked the picture of success – debonair and immaculately turned out. One night when we were debating the Firearms Bill, which was taken through its stages by Douglas Hogg, there were endless votes led by Dennis Skinner. In order to avoid the continual procedure of members going through the division lobbies, a rarely used mechanism was employed to enable members to vote by standing up in their Commons seats.

During that long night I sat next to John and spent a lot of time chatting to him about all manner of things. Never during the course of the conversations that we had did I think for a minute that anything was wrong. Yet only a week later, the news

70

broke that he was found dead in his Jaguar, at a remote chalk pit with a hosepipe sending noxious exhaust fumes into the car. It transpired that he had been on the verge of financial ruin. If only we could have talked to him about his problems and tried to help.

Perhaps the most extraordinary death involved Stephen Milligan, Member for Eastleigh and former Telegraph journalist. My then secretary, Sally, lived next door to him. One evening we were about to leave for the Blue Ball when Sally took a call from her mother. She told her to turn on the TV, 'There are media crews and police camped outside your house!' It was only later that we found out Stephen Milligan's body had been found in his property, an orange stuffed in his mouth and a ligature around his neck.

While most political careers do not end in death, they do tend to end in tears. Harvey Proctor would be a case in point. He was my parliamentary neighbour in Billericay. When they were choosing a candidate for Basildon, he was apparently promoting our then number one tennis player, Buster Mottram.

He was presumably disappointed when they chose me rather than Buster, but he never showed it and was very supportive. He lived with his mother in a modest property in Jackson Lane. He didn't drive, which was symbolic of how unmaterialistic he was, especially for a Conservative Member!

Smartly dressed but a man of simple taste, he had a reputation as a first-class constituency MP. Politically he was very much to the right of the party. Some even accused him of being aligned with the National Front – he certainly was not. He was however a devotee of Enoch Powell, believing in strong controls on immigration, very much a Brexiteer (not that the word existed back then) and intensely patriotic. Yet his sudden departure from parliament came about as the result of a so-called sex scandal. He was accused of gross indecency. History will show that he was falsely accused, complete and utter slander that ended his entire career.

The timing of the revelation had not been helpful (I imagine deliberately so) and coincided with the announcement of a general election. The ensuing row resulted in in him resigning one week into the campaign and being replaced with Teresa Gorman. Harvey had no financial means and was thrown to the wolves. He was humiliated and personally ruined. A group of colleagues led by Michael Heseltine eventually financed a retail business which Harvey would run. He sold ties, shirts and gentleman's accessories. It was a very kind gesture and gave Harvey some self-respect back.

Ron Davies, whose ex-wife – a lovely lady – is now an MP, served as Secretary of State for Wales. I did not know him at all. My only encounter with him was when walking with Ann Widdecombe to catch a taxi at member's entrance following a late sitting. Worse for wear, Mr Davies uttered unflattering expletives in Ann's direction. Some weeks later, he stood down from Parliament having been found on Clapham Common in a compromising position with a Rastafarian gentleman. It was later described by him as a moment of madness.

More recently, Andrew Mitchell had perhaps the shortest career of any Chief Whip. No sooner had he been appointed than he was accused of calling a police officer a pleb while riding a bike through the gates of Number 10. The whole issue as to what he did or did not say was neither proven nor satisfactorily resolved. The case dragged on with various police officers being found guilty of police misconduct and dismissed. However, the whole incident cost Andrew his job and a great deal of money.

By the time of Chris Huhne's downfall, I did not think that anything could shock me anymore, but it did. Huhne was within a fingertip of becoming Leader of the Liberal Democrats. Yet his demise was brought about by a bizarre love triangle. The precise sequence of events is unclear, but he left his wife Vicky Pryce for his PR adviser with whom he had been having a long-term affair. Angry and keen for revenge on her husband, Pryce contacted journalists to let it be known that some years earlier she had taken points which had been given to Huhne for speeding, in order to avoid him losing his licence. The result of all this was that not only did he go to prison, but so did Pryce, both given eight-month sentences. The cherry on top was that Constance Briscoe, a judge involved, also ended up being convicted and going to prison. All very bizarre!

The theme of this book centres on change and the nature of scandals has most certainly developed thanks to social media. The most obvious example is that of the so-called Westminster Sex Scandal.

The Westminster sex scandal

As a self-confessed dinosaur, I do not fully embrace social media and have little understanding of it. So, I was quite taken aback when I learnt of a WhatsApp group made up of a number of members of parliamentary staff who had drawn up a list of MPs to be avoided. I cannot help thinking that if this was a truly honest and representative list then it would be a long one! Apparently in this example, the list was restricted to members who should be avoided because they were sexual pariahs.

As expected, a redacted spreadsheet of allegations soon became unredacted and before you know it, the media had access to it. Panic, whether rightly or wrongly, broke out amongst colleagues as to whether or not they had made the cut. The simple thrust of the contents accused multiple MPs of being unable to control their sexual urges, no matter what way inclined they were. I do not know if there is any truth in the allegations, however stress levels rose dramatically and yet again reputations were destroyed on the basis that there is no smoke without fire.

Backbench Bills

After learning of some of the more dubious activities to have occurred in the Westminster Village, you may be forgiven for thinking it a good thing that it can be difficult for backbench MPs to pass their own legislation. I couldn't disagree more and believe absolutely in the power of Parliament and of backbenchers in making their voice heard.

It is sometimes claimed by colleagues that you can only 'get things done' if you are a minister in terms of piloting legislation. That is simply not true. It is perfectly possible for the humblest of backbenchers (if any of us are) to successfully legislate. Let me explain how...

Private Member's Bills

Private Member's Bills (PMBs) are perhaps the best-known method. Every year, there is a ballot for 20 PMBs. This is hotly contested: a book is placed in the No lobby, which you have to sign, and then on a specific day at a specific hour, members are invited to attend a meeting in Committee Room 14 where the Chairman of Ways and Means draws the ballot, naming the lucky 20 winners. The higher you are to the top, the more chance you have of your bill becoming law, unless you are driving a completely uncontroversial, innocuous piece of legislation and then it does not matter where you are in the draw. It is all a question of the parliamentary time available.

Having faithfully entered the ballot every year, it wasn't until my 16th attempt that I was successful. I was drawn number five, which in effect meant that I had a realistic chance of success. Experience has taught me that the fundamental difficulty of passing a PMB is getting to grips with the correct parliamentary procedure. If only my peers took a little time to ask our wonderful parliamentary clerks, most of whom are far more intelligent and learned than the average member, how things ought to work. They are invariably helpful and act as a mine of useful information, never failing to guide us in the right direction.

On the day of the PMB ballot, there is usually a great deal of media interest. So, no sooner had my name been drawn that

I began to receive telephone calls from various lobbying organisations asking me to adopt their particular bill for all manner of reasons. I became engulfed by lobbyists and took tremendous difficulty in making my mind up as to which good cause I should choose. It was really at the eleventh hour that I decided to work with Friends of the Earth and National Energy Action. In fact, I made my decision with only half an hour before the deadline for submission.

In an ideal world, I would have adopted a bill to deal with the emotional question of abortion. After all, I was widely known as a pro-life MP and the lobbying organisations had very much wanted me to try and introduce a measure which would reduce the term limit for which an abortion could be obtained. However, I knew only too well that the House was deeply divided on this issue and that through introducing such legislation, you could open a can of worms and make the time limit even more liberal. I must confess to feeling guilty at not going with a pro-life bill, but I wanted to make a real difference to people's lives by ensuring that I achieved something for them.

Anyhow, I was presented with potential legislation which would, according to them, end fuel poverty. A particularly harrowing incident in my constituency had been playing on my mind and in hindsight certainly played an important role in my decision. A Polish man was found dead in his property, hypothermia had been given as the cause of death. I could not believe that this had been allowed to happen in this day and age, and it motivated me to ensure that no one would ever again perceive themselves as not having enough money to heat their own home.

Now, let me say at the outset that I had absolutely no expertise in energy matters. Attempting to end fuel poverty was not an issue I had ever really been involved in and possibly a somewhat unlikely one for a Conservative to be associated with. Nevertheless, I was impressed by the presentation given to me by the two groups. They made persuasive cases for my supporting them and perhaps more importantly promised to give me all the secretarial support that I would need throughout the bill's journey.

Unfortunately, but inevitably, this bill would not pass without controversy. I had been aware of the dual opposition of two of my colleagues, the late Eric Forth and David Maclean, now Lord Blencartha, to PMBs and what they perceived to be unnecessary legislation per se. (This is an issue that still hits the headlines today, usually in the form of Sir Christopher Chope and Philip Davies. Christopher recently objected to the implementation of a PMB regarding the criminalisation of 'upskirting', an offence which had broad Government and public support. This provoked widespread uproar and once again shone the limelight on the practices of members who fundamentally disagree with the premise of PMBs). What I hadn't bargained for was the year long dispute I found myself involved in with these two colleagues. It really was a war of attrition, but one that I was determined to win. I managed to gather solid all-party support for the legislation and the second reading of the bill was very well attended. However, during the course of the debate, it was clear that Eric and David would be opposing the measure. There were no two better Parliamentary performers or tacticians than those two. These colleagues and others would use Erskine May to its full effect and frustrate bills which they didn't like from becoming law. They would religiously attend on Fridays, when many would be in their constituencies, to ensure that legislation, whatever its merits, was properly scrutinised. Their attitude could best be described as absolutist. I very much understand the way they operate and why shouldn't they use the rules to what they believe to good effect? However, I'm not sure the general public understood their reasons for delaying bills.

The idea of my bill was to alleviate fuel poverty by providing domestic insulation and other energy efficiency measures. The magnitude of this would be that, if passed, it would be the first time that the government would commit to ending fuel poverty. Like any other MP in my position would have done, I extoled the virtues of the legislation from various perspectives, writing the following piece for *The House* in January 1999 in a last-ditch attempt to persuade any MPs that had not yet made up their mind:

> Over the Christmas holiday, *The Independent* reported that the number of 'excess winter deaths' rose last year to 49,000, the highest in ten years. The major reason for this? In Britain some ten million people struggle to heat their homes each winter because the heat 'leaks' away through draughty windows and poor insulation. Evidence from overseas shows that this increase is preventable; winter in Norway and Sweden are much colder, yet their winter death rates has only increased by a third of that in Britain.
>
> The Warm Homes and Energy Conservation Bill requires the drawing up and implementation of a solution to this problem. This would end 'fuel poverty' by fitting decent insulation, and where necessary, an efficient heating system, to all affected homes. Such a scheme will have many benefits. Firstly, it would dramatically cut the illnesses and deaths caused by cold, damp homes – saving the NHS £1 billion a year. Secondly, the home improvements would generate almost 30,000 new jobs. Finally, the government research suggests it could save £1.25 billion a year in the management and maintenance of public sector housing. At this year's Labour conference, the Prime Minister himself admitted that the number of elderly people shivering in winter kept him awake at night. Other ministers have called fuel poverty an 'obscenity' and a 'preventable scourge'.

The idea of eliminating fuel poverty was incredibly ambitious. Quite how we achieved success I will never know, but by using parliamentary procedure to my own advantage, I managed to take my opponents by total surprise one Friday and amend the bill, inserting a different clause that sought to define fuel poverty. The trick of it all was to find the Parliamentary time and not allow the bill to be ruined by filibustering. While some people criticise the notion of this tactic, I see it quite differently.

We got the bill through Committee Stage, Report Stage and then finally there was just enough time for it to go through the House of Lords. It was an absolute delight when the Bill received Royal Assent. The campaign groups held a party on a boat on the River Thames. As I looked around the boat, it was a joy to see those who, in contrast to a Johnny-come-lately like myself, had worked for so long in order to make this legislation possible.

History will show that the bill which allowed people to have their lofts insulated and walls and doors draft proofed, was the most expensive (in terms of ultimate cost) PMB ever. And while the succeeding government tried to circumvent the definition of fuel poverty – something I am currently working on – I am really pleased that thousands of people have benefitted as a result of my simple measure. This proves that you don't have to be a Minister in order to get life changing legislation onto the statute book.

Ten-Minute Rule Bills

The Ten-Minute Rule Bill is another useful mechanism for back-benchers. I learnt quickly that Ten-Minute Rule procedures are a splendid way of highlighting a political issue which you want in the public domain. I have promoted countless numbers of them and successfully turned one into law.

I have a strong interest in animal welfare and hit upon the idea of promoting a law which would prevent horses, ponies and donkeys being cruelly tethered. I was inspired by a group of constituents living in Vange. They came to see me at a constituency surgery and were complaining about the animals being tethered and then rounded up at the dead of night, taken in lorries, killed and used for animal feed. As someone who has spent his whole parliamentary career campaigning for the better treatment of animals, this was something that I found particularly cruel and upsetting. I made it my mission to do something about it.

To secure a Ten-Minute Rule Bill now is a rather simple procedure. The whips hand them out willy-nilly to whoever they deem to be most deserving at the time, or indeed just to members who have asked for one, whatever its merits. The same cannot be said back in 1988. It is among the traditions we have lost which I regret the most. Gaining this slot in the House was extremely competitive and you would have to be the first in the queue in a room outside the relevant Clerk's office at 10am on a specific morning. This would involve sleeping overnight in the room opposite the Clerk's office.

I've lost count of the times I have slept in the same room as Ann Widdecombe and others. As unappealing as the practice may sound, the great sense of satisfaction achieved when you were given the opportunity to present the bill was well worth the effort. But that was only the beginning. As soon as you got your spot, the hard work really began.

I knew that for a motion of this type to be successful, I would need to gain a good amount of positive press coverage and get members talking about my campaign. For this reason, I couldn't think of a better way of launching it than arriving on College Green – a small public park adjacent to Parliament – on the back of a horse. The campaign took off instantly.

The essence of getting a Ten-Minute Rule Bill onto the statute book meant that you had to persuade every colleague to remain silent when your bill was moved, and if anyone objected that would be the end of that. The Minister whose department would in effect be dealing with the measure was Douglas Hogg. I asked if he would have any objections to which he said, 'Go and see my civil servant about the matter, if she has no objection nor do I.' So that is what I did. I gained the Department's support and when it came to the Friday and the Bill being moved, no one objected, in spite of the late Lord Tristan Garel-Jones doing his utmost to convince someone else to. Lord Houghton of Sowerby took the Bill through the Lords and so I put a Ten-Minute Rule Bill onto the statute book.

More recently, again through getting no one to object, I successfully piloted two further measures. A technical one dealing with the registration of driving instructors and another to stop security printing equipment being produced except under licence, which could potentially falsify such documents as passports, birth and death certificates and the like. While it is true that I have promoted many pieces of legislation which have not become law, many of them have been incorporated in various pieces of government legislation.

* * *

Whether I have mellowed or not is for others to decide, but I now absolutely understand what is meant by the expression 'politics is the art of the possible'. I am no longer idealistic about what one can achieve and take great pleasure from the fact that a number of my ideas have found their way onto the statute book. The irony is that it is rather easier to get bills which one feels strongly about into law as long as they're not too controversial. I say that because the House is no longer so well attended in terms of numbers who might speak against legislation and in any case, the skills needed to frustrate legislation no longer seem to be around.

In the same way that the Chamber has lost its ability to legislate and scrutinise, I have witnessed a slow and steady decline in the power of ministers and of the ability of Members of Parliament to achieve things and make a real difference on behalf of their constituents. When I first became an MP, it seemed to me that Parliament was sovereign in so many ways by which I mean, it made laws which affected the lives of all of us. Over the years however, much of its power has been taken away and in fact undermined by the endless quangos introduced by Tony Blair. These unaccountable and unelected organisations, often with highly paid senior staff, increasingly have become the real sources of power of so many things which affect our everyday lives. These bodies are more than happy for politicians to take the blame when things go wrong.

Ministers used to have much more power. So often now, you're waiting for a ministerial response which when you actually receive it amounts to a meaningless lot of waffle prepared by the Civil Service. This loss of authority can best be illustrated by my own experience as a constituency MP. During my 15 or so years as the MP for Basildon, I was able to make a huge difference to people's lives. For instance, I stopped three school closures, I prevented a silver birch forest being razed to the ground, I persuaded the then Housing Minister John Patten to repurchase 10,000 properties which had been sold to tenants under the Right-to-Buy, but had been found to be uninsurable because of clay heave. With two days to go before Basildon A&E was to be closed, on the advice of a completely misguided health bureaucrat, by having a robust exchange with County Councillor Joan Martin, Chairwoman of the local Health Authority, I was able to stop the closure. The list is seemingly endless.

Today, I would struggle to repeat any of those successes as a constituency MP. My influence is often at the margins, with real power lying with some unelected body. Underpinning all of this has been the inexorable rise in the power, and interference, of the European Union and its impact on Parliamentary legislation. I remain optimistic that as a result of the historic vote of our country to leave the EU, in time the sovereignty of Parliament will be restored and with it that of our Ministers and of Constituency Members of Parliament.

Moving out – The future of Parliament outside the Palace

The most recent change to the Houses of Parliament was the decision made by MPs to leave the building in 2025. As a member of the Administration Committee – responsible for the services provided for Members, Staff and Visitors, I was invited to climb the Elizabeth Tower and see for myself how urgently repair work was needed.

I had not before thought about how much of a nuisance it was to not have a lift. If anything ever needed repairing, it had to be winched up the side of the building. The wear and tear was so bad that every time it rained, water was pouring into the building through the clock faces. As a result of what we saw, the Elizabeth Tower had to be closed for remedial work. This has now happened and will last for four years while repairs are carried out and a lift installed. I am sure thousands of tourists will be disappointed in the interim period, but the repair work is vital.

Fierce arguments have surrounded the restoration and renewal of the Palace of Westminster. In recent times, numerous debates have been held in the House, against the background that serious and urgent works need to be carried out on the building, which has slowly become a fire risk.

When you have worked in the building for as long as I have, these things are not always as obvious as you would think. The main chambers are well maintained enough, but I do now understand the seriousness of the current situation. The root of the challenge has been dealing with the increased footfall coming through the doors. Due to lingering concerns about the political engagement of the population, and in an attempt to increase understanding about what MPs do, Parliament has been subject to a surge in outreach programmes. These range from increased availability of guided tours to partnerships with schools all across the UK. This is undoubtedly an integral part of the future of our democracy but has had negative consequences for the buildings themselves.

One bugbear of mine has always been the criticisms levelled at Parliamentarians for the long summer recess. In response to public outrage at their length, Parliament has started to sit for two weeks before the Party Conference season in September.

I regard Party Conference as a complete waste of time in any case. Very little is achieved in these two weeks in terms of business and it has a major effect on the ability of maintenance staff to refurbish and restore the Palace. From what I have seen with my own eyes, this has had a dangerous and debilitating effect on Parliament, contributing significantly to the accelerated timetable for a full decant.

The Palace is a symbol the world over, and the envy of most other countries, but behind the facade, there is severe decay. The sewers are no longer functional, and you only have to visit the cellars to realise the very real fire risk from the miles of electrical cabling. Various parts of the roof are leaking, stone masonry needs restoring, and so do many of the stained glass windows, not to mention the asbestos. So, I accept without reservation the need for action. What I remain unconvinced by is the proposition that the elected House should move out of the building.

When Parliament debated and voted on the issues, we were faced with the choice of a part decant or a full decant of the building. Robust arguments were deployed either way with the latter option prevailing. I hope I am wrong, but I think this decision is a great mistake.

My fears are as follows: I believe that Parliament may never return, in spite of all the guarantees given, because we know that one Parliament does not bind the next. I believe this primarily because with every new intake, the building is seen in a different light.

Some would prefer a more modern building and one not necessarily in London. Some of them feel our traditions are an anachronism, for instance why go through lobbies to vote when one could easily press a button. Change in this sense has already occurred with the advent of proxy voting.

Others believe the chamber itself to be outdated, perhaps even too confrontational. They would prefer a hemisphere type structure with members having a dedicated seat and making their speeches from rostrums not benches. None of these people suggest the building being razed to the ground (not yet at least) but they much prefer the idea of it being turned into a full-time tourist attraction.

I reject these proposals as being a denial of our history and the way our democracy has evolved. The traditions of the House and British politics itself, are embedded in the very fabric of the building.

The magnificence of Westminster Hall conjures up the image of Henry VIII running the country, the Gunpowder Plot – which was hatched in the bowels of the building – and Guy Fawkes, the trial of Charles I, Thomas More's condemnation to death and Winston Churchill laying in state.

The floor of the Commons has heard so many historic moments: Cromwell's dissolution of the Rump Parliament, William Wilberforce's fight for the abolition of slavery, Stanley Baldwin's stance on the abdication and Sir Geoffrey Howe's use of a cricket bat to stump Margaret Thatcher.

Moving to the other end of the building, the House of Lords is simply spectacular. The grandiosity of the throne, the exquisite Royal Gallery, depicting the famous triumphs of Trafalgar and Waterloo and the symbolism behind the robing room, reserved for the Queen herself.

The essence of what I am arguing is that no other Parliament has the privilege of experiencing these unique, somewhat eccentric, but most importantly constructive and productive methods of working, which have evolved over centuries. The use of the Palace of Westminster as the home of our politicians is far more important than any figures or reports, and far more emotive than any Committee can countenance for. It touches upon the very heart of our heritage, of our democratic culture, what it means to be British. It is the gatekeeper of British liberty, the creator of all our laws and has withstood a civil war, two world wars and ten years of a Tony Blair led government.

Joking aside, I see no better place to hold members to account than under the watchful eye of those who came before us. Let us learn from our past rather than run from it.

And this leads me to the last point I want to highlight. Brexit. Do we wish to spend our first years as an independent United Kingdom based in the Department of Health? In a world where soft power is significant, would we rather welcome foreign dignitaries to Richmond House or Westminster Hall? We must project an image of strength and the Palace of Westminster is the best place to do that from.

So while I am sad about the decision to leave, and sceptical regarding the long-term intentions of MPs, I am sure that rational argument will hold out in the end despite the initial decision which I am not convinced has been fully thought through at all.

PART 2

Elections

NO MATTER WHAT I think of the current state of the Houses of Parliament, it would be impossible for me to influence the home of our democracy without possessing the ability to win an election.

I wouldn't pretend for one moment to have all the answers about winning an election. After all, events, often way beyond one's immediate control, ultimately have the most significant impact on any campaign. However, I was elected in Basildon in 1983, 1987 and 1992, at all times the odds were firmly stacked against me. I have represented Southend West since 1997. As a result, I have won ten general election campaigns and lost just the one, when I stood for election in Newham North West in 1979 – the area that returned the first ever Labour Member of Parliament James Keir Hardie.

I have always worked on the maxim that in an election campaign, leadership must always come from the candidate. If he or she works hard, the others will follow. If the candidate is innovative and inventive, others will respond accordingly, and the campaign will invariably create momentum (as unfortunate a word as that may be in the current climate). So, I very much believe that all those working around the candidate feed off their energy, their drive and their determination. You must lead from the front and take others with you because, believe you me, it is not always the most rewarding hobby to go canvassing and knocking up on behalf of a politician. If you suspect the campaign is going against you, you must never ever let it show – positive, positive, positive!

I have received so much advice from predecessors, colleagues and constituents alike, but three pieces in particular
have moulded my interaction with voters. I have no doubt that
they play an important role in my success on election day. Jack
Aspinwall, Member of Parliament for Wansdyke and Sir Rhodes
Boyson, Member for Brent North are both now deceased. The
former, besides being an unlimited fund of jokes, advised me to
send an 18th birthday card to everyone celebrating their special
day in the constituency. The latter took me to one side and said,
'David, whenever you go to a social event, lunch or dinner, make
sure you meet everyone.' So, I always go around tables during
the various speeches and between courses. The final wise words
that I took particular note of were from Janet, now Baroness,
Fookes. She recommended that I have a Christmas card list.
I subsequently send a card to everyone who writes to thank me
for something I might have done for them throughout the year.
These three pieces of advice are admittedly very difficult to put
into practice when seeking election for the first time. However,
when seeking re-election, these are important tasks that contribute to flourishing personal relationships between yourself and
your constituents in that five-year interlude. They help you keep
in touch, understand what people need and form human relationships in the constituency to help fight against the perception
that some Members use the Westminster bubble to hide away
from the local issues of the day.

They also tie in with what I believe to be the most fundamental part of any campaign, personal contact. I fully accept
that campaigning has taken a turn for the worse and has, in the
main, switched to social media. Long gone are the days when
MPS held umpteen public meetings in various venues dotted
around the constituency. However, there is no substitute for
looking an individual in the eye, eliciting from them how they
intend to vote and then ensuring that if they are a supporter,
they do vote on the day. For similar reasons, you must be able
to have a strong set of opinions that you are happy to justify

when challenged. These beliefs may not be the most popular, but I do think that the general public respond better to politicians who have convictions. A number of commentators have remarked on some Members of the new intake having had their views anaesthetised and appear passionless – I think that's a bit hard. Personally, I always begin my campaigns with an open-air rally. Don't get me wrong, hardly any members of the public turn up, but I can rely on my doughty supporters. It gives me the opportunity to air my views, get my message across and enthuse others, while not giving my political opponent the platform they would profit from in a debating scenario.

We have certainly had to adapt. The tools and rules of electioneering have changed. Telemarketing is so much more sophisticated. Big data (as people are finding out to their dismay) leads the way. Targeted letters and literature can be sent to various groups of constituents, depending on a number of factors. For example, senior citizens may receive a leaflet about the health service and pensions and young people may hear about education and job growth, etc... When I first campaigned for national office, these tools really were unimaginable. The iconic posters of the Thatcher years ruled supreme. No one who was around at the time will forget the image of queues of unemployed people above the slogan 'Labour isn't working'. It was a lot of fun persuading constituents to put these up in windows and at prominent local locations. Nowadays though, they are hardly worth the effort. Other than helping morale amongst your supporters, they don't sway the electorate. I hardly think the modern version of this, the deployment of vans and lorries with advertising boards on the sides of them, makes one iota of difference either. Other than that, it is no news to anyone that party-political broadcasts are now just another opportunity to put on a cup of tea, and most people wouldn't even recognise many high-profile politicians if they came to visit the constituency.

So, all in all, I am not sure there is anything special that establishes electoral success, but it is perhaps more of a combination of important factors. A strong national leader is certainly becoming more important. While we are not quite at the Presidential stage, an uncharismatic, ineffective and incompetent leader is simply not going to win an election.

But what I can say is that I have won ten of them. In all ten I have interacted with as many people as possible, I have had a core set of beliefs and I have stuck to what I know best (rallies, canvassing and the song). Stick to your guns, be true to yourself and listen to your electorate.

One final piece of 'wisdom' that it would be a shame not to impart regards canvassing. The best canvassing story I ever heard was shared with me by my good friend Lord Stockton, Harold Macmillan's grandson. It went: 'I was canvassing when someone invited me into their house. The gentleman said, "Would you like to see my grandmother?" To my surprise, I was taken upstairs to a room with drawn curtains and there lay said grandmother, stiff as a board in a coffin. The gentleman then proceeded to tell me "She's been a lifelong socialist and I have been given her postal vote which I marked your name on, so you even have a vote from beyond the grave!"' On a more personal note, my own canvassing stories have revolved around gaining as much attention as humanly possible. Back in my Newham days, I turned up to the council offices, which had been built like pyramids, with a crowd of supporters dressed in Egyptian clothing – someone as Cleopatra and a camel to boot. Just a week before the 1979 election, I first attached a loudspeaker to the car and blared out the tune 'Maggie May'. This was followed rather grandly by me in a chariot and Miss Bluebell on a float. I will never forget the expression on East Enders' faces when I drove past asking for their vote! So, I certainly have been prepared to put myself out there, kick up a fuss and get people talking about my election campaigns and have learnt to always expect the unexpected when knocking on voters' doors.

At this stage, I thought it may be useful to recount three of the most exciting elections I have been a part of since my involvement in mainstream politics.

Basildon, 1992 – Against all odds

When I am lowered into my grave, because I intend to be buried and not cremated, I will probably only be remembered, if indeed I am, for the 1992 election campaign. Any number of people only discovered me at that election. That was entirely because of the publicity that I attracted.

The truth however is that my greatest parliamentary election took place some nine years earlier. In 1983, standing on a podium in a building which had once been a zoo, I never expected to win Basildon – but I did. My childhood dream came true. I was the first MP to ever be elected with no county or district Councillors of his own party in the constituency. In the local elections four weeks previously, the Conservatives had only attracted 28 per cent of the votes. I had pulled off the most unlikely victory that summer, but nine years later, the big question was whether I could do it again.

Much had happened in the interim period. Margaret had been brought down in a cruel and cowardly manner. John Major had taken over as leader. The contrast in styles could not have been more obvious. We turned away from a radical and towards a consolidator, having brutally cast aside the very woman who had successfully fought three general elections and transformed the party's fortunes.

As a result, I entered the 1992 campaign feeling rather sheepish about my chances. By that time, I had established myself as Mr Basildon and could point to any number of tangible achievements. However, my party was seen as divided and that is not something that the electorate admire. Furthermore, we had been in power since 1979 and some pundits were suggesting that the Government had run out of steam. I was sitting in my office and the telephone rang...

It was David Dimbleby. He wanted to be the first to interview me on the night of the election. Another call followed from the BBC's Anna Ford asking the same question. I was taken aback by these enquiries. Why was I, hardly a national figure of importance (just remember how no one had been there in 1983), suddenly becoming the focus of the media's attention?

I soon found out that the Labour council had decided to employ at least 100 Barclays' bank tellers to conduct the count. They had told the media that they should come to Basildon as the count would be concluded within an hour. This would ensure that they would capture the first Conservative election failure of the evening and that my humiliation would be enjoyed by a rather large audience. My demise was being plotted and the organisers hadn't even had the courtesy to invite me onto the Planning Committee. Unfortunately, the local Labour Party were not the only ones enjoying the mouth-watering prospect of my loss. Every time I addressed the House in the lead up to 1992, my colleagues on the opposite benches would wave and shout 'Goodbye'. Upon reflection, a little bit of humility goes a long way in politics. This is a lesson I had learnt much earlier in my career, and one that those smug plotters would soon learn themselves.

By that time, I was a very experienced and battle-hardened campaigner. While I needed an agent for technical reasons, I felt more than capable of taking the lead myself. As it turned out I could not have wished for a finer, more hard-working or dedicated agent than Barbara Allen. I adored her, and I think the feeling was mutual. Ironically, she lived in Prittlewell (in my soon to be constituency of Southend West) and had previously masterminded many a campaign for the MP for Castle Point, the late and great former Father of the House, Sir Bernard Braine. I really do have so much to thank her for.

I mentioned my constituency almost every time I stood up to ask a question or to make a speech and truly was Mr Basildon. So, unlike in 1983 and 1987 and thanks to two terms in office, I had Ministers queuing up to come and support me in the campaign. Chris Patten was Party Chairman and I had fully expected that he would arrange for the then Prime Minister John Major to visit the constituency. I was also very excited to learn that Margaret intended to come and support me.

My supporters were absolutely ecstatic at the thought of a visit from the Lady in Blue.

My tactics for engineering a successful election campaign have never wavered. The tried and tested formula includes lots of razzmatazz, plenty of posters, milking the incumbency factor for all it's worth and, most importantly, knocking on as many doors as possible. You need to meet every constituent you can and record whether they will vote for you or not. If the answer is affirmative, you record it and make sure you get them out on the day. Moreover, the public need to see and hear you, so I was constantly out and about. I could always be seen standing on a small step ladder shouting through a loudspeaker about why constituents should vote for me. I believe this strategy demonstrates elements of pride and bravery which, by and large, is much appreciated.

Two key tools were prominent in my campaign. Firstly, there was my motorhome, which doubled up as a mobile surgery. This was clad with Amess paraphernalia, leaving people in no doubt as to who I was. Second was what I believe to be the killer punch. It was my signature campaign tune, first recorded in 1983 and used in every subsequent election to date. It goes something along the lines of:

> Vote, Vote, Vote for David Amess, David is the man for you.
> If you want to be true blue, and to air your points of view,
> Then David Amess is the only man for you.
> David Amess is the only man for you.

During the three-week campaign, the tune became so famous that locals would actually start singing it aloud when the motor home drove past. Despite *The Times'* assertion that my 'campaigning was in the manner of an ice cream vendor', I think it worked wonderfully in sending my message out across the town.

The tune was a particular hit with Douglas Hurd when he visited. Other prominent guests included Norman Tebbit, Baroness Blatch, Baroness Young and the boxer Sir Henry Cooper, who galvanised the locals at Pitsea market. His visit prompted a plethora of boxing pun related headlines the following day – my personal favourite being 'Enry Delivers Knockout Blow'. Nearly all the cabinet came to support me at one time or another.

Supporters tend to get very excited when the words 'media coverage' are mentioned. In reality, the media can often be a double-edged sword. You can invariably spend a lot of time preparing for an interview which boils down to perhaps a minute or a minute and a half of actual airtime. In 1992, I not only had local media following me around, but national and international news outlets too. While it might be fascinating to give interviews to *Gujarati News* or the *Honolulu Advertiser*, it does you absolutely no good in terms of securing a parliamentary majority. That is down to straightforward hard work and commitment.

I got on the phone to Jeffrey Archer to ask him when John Major would be visiting – a great opportunity for some excellent coverage. He said, 'David, I don't think he will.' We had always assumed that he would make his last campaign visit to Basildon, particularly as it was so near to Westminster. I was incredibly disappointed and couldn't quite decide whether it was because his team thought we would lose or that he didn't think we needed his support as they were so certain of our victory. Whatever way it was I did not relish breaking it to my team.

My agent was as magnificent as ever. There she was, sat in our campaign headquarters at 38 Rectory Road, papers strewn everywhere; to some it might have seemed chaos, but she knew where everything was. With a cigarette in her mouth, she shrugged her shoulders and said, 'Don't worry David, you will win in spite of it.' I hoped she was right. Although my supporters were naturally disappointed and indeed mildly angry that the PM wasn't visiting, we still had one trump card up our sleeve, the visit of former PM, Margaret Thatcher. So, when the great day came there was enormous excitement.

She arrived in typically grand style. Together we drove around Basildon in her blue Jaguar Daimler, waving to the crowds that had gathered. We visited Marconi's, one of the town's many defence companies, where some of my relatives worked. My own family were waiting on the doorstep clutching roses to present to the great lady. This was one of the places that the council had previously tried to discredit by claiming that Basildon was a 'Nuclear Free Zone', going so far as to put signs on the approaching roads to reinforce the message. We swept past the signs which much amused her.

There were plans for Margaret to address a rally in a function suite above the Bullseye. As ever, she received a rousing reception from the assembled supporters and made a stirring speech in which she told everyone how marvellous I was. I'm not sure my wife agreed, but the crowd loved it all the same. I must confess to thinking, if only she was still Prime Minister. I was then allowed to travel with her alone when she was driven out of the town and I picked up my car. I remember asking her how she thought the election would go, to which she responded with a hand gesture indicating that it was on a knife edge. I was elated at her visit, as indeed was everyone else. I would never have won my seat in the first place without her leadership and now she had come to save me.

Not only did I have a brilliant agent, but I also had a most effective campaign manager who I dubbed 'Little Hitler' (now known as The Rt Hon Mark Francois MP). Not, I might add, in terms of his views, but because he was short of stature and very, very bossy. This was an enormous advantage in terms of running such a high-profile campaign. So, while I was being stalked, literally, from door to door by the media, he ensured that our growing list of supporters kept up the momentum in terms of canvassing.

There were a number of journalists covering the election campaign who clearly wanted to follow an MP who was about to lose their seat. *The Guardian* decided to run a daily piece on Basildon, which was nothing more than a mickey take of the townspeople by a middle-class newspaper looking down its nose at us. One particular journalist even wrote to me after the election saying, 'I am sorry for how I was during the campaign, I gave you such a hard time and I got the result completely wrong, you were deservedly re-elected'. I was touched by his apology.

The local newspaper, the *Evening Echo*, appeared not to be too keen on me. I could never understand why, but I speculated that they had never forgiven me for winning the seat in 1983 when they had hoped Buster Mottram would be selected as the candidate. So the local newspaper gave great prominence to the Labour candidate. On this occasion it was a particularly ghastly man and leader of the Labour council, John Potter. They even brought out a local opinion poll the night before election day suggesting that I would lose. This of course did not help morale, but I have always followed the maxim that the only poll that counts is the actual poll itself – something that rang very true in 2017.

At least we had *The Sun* onside, who ran the famous headline: 'If Kinnock wins today will the last person to leave Britain please turn out the lights'. This paper was also the first to catch on to Simon Heffer's notion of the 'Essex Man'; the displaced, working-class Londoners that had settled in Basildon, yet who held strong middle-class aspirations. Despite this chink of light, the media campaign run against me was in general negative and personal. This is best exemplified by the leaflet produced by Labour suggesting that I had voted in favour of fox hunting, which given my well-known love of animals was quite absurd.

I really was very angry with this Labour ploy. What was unforgivable is that the then County Councillor who later became the MP for part of my old constituency was the Secretary for the Campaign Against Cruel Sports and had been writing to me specifically on the issue of fox hunting. Disgraceful. Nowadays the expression 'fake news' has become commonplace. I'm not sure I used to think of telling a pack of lies as fake news, but that is what it amounted to. My election agent threatened legal action – Labour backed down and issued a grovelling apology and made a donation to an animal rights charity. I lost count of the battles I had in correcting misreporting about myself. In that sense not much has changed, but modern technology means it is now far more difficult to keep up with.

John Major had only been the Prime Minister for two years and in that short space of time had shown himself to be an honest and straightforward man, which were two qualities admired by the public. Nonetheless, the polls indicated that he would lose narrowly. His Labour opponent, Neil Kinnock, was nicknamed the Welsh Windbag. He had done a valiant job in taming the extreme left of his party. He, however, had a reputation of using a dozen words when one would do, and made the historic mistake of appearing at a rally in Sheffield in which he strode onto the stage like a drunken pop star, drowning in the elixir of hysteria, giving the impression to the British people that the election had already been won. Adoring activists shouted his name and there were orchestras, celebrity endorsements and even an arrival by helicopter for the headline act himself. The arrogance of it all would rebound badly in the end.

On 8 April 1992, the day before the biggest fight of my political career, bets were being taken at William Hill – most of these were predicting my demise. Labour MPs were making predictions: 'The one thing we can be pretty sure of is that this election has been lost by Mr Major and the Tories. That means Neil Kinnock in Downing Street' claimed Bryan Gould.

Despite the intense scrutiny and speculation, I embarked upon my usual election day activities. I got up early in the morning and cast my vote alongside my wife Julia. I visited every polling station and all our committee rooms thanking those in attendance. I always visit every polling station, not just because it gives me something to do but I think it is right that you should be seen to show an interest in the physical operation that happens when a vote takes place, and also to get a feel of the turnout. In spite of the inevitable Conservative defeat that most major outlets were reporting, Basildon's Conservative Association stayed positive. As the day wore on, a last minute 'knocking up' campaign ensued. Given the advice that there would be an early declaration of the result at my count, I had to get there more or less right at the beginning. As a result, our efforts to drum up last minute support to get people to the polling stations were particularly frantic.

When the time finally came and we entered the hall, the atmosphere was electric. There were throngs of local, national and international media, and people worked to the low buzz of the anticipatory, excited chatter. Events began to unfold so quickly that I could hardly take them in and before I knew it, the time for the results had arrived. Our Labour opponent had his victory speech ready and the Chairman of the local council, Dave Marks, had his script prepared. When a count is being conducted in just an hour, it is difficult to get a sense of how the votes were shaping up, but it was clear that there had been a huge turnout, 79.8 per cent in the end, and I could gauge that we were doing well.

Julia noticed some commotion amongst my supporters. They were all congratulating one another. As the Returning Officer called us to the stage, she told me that judging by the reaction of my group, I had won. I refused to believe her, thinking instead that a recount had been ordered. Yet at that moment, I was able to glimpse what was written on the Returning Officer's paper. What I saw made my heart stop and confirmed what I had refused to believe. Written in plain black and white was the news that nobody outside of my circles had expected: I would be returning to Westminster as MP for Basildon for the third time. As I stepped onto the stage, I had to keep a straight, expressionless face as the result was announced. Sarah Hogg and Jonathan Hill describe John Major's reaction to the Basildon declaration in their book *Too Close to Call*:

The candidates were lined up on the platform waiting for the result to be declared. All eyes were on their faces, looking for clues. The Conservative candidate, David Amess, looked gloomy, his wife shattered.

'Look at her face', Sarah said. 'He's lost.'

'Look at his face', the PM said. 'He's won'. The PM recognised the signs of a successful candidate struggling to keep his face set and expression grave. Then the result. The PM leapt to his feet.

'That's it. We've done it. We've won the election.' He went through to the other room where the rest of his family were sitting. He punched his fist triumphantly into the palm of his hand.

The look of horror and shock on my opponents' faces was an absolute delight to behold. I will always remember the smiles of the policemen in the room. I was swept on to the stage and couldn't help noticing a number of people smiling with delight. Councillor Marks, with a face like thunder and his hands trembling declared, 'David Amess has been duly elected as the MP for Basildon.' The crowds and audience went wild.

At this point, I am sure that the local Labour Party were much regretting their decision to put me in the spotlight. I took the microphone, which was being filmed by all national and international outlets and spoke the following words from my heart.

> Rejoice, rejoice, rejoice; let this message go out across the country. John Major has been re-elected as Prime Minister of this country and in four weeks' time I would like local residents to go and vote this rotten Labour council out of office.

That is indeed what happened; four weeks later every seat was won by the Conservative Party with huge swings and a Conservative council came into being.

I have fond memories of that celebration, one of which was purchasing wire clippers and cutting down one of the nuclear free signs with my supporters which I saved as a trophy.

Anna Ford did indeed conduct the first interview. The best that I can say is that she was adept at changing the script that had clearly been written for the first defeated Conservative candidate. The rest of that evening was a blur as Julia and I triumphantly went to a tremendous celebration at the Bullseye. We went on to Raquel's discotheque to dance the night away to a live performance of Rose Royce singing 'Car Wash'. *The Sun* came out the next day with the headline 'It was The Sun Wot Won it'. Well, for me it was Maggie and as she left the country for a short trip, she gave a touching interview saying how pleased she was by my victory.

For the next few days, wherever I went people came up to me to shake my hand and congratulate me. The messages I got as a result of my international media coverage meant people were so confused that they thought it was me alone who had won the election. I enjoyed my couple of minutes of fame and even if that is all I am remembered for when I die, it was worth it just to see the look on the faces of my defeated opponents.

Southend West, 1997 – The landslide

The 1997 election could not have been more different to 1992. Eighteen years of a Conservative Government had taken its toll on the patience of the British people. John Major's cabinet was seen to be at loggerheads over the European Union, and everyone knows that divided governments do not win elections. Adding fuel to the flames, the party had been hit by a number of 'scandals', invariably of a sexual nature. We had become known as the sleazy Government. On the back of these, it was not difficult for the press to come after us.

John was accused of dissolving Parliament early to prevent the publication of Sir Gordon Downey's report into the Cash for Questions Affair from affecting the election result.

This was utter rubbish, but nonetheless the reporting gave the impression that the PM was trying to protect Neil Hamilton. Hamilton's fierce denial of the allegations only attracted further negative publicity, especially when Labour and the Lib Dems chose not to oppose him in Tatton and persuaded Martin Bell, a BBC journalist and war correspondent, to stand as an independent on an anti-corruption ticket. Piers Merchant, the former MP for Beckenham, was found to be having an affair with a 17-year-old Soho nightclub hostess. Allan Stewart, the former MP for Eastwood, and Sir Michael Hirst, the former MP for Strathkelvin and Bearsden, both resigned over revelations about their private lives.

Legislatively, the Government was seen as running out of steam. Underlying all that, however, was the arrival of a new Labour leader. Tony Blair, nicknamed by some as Bambi, had replaced Neil Kinnock. He was portrayed as the new moderate face of socialism and indeed reinvented the Labour Party to such an extent that the party was now called New Labour. They even had the gall to steal the red rose as the party logo.

I was no longer the candidate to be re-elected for Basildon, but was the prospective parliamentary Candidate for Southend West. Boundary changes had meant that my former constituency was being split into two. One part joined Thurrock and the other part joined Billericay, so I had to face the dilemma of whether I should secure and defend either new seat or look for somewhere else. After much agonising with my family, I decided the latter.

My Labour opponents made hay with my decision, not for a moment being worried about the facts, which were that very significant boundary changes had come into effect. They left me with two options if I wanted to continue to represent my beloved Basildonians. My first was to contest against Teresa Gorman. The rules allowed Members who had a certain proportion of their old seats in a newly created patch to apply for consideration. The second was to fight a seat that was part Basildon, part Thurrock.

I decided that neither appealed to me. I did not relish going head-to-head against my parliamentary neighbour and friend Teresa. The media would love it, but I thought that it would attract controversy and unwelcome publicity. In any case, given that the new seat comprised more of her old constituency than mine, I thought she would be likely to be selected. The second seat had crazy boundaries. If elected, I would be dealing not only with Essex County Council but with Thurrock Unitary Council. It seemed incredibly ill-conceived to me.

I notified Central Office that I was looking for another seat, and to my surprise was called to interview for three seats which were all, at that point, staunchly Conservative: Southend West, South Cambridgeshire and Mid-Sussex. The selections for Southend West and Mid-Sussex took place over the same weekend – not an ideal situation. I went along to Mid-Sussex fully realising that there was no way I was going to be chosen instead of Nicholas Soames and that turned out to be true.

The local media did their best to broadcast the fact that I had been rejected and that Southend West was my second choice. Unbeknown to me, there was a real split within the local Conservative Association regarding the merits of my candidacy. The general attitude seemed to be along the lines of, we don't want that chap from Basildon! When my wife and I drove up to Belfairs School, where the selection was being held, we were flabbergasted to find cars queuing up to get in and someone directing the traffic. It was obvious that the forces for and against had been mobilised.

The choice had been whittled down to Eleanor Laing and me. From the moment my speech ended the hostile questioning started, so when the ballot took place and I joined Eleanor in the green room, I congratulated her on her victory. I was staggered when Vera Playle, the wife of the Chairman of the Association, summoned me back into the room as the victor. Unbeknown to me, Ron and Vera had been against my selection, but I couldn't have wished for two more staunch supporters once the decision was made.

Back in the House of Commons, every time I was called to speak, various Labour Members began to cluck as I stood accused of going on the chicken run. So, in 1992 it was waving and 1997 clucking, what a unique challenge to face in the workplace! I had been drawn to ask a question to the Prime Minister and decided to tackle the situation head (beak) on. I was ready when my name was called so I took a plastic bag from my pocket containing chicken corn. I held it up and pretended to scatter it across the Chamber as if feeding the chickens. It did the trick and I was never again subjected to clucking noises.

I was of the view that the Conservative Party was in dire peril of not only losing the election but losing a considerable number of seats. Looking back on it, I suppose that my years fighting for a highly marginal seat always made me fear the worst come election time. There is no question that many of my colleagues who lost their seats, many of whom had previously had large majorities, did not prepare themselves for the worst. There was a disturbing difference between the two major competitors. Labour had reinvented itself. The party had become moderate, full of fresh ideas, miles away from the old ideologies of socialism and had completely rebranded. They attracted vast numbers of 'Bright Young Things' and showed off their new headquarters at Millbank Tower.

In contrast, the Conservatives were perceived to be tired, old-fashioned and to have run out of ideas. While its leader, John Major, was still popular, and a thoroughly decent man, the brand had become toxic. It was associated with privilege and sleaze and was seen as being out of touch with the hopes and aspirations of many people. Tony Blair, and his partner in crime Gordon Brown, had very carefully gone out of their way not to attack Margaret Thatcher – in fact they let it be known that they admired so many of her qualities. The media had also turned. Not long ago so supportive of the Conservative Party, they were now excited by the prospect of change. It was no longer 'will the last one left turn out the lights' but more 'give change a chance' emblazoned across the front page of *The Sun*.

Major used the tried and tested advertising agency Saatchi & Saatchi, but the political landscape had changed, and fear of a socialist government no longer felt so real. A dour Gordon Brown came across as frugal and trustworthy rather than the unhinged revolutionary of old. It is somewhat ironic when you look at the last leadership of the Labour Party. You have Jeremy Corbyn, a completely unreformed socialist, holding on to his idealistic principles. The real brain behind the operation was probably Jon Lansman of Momentum and in parliamentary terms, John McDonnell. Yes, he's a sharp dresser but be in no doubt at all, he is serious about a 'revolution'.

The irony of course was that the Government had been in very choppy waters economically when we decided to enter the Exchange Rate Mechanism, something that Margaret had always been emphatically opposed to. The experiment was a calamitous failure and had a severe impact on inflation, interest rates and, perhaps most importantly of all, the burden of public debt. Managing the economy well had always been a great hand to play, but we had undermined our own strength. It was most bizarre to see the Labour Party campaign based on fiscal competence and being 'tough on crime, tough on the causes of crime'. Two extraordinary reversals that stole the middle ground from under our feet.

On a more local level, the Labour campaign was irking me further and further. I make no apologies for my association with raising the profile of Basildon. In a curious way the opposition assisted me in doing so, particularly in 1992. However, what was particularly galling and undoubtedly disingenuous, was my opponents and the media pretending that the Basildon constituency had not changed. The narrative was that I had run away from the seat expecting to lose and for the Government to be defeated. My decision was being used relentlessly by the Labour Party for political capital, based on an absolute pack of lies. Ironically, the Labour candidate for one Basildon seat was living in Southend West but did not choose to fight the election there. She was a County Councillor in an area which included Billericay but didn't choose to fight the seat there either. No, instead of all that, she wanted to fight a seat where she thought she had the best chance of winning. There is nothing wrong with that – it is just a case of being pragmatic. But the reality of my own circumstances was never explained truthfully and worse, used against me hypocritically.

Labour decided that they would launch their campaign by Tony Bair arriving in a cavalcade at Vange Working Men's Club, covered live on TV. The very idea that Tony Blair, given his background had anything in common with a Working Man's Club was truly laughable, yet the media bought into the lie. The TV showed Blair and the Labour candidate for one of the two Basildon constituencies glad-handing members of the Club. As the campaign progressed it became obvious that New Labour were extremely adept at projecting false messages and that was very much the case with their visit to the Basildon Club. They found people who would say live on camera that they had been Conservative but would not be supporting the party anymore.

Despite my frustrations, I had other things to worry about, namely retaining the Southend West constituency for the Conservative Party, something that had always been seen as a foregone conclusion. Southend West was regarded as a rotten borough, having been represented by the Guinness family for over 100 years starting with the Earl of Iveagh. The list of MPs to follow him is not long – his wife Lady Iveagh, the celebrated diary columnist Henry 'Chips' Channon and finally his son Paul Channon, who had been the Member for some 38 years.

There was some irony in having chosen someone like myself. Four generations of the Guinness family had represented the town and now the baton had been passed to me, not of blue blood and with no dynastic ambitions. However, many members of the Association had decided that in these tough political times a street fighter was needed, and in that respect, I fitted the bill. The members of the Southend West Association found my style of campaigning very different to that of my predecessor.

While the impression was given that as the seat had always been Conservative and I could take a fairly relaxed approach to campaigning, I decided that I would not follow suit. I felt strongly that because of the perceived, and what turned out to be real, unpopularity of my party even a so-called safe seat like Southend West had to be fought as if it was a key marginal. When I began knocking on doors, I soon found out that my judgement had been spot on.

I had been used to relatively straightforward engagement with the electorate in Basildon. If I knocked on a Labour door, they were straightforward in telling me so. Sometimes this message was mixed with a few expletives, but I knew where I stood with people. The battleground was occupied by the Labour and Conservative Parties. In simplistic terms, capitalism versus socialism, others barely got a look in. How very different it was in Southend West. I found my main opponents to be the Liberals. I had often heard colleagues discuss how they preferred a battle with Labour rather than the Liberals and now I understood why.

They were poisonous beyond belief. Someone said to me that their parliamentary candidate must have woken up in the morning, put on her witch's gown and grabbed her broomstick as she went around the constituency spreading lies about me. My supporters believed that she had no regard for the truth, lie after lie after lie. It certainly was the case that if you tell enough untruths regularly, they begin to stick – a character assassination was playing out before my own eyes.

I lost count of the times I was greeted on the doorstop by 'not you, we don't want someone from Basildon. What do you know about the area? We want a local candidate.' So I had my battles, which I had not been prepared for, to secure the selection as a Conservative candidate in the first place and now as a result of my reception on the doorstep I was beginning to regret that I had ever set foot in the place!

It was the worst kind of elitism I have ever encountered. Anyone would think that Basildon was another country, when in reality it was just a short drive away. There was undoubtedly a snobbish element to the abuse I received. Some residents clearly looked down their nose at the town of Basildon, regarding it as full of rather uncouth, rough East End people. I will never forget when the Chairman of Southend Rail Commuters Group visited one of my surgeries held at the Triangle in Langdon Hills. He had the audacity to lobby me and argue that certain trains travelling from Thorpe Bay to Southend should not stop at Basildon. I couldn't quite work out whether it was because he didn't want 'common people' mixing with commuters from Thorpe Bay or if it was that he didn't want trains delayed in picking travellers up from Basildon, or a combination of both. Whatever his reasons were, it was a bloody cheek; so I had encountered this mindset before even setting foot in my new patch.

In reality, the residents did not understand the surrounding towns and countryside. Not everyone lives in tiny little boxes. I had 28 farms in Basildon but not one in Southend West. We had a country park with the highest point in Essex, Westley Heights. We even had thatched cottages in Dry Street. During my time as MP, not one person was murdered, whereas in Southend we are well into double figures, albeit often caused by visitors from London. The list of misconceptions was endless, and I wasn't having any of it. After all, it had been my very happy home where my five children were born and educated.

On a national level, the signs were not positive. While by-elections do not always accurately signal the outcome of general elections, the ones leading up to a general election are a good indication of the direction of travel. In that regard they made grim reading for us. Fortunately for me, the Liberals were my main challengers. They were not polling particularly well in the country as a whole, but their technique to concentrate on particular constituencies – which they did in Colchester, Chelmsford and Southend – meant their stretched resources could make a real impact.

On the doorstep, the responses I received were light years away from that which my predecessor Paul Channon had experienced. He was unfairly criticised for being wealthy, detached, not living in the constituency and not having a high-profile locally. These charges, heavily worked up by the Liberal Party, were grossly unfair. Paul was an honourable man, who undoubtedly did his very best to work on behalf of his constituents and assist them with their various problems. However, for many years his time was taken up with Ministerial duties. When you are a Secretary of State your time is spent attending to things all over the country and abroad.

Everywhere you looked in the constituency, you saw Liberal posters and Liberal boards – we were swamped. I was mentally preparing myself for the unthinkable – defeat in the Southend West constituency after more than 100 years of Conservative rule. I knew the fight would be tough and regardless of the national decision I fully expected to be blamed for the local defeat on the basis that I had come from Basildon.

Come election day, I did my usual tour visiting every polling station. Being my first time in Southend West, I did not have much to compare with, but the turnout certainly wasn't on a par with 1992. I recall asking myself whether this meant that traditional Conservative supporters could not bring themselves to vote for me or whether the anti-Conservative vote had not been mobilised that effectively.

When the polling stations closed, I returned home to wait for a call from my agent as to when I should best arrive at the count, which was held in a sports centre called Garrons. Somewhat naively, I had assumed that the count would be conducted in a similar fashion to that which I had grown accustomed to in Basildon, by which I meant very quickly and very efficiently. It got to 1am, no call. It got to 2am, still no call. While I was waiting, I was glued to national TV – the exit polls had realised my very worst fears.

It forecast the Conservatives losing heavily and Labour winning with a landslide. Declaration after declaration showed long-serving colleagues, who had previously held five figure majorities, losing drastically. The expressions on their faces said it all – they were shocked. As the night wore on and the results for the Conservative Party got worse and worse, I feared for the outcome of my own seat. I knew that I was a target for the Liberals and the 'swingometer' showed seats falling to the Labour Party and some to the Liberal Party, well within the target range of Southend West. I looked at my wife Julia and said, 'I think I have had it this time, I may well be looking for another job.' She remained positive and reassured me that I was over worrying. I hoped and prayed that she was right, but I had serious doubts. I had phoned and spoken to one of my campaign team, Andrew Lee, to find out what was going on. He said he had never seen such a slow count before. He thought that we were ahead, just.

Eventually, at around 3.30am, the call came that the formal part of the count was nearing its conclusion, with ballot papers verified and bundle counts taking place. Julia and I jumped in the car and left the children in the care of my mother-in-law. When we arrived at the count and I walked into the hall, there was a somewhat strange and subdued atmosphere. This was in stark contrast to the scenes at the Basildon count, which were always very lively and vocal events. The Liberal candidate had not arrived; I understood that she had been given intelligence when the polls closed that she was a dead cert to win. The arrogant Liberal candidate, according to one estate agent, had already been viewing properties in the Chalkwell ward of the constituency. As it turned out she had counted her chickens a little too soon.

Liberals were striding around the hall with clipboards, anxiously looking at the votes. The members of my team acting as scrutineers looked exhausted. A couple of members, Norman and Hilda Clarke, even fell asleep slumped over the tables. Eventually my opponent arrived, but not to the reception of adulation that she had perhaps envisaged. She was surrounded by her agent and others and then went over to the area, which was sectioned off, containing the actual ballot papers which were being bundled up according to the political party that had been voted for. The blue bundles looked to be ahead but not by a huge amount. Unbelievably, it was alleged that when it came to checking the bundles of votes, one or two of the Liberal scrutineers were actually trying to handle some of them. My agent was not best pleased. The Returning Officer, Douglas Moulsham, looked somewhat jaded after a long night but let me know that as far as he was concerned, I had won.

The declaration was eventually made at around dawn. Even though the Conservative majority had been slashed to 2,615, I was mightily relieved. I managed to produce a laugh when, in my victory speech, I said it was the largest majority I had ever had, which it was! The Liberals lost three seats since the previous general election. The Labour vote had surged with one of their biggest votes ever in the constituency and Conservative voters had stayed at home in their droves. Even my re-elected parliamentary colleague Sir Teddy Taylor was returned with a greatly reduced majority.

So, as dawn broke and the birds sang, we gathered in the car park outside the sports centre feeling mightily relieved. For a brief moment, we had been able to escape the bigger picture. We had a new Prime Minister and a new Government with a landslide majority, nearly 400 Labour MPs and just 165 Conservatives left. We had suffered a damning defeat and faced political meltdown.

2017 – Not again?!

It had taken 18 years, 13 of which had subjected the country to successive Labour Governments, but the Conservatives had finally been able to govern with a majority as a result of the 2015 election.

Cameron, Miliband, Clegg and Farage had dominated the airwaves. The election took place at the end of the fixed-term Parliament, so no one was taken by surprise. The burning question was how would the coalition partners fare? Would the Liberal Party's support of the Conservatives be damaging?

They had been unable to shake the tuition fees issue and Clegg was hammered in the media and on the doorstep. Miliband polled well, but ultimately was too awkward and became embroiled with some unfortunate publicity stunts. The EdStone was rumoured to have cost approximately £10,000. In a biblical scene, Labour had carved six pledges onto an 8-foot-high stone tablet 'to prove' that they would commit to their promises, unlike the Liberals. It was very strange, or as Boris put it better 'some weird Commie slab'. Cameron, for his part, had proved that he was a strong leader. He somehow managed to keep the coalition together and dominated Parliament. It was not foreseen that his nemesis would be Nigel Farage, UKIP and the promise of a referendum.

The Conservatives swept to power and Miliband resigned. As his brother had already departed for a plum job in the US, Jeremy Corbyn emerged as Labour leader. At the outset, he couldn't even get enough sponsors for his candidacy and had to be lent votes by MPs who would have supported other candidates. It was an extraordinary turn of events. After all, the least likely and most disloyal, in terms of support for his party, candidate had won. Not, I might add, with the support of fellow Parliamentarians, but with the support of party members, the numbers of which had been hugely inflated by fixing the membership fee at the small amount of £3. We could not believe our luck. Not only were we the surprise victors of the general election but now we faced a lame duck opposition leader.

So it was against this background, and the 2016 referendum result, that constant questions were asked about the new leader, Theresa May. Many questioned her mandate to govern, but the party line had always been 'We've only just had a general election, which has secured a majority for the party, and as Theresa had been a candidate in that election there was no need to seek a fresh mandate.' It seemed logical and we all believed it.

MPs had not known that a very small group of individuals had been advising Mrs May to call a snap election. The reasons for this were: the complexities of Brexit and the timescales involved, as well as the need for a fresh mandate to ensure what type of Brexit ought to be delivered. What wasn't said was that in a short space of time, Corbyn had established himself as the worst ever leader of a political party.

He didn't shine at the despatch box, even against, at times, an uncertain PM. He adopted the style of reading out letters from what may or may not have been constituents asking the PM about various issues. It was a little bit like a reader's letters page and Theresa had a field day dealing with the weekly clash. Not only was his performance poor in the House of Commons, but the Labour Party was deeply divided. In essence, the parliamentary party had a leader they just did not support. Many of them were supporters of Tony Blair and Gordon Brown. They were certainly not taken in by someone who, in his whole time in Parliament, had been a critic not only of the Conservative Party, but very much the Labour Party. It is incredible to think that he voted against the whip 428 times during the most recent Labour Government.

He was regarded as being on the extreme left and a Marxist. His chief adviser appeared to be John McDonnell. He might cut a picture of sartorial elegance, but behind that facade he's a brilliant hard-left organiser. Corbyn struggled to form an opposition Government. For the most part, anyone of substance and experience refused to serve, and he found himself relying on MPs who had only been recently elected. Over a 15-month period between December 2015 and February 2017, Labour had four Shadow Business Secretaries, four Shadow Defence Secretaries, four Shadow Welsh Secretaries and four Shadow Culture Secretaries. It was a complete and utter farce. A merry-go-round of political opponents – great fun for all of us on the Government side of the House.

So, it was for these reasons and no doubt more, that the PM was advised to hold a snap election. It transpired that they were not only persuaded by the large lead in the opinion polls but by the fact that their own private polling indicated that the Labour Party would lose heavily in the Midlands and the North of England. Analysis showed that they were not only vulnerable to Conservative candidates, but in many areas to UKIP ones too. It appeared that the election would see a seismic shake-up of the political system. In hindsight, it was this narrative that the Conservatives were seeking to take advantage of – a weak opposition that would anger the electorate.

When I drive to Westminster on a Monday morning, as is my habit, I catch up with my secretary on my hands-free device. On this particular Monday, while dictating her a letter, she suddenly screamed. I wasn't quite sure whether she had been murdered or what else could have possibly happened. After I had asked what was wrong, she said, 'Bloody hell, Theresa May's called a general election.' At this point I nearly crashed the car. My first reaction was what an absolute nuisance, with all the engagements that were already arranged in my diary. That was before I even began to consider getting ready to fight an election!

Once I got over the initial shock of the election being called, I came around to the view that it was perhaps a masterstroke that I should embrace. I recalled that when Gordon Brown was PM, he had an opportunity to go to the country early when it appeared that he would be returned with an enhanced majority. All the preparations were made for the election to be called, but at the last minute Brown changed his mind. He lived to regret it. So on the basis of recent history, we could see where she was coming from. Former PM David Cameron even tweeted the message 'brave – and right – decision by PM'.

So while, dare I say, it was a nuisance to have the election and unpick plans which were well advanced for the coming weeks, not to mention upping camp and basing myself full-time in Southend, I soon came round to the mindset of being an enthusiastic supporter of this surprise call. I had anticipated that my party would have made sure that a great campaign was planned and augmented by a bold and popular manifesto. How wrong could I have been?

I took part in the usual rituals which take place when Parliament is dissolved, and managed to have a new photograph taken with the PM. I had decided very quickly that this PM would be an asset in the campaign; she was clearly popular in the country, had Prime Ministerial bearing and was widely respected. I resolved to ensure that some of her gold dust rubbed off on me. I had not always been as enthusiastic to have my party leader standing shoulder to shoulder with me in my own election material, but this time it was going to be different.

I was in touch with some of my Essex colleagues throughout as I was anxious to compare notes as to how they were faring. I've never taken the view that there is such a thing as a safe seat. In 1997, I graphically recall watching some rather 'safe' colleagues fall – Rifkind, Portillo, Lamont, Forsyth, etc... Nevertheless, if you were to believe the betting odds, my seat was seen as being a comfortable hold for the Conservative Party and I was asked to assist my good friend Jackie Doyle-Price in Thurrock. From the very outset of the campaign, the pundits regarded the result as a foregone conclusion. There would be a landslide and Corbyn would be humiliated. From the very first moment I began canvassing, while the response was quite good, it never felt that one sided to me. Indeed, each day it seemed to be getting a little worse and I kept saying to my office, when are we going to get the manifesto?

Corbyn toured the country and met growing crowds of people known as 'Corbynistas' who gave their leader an evangelical welcome. Theresa never did that. There seemed to be very little contact with real people, instead there would be contrived situations where she would address hand-picked groups often in workplace settings. Her campaign came across as rather wooden and old-fashioned. The polls seemed to reflect a narrowing of the previously gigantic gap.

Something that seemed to be contributing to this was Theresa's refusal to take part in a leadership debate. For me, these really are a throwback to American Presidential elections and are most un-British. In this country, we had never concentrated on a candidate's personality. I believe televised debates are most unbecoming. I suppose I have a natural prejudice towards television and the way it portrays politicians. It somehow seems to me that these debates are very much like a show. I really don't think they give a good account of accurately portraying the people who run the country or aspire to do so. The interaction with the audience, for instance, hardly engenders statesman-like responses, no matter how well-disciplined the Chairman is. Nevertheless, I fully accept that, in the modern times which we live, these ghastly debates are probably here to stay.

The PM held firm to the view that she would not take part in a leader's question time debate but would instead appear on her own and take questions from the invited audience. Initially, the decision had seemed a good one, to not give opposition Members a platform, but increasingly it appeared to be a sign of weakness rather than strength and made a mockery of the national campaign slogan 'Strong and Stable Leadership'. Theresa was completely outmanoeuvred by Corbyn. Originally, a debate had been scheduled for all major parties other than Labour and the Conservatives. Amber Rudd was sent on behalf of the PM, just days after the death of her father, and did a fantastic job. Having said that, Theresa was hounded for not turning up. Corbyn's office had convinced him to take part himself at very late notice and this played to the theory that Theresa was not willing to answer the tough questions.

As I continued with my doorstep canvassing, supported by my loyal hard-working band of volunteers, I noticed a continual loss of support. I experienced some ugly moments which I had not seen since the '70s. It is a long time since I had knocked on a door and been greeted with profanities just because I was a Conservative. Not only that, I recall one or two incidents where the person answering the door had been not only rude but aggressive. Likewise, my supporters and I were taken aback when a seemingly middle-class lady in her 70s turned up at a canvas session to stalk me as I went knocking, shouting, 'Don't vote for him, he's useless.' She then turned on my supporters near the railway station. This went on for what seemed like hours, but in reality was probably nearer 30 minutes. She refused to stop following me and I had to call the police! While not the most serious of incidents, for a seat like Southend West it marked a real shift in tone from what I had experienced since arriving in 1997.

My impatience for the manifesto to be published finished on 18 May, but I cannot claim to have realised its full impact. Gone were the days when the manifesto was delivered in a hardbound copy. Now, they are available online. I was increasingly frustrated by the central office campaign which seemed ill-prepared. Previously, we had always been able to access literature and have it delivered speedily. Furthermore, a comprehensive campaign guide had been offered to all candidates which in essence indicated the line which should be taken on more or less every conceivable issue. None of this was available in 2017. It didn't take long, perhaps just a couple of hours, for the first angry email to arrive. The emails did not arrive just from opposition voters, but in large numbers from our very own. They were angered by what they saw as an attack on their way of life. They felt penalised for having carefully managed their earnings over so many years. A media storm developed, and our poll ratings plummeted dramatically. I couldn't believe that our manifesto, far from being a boost to our campaign, had delivered a mortal blow with an attack on our own supporters.

In the election campaign, no Cabinet Members featured much at all. When Theresa did do a walkabout with our candidate, she found herself involved in a confrontation with a member of the public and looked ill-at-ease on the trail. Much has been made of how brilliant a campaigner Theresa had been in her locality but, as she was finding out, leading a national campaign was a whole different ball game.

The pledge to abolish the winter fuel allowance for certain pensioners and the poorly explained changes to the costs of social care seem to have aggravated the electorate and derailed her campaign. Furthermore, the media lampooned her when she answered what the naughtiest thing she had ever done was 'run through a field of wheat'. She was quickly being transformed from a steady hand into a figure of fun.

Labour had its own difficulties in the form of Diane Abbott. Most people can remember, in 2015, the then leader of the Green Party being challenged on her housing plans by Nick Ferrari and falling apart when put under pressure. The fallout was so severe that she ended up apologising and blaming it on brain-fade. Well Diane Abbott conjured up a gaffe of larger proportions. She got tied up in knots when asked about the cost of the increased number of police which had been pledged. With claims that she had been ill, she was swiftly removed from the campaign. This was one of several high-profile gaffes, including Tim Farron's failure to answer a question about sin and gay sex, Corbyn's inability to manage childcare cost figures and Paul Nuttall's inability to recall Leanne Wood's (the then leader of Plaid Cymru) name during the leadership debate.

I don't know whether it happens to us all as we age, but it seemed to me that the newest intake of politicians were not as adept at electioneering. They were less savvy at campaigning generally, were inexperienced in dealing with the media and had little or no answer to cope with the advent of social media.

This general election campaign, perhaps like no other, saw social media gain huge importance. For so many elections, it had always been the case that young people did not vote in such large numbers as older people did. All of that was about to change; the youth vote had stirred, and the false dawn of tactical voting had at last been realised. So it was then that I sat in my lounge at home, having finished touring the constituency, to wait for the exit polls. I told my wife that while the opinion polls were in many respects meaningless, the exit poll was a different matter. I vividly recall how I felt when on the stroke of 10.00pm, David Dimbleby announced the result that the Conservative Party would be the largest but with no overall majority. In short, it was a disaster and a humiliation. I had privately told my fellow Essex MPs that I had feared the worst, but I wanted to be proved wrong. They were for the most part confident that we would be returned with an increased majority. I much regret that I was proved correct.

The rise and fall of leaders

I have seen many political careers begin and end before they even got started. Others cruise on a tide of popular support before brutally crashing back to reality. What I do not have any memories of is an incumbent of the highest office stepping down on his or her own terms and at the right time (from their own point of view).

John Major

Where John Moore had once been Margaret's favoured candidate to succeed her, the dapper Secretary of State for Health and Social Services began to lose his charm. At one point destined to be a future leader, Moore rather suddenly found himself behind John Major, the new chosen one. In just a matter of months, Major was Foreign Secretary, Chancellor of the Exchequer and then Prime Minister. With the trauma of Margaret's resignation, John Major kept his nose clean by not being available for interviews because of dental problems. At the back of his mind, he must have had a plan to become leader, how else could he have assembled a campaign team so quickly? While the media did nothing other than talk about Michael Heseltine, or Tarzan as he was known after seizing the Commons mace and swinging it above his head in 1976, Major made his move. The Chairman of the '22 opened nominations for candidates. Major immediately appeared on the steps of the Treasury surrounded by supporters and declared his candidacy.

John portrayed himself as the antipathy of Margaret. He was working-class, had left school at 16 and was born in

Brixton, not the most affluent part of London. At the same time, he was tall, wore glasses and was very conservatively dressed. He wanted to be seen as ordinary and in part he achieved that. Unlike Margaret, he wasn't going to have elocution lessons, he wasn't going to have contact lenses, he wasn't going to go anywhere near Grecian 2000 and he wasn't going to abandon his pinstripe suits. Having said that, in the two years that he and Neil Kinnock faced one another, Neil grew in confidence clearly believing he had found himself an easier opponent.

There had to be an election by 1992 and some Conservatives judged that with a new leader they stood a far better chance. We moved towards that fateful election which turned out, in a very small way, to be historic for myself. As the campaigning started and leaders' battle buses toured the country, Neil's momentum grew. John's campaign though had struck a chord with many. He decided that he had nothing to lose and so should take the fight to the enemy. He did this magnificently by developing a style called the soap box. Assisted by his loyal lieutenant, Graham Bright, he turned up all over the country and made speeches standing on a box with a loud hailer – a trick he must have stolen from me! What a contrast to how elections are fought today, whereby it seems the last thing the leaders want to do is meet the general public. They surround themselves with sycophantic, banner-waving supporters, which I have always thought is rather puerile.

The Blair years

Tony Blair, Gordon Brown and I were all elected on the same day, 9 June 1983. We didn't know each other and barely exchanged words in those early years. Having a huge Conservative majority meant I didn't much notice the new Labour Members as I was far too absorbed in my new life as an MP and the shock of it all.

The House of Commons was stunned by the death of John Smith, who had made Labour electable again. Tributes were immediately paid, and the planned sitting was suspended. He had died young and was undoubtedly a loss, not just to the Labour Party, but to the country. The late Lionel Altman, who I owe so much to, ran my office at the time and was a City of London Councillor. His flat was near to the block where John Smith lived and so quickly alerted me to what had happened. John had been due to visit Basildon on that very day but had suffered a heart attack while in the bath.

Politics is a cutthroat business and Members are very resilient (critics might say mercenary). No sooner had John Smith died than campaigns to replace him as Labour leader were put in motion. It quickly emerged that the main candidates would be Tony Blair and Gordon Brown. Much has already been written about what actually happened between them regarding the day that followed Smith's death, but it would seem there was some sort of agreement that Blair would succeed him and after a number of years had passed, the leadership would be handed over to Brown. I am not sure of the truth of the matter, but Blair quickly emerged as Smith's successor. Rather than being a contest, it felt more like a coronation.

He was a formidable opponent of John Major at the despatch box and as time went on and John's Government became increasingly fractious, the contrast between the two was very sharp. Tony Blair had popped up in the right place at the right time. His fresh face was surrounded by adoring supporters and a whole new generation of luvvies sailed into Downing Street on the back of a tide of support for change. Who can ever forget Labour celebrations at Millbank Tower with the tune 'Things Can Only Get Better' blasting away in the background? The irony was of course that Ken Clarke, the outgoing Chancellor, had managed the country's finances astutely so Blair inherited a growing economy with inflation very much under control.

I look back on the Blair years with complete and utter disdain. I always thought the claim that he was actually another Margaret Thatcher dressed up as New Labour to be totally disingenuous. He was a very clever PR guy. For the cameras, he quickly invited her to Number 10 after which she made the statement that he wouldn't damage our country. It is not often that I disagree with Margaret, but this was one of those occasions. How wrong she was. Many regarded him as the biggest charlatan and con artist of the time. He would claim that he was the saviour of the Labour Party and did enormous good, but I totally disapproved of many of his decisions.

For instance, he broke up the United Kingdom and I would blame him for many of the difficulties which we now experience in Scotland. He interfered with the House of Lords by removing the Hereditaries, yet fundamentally failed to reform the foundations on which the revising Chamber was based. I blame him for the way he dealt with immigration generally and for changing the face of London with no regard for social cohesion. Above all, I blame him for the way he misled Parliament over the war with Iraq.

As far as I am concerned, he really does have blood on his hands as a result of his taking British forces into the ill-judged war and agreeing to support the Americans without any sort of plan for regime change. He brought terrorism to these shores much more quickly than would otherwise have been the case, and ultimately world order was destabilised. He never recovered from this huge mistake and his departure from office was undoubtedly precipitated by this dreadful deceit.

Gordon Brown had become frustrated at Number 11. He began briefing against the PM and was clearly unhappy that Blair seemed to be reneging on his promise to honour his commitment to resign after a certain number of years.

On the day of Blair's last performance in Parliament, I found myself thinking how much of a contrast it had been to Margaret Thatcher's. Margaret was removed from office through the treachery of some of her colleagues, but Blair left office as a result of his own. When he sat down with the usual Cheshire Cat grin on his face, David Cameron encouraged colleagues to stand up and give him an ovation. I and others steadfastly refused to do so.

I much preferred Gordon Brown, even if he was so utterly miserable. In hindsight however, his premiership was a tragedy as it came too late. It was lovely that he found happiness with his wife Sarah but a tragedy that they lost their baby, Jennifer Jane. In all honesty, he was neither suited to lead the Labour Party nor to be Prime Minister. He lacked the qualities that were needed and was unable to heal the rifts which had been laid bare by Blair between Labour MPs and the country at large.

2010 – Cameron, Clegg and the coalition

The argument surrounding the timing of Blair's departure and the question of when Brown would take over helped Cameron improve his own standing not only among the party, but also in the country. Nevertheless, for the Conservatives to win would be a very big mountain to climb and the opinion polls forecasted something that had not been contemplated for many a year, a hung Parliament.

But while all this was happening, the Liberal Party was undergoing something of a renaissance under their new leader, the slick Nick Clegg. Charles Kennedy had been a formidable and popular leader of his party but retired prematurely under sad circumstances. In hindsight, because of what eventually happened to Chris Huhne, it was as well that the party chose Nick. They were riding high in the opinion polls, not least because they had been the only political party to come out firmly against British involvement in the war to replace Saddam Hussein. Nick was also a seasoned campaigner, so when it came to the televised debate, which Gordon Brown unwisely agreed to, Clegg came across well playing the honest broker.

When all the votes were counted, no political party had an overall majority and there was much speculation as to what would happen.

Following days, if not weeks, of drama, the new Government was formed, and it was to be a coalition government headed by David Cameron as Prime Minister with Nick Clegg as his deputy. Clegg had been an MEP before arriving at Westminster. He and his wife Miriam were young and presented themselves extremely well, but for me Nick was always far too smooth for his own good.

I was very much against going into a coalition with the Liberals. As far as I was concerned, they fitted much more closely with the Labour Party, and in many respects they were more left-wing. A number of their MPs had actually been members of Labour, the most prominent of whom was Vince Cable.

The negotiations resulted in Labour rejecting a coalition. Personally, I much preferred the possibility of forming a minority Conservative administration. It would then be left to the House to decide whether or not they wanted to vote measures down. I also judged that there was no real appetite for another election, not least because there was no money to fund campaigns.

I vividly recall being summoned to Committee Room 14 for a meeting called by the 1922 Backbench Committee. Conservative MPs had been told all along that they were being consulted about the possibilities. Experience told me that this did not mean what it implied. The reality was that we would rubber stamp David's suggestion. Even from my school days I had been taught that coalition governments were formed in times of war, and 2010 certainly didn't seem like wartime to me. Nevertheless, the Coalition was billed as being formed at a time of national economic crisis. We certainly did face a very difficult economic situation thanks to the outgoing Labour Government. Therefore, it was felt that we needed a Government of national unity tasked with delivering difficult policies, otherwise known as heralding a decade of austerity. The British banking system had virtually collapsed, and the public debt consequently soared. It was the Coalition's job to restore confidence in our country.

A packed parliamentary meeting gathered and the Chairman of the '22 welcomed the party leader to address the meeting. I stood at the back with a number of like-minded colleagues. Cameron declared that he was forming a coalition Government. The room exploded with joy and new Members were particularly enthusiastic at the announcement. There was wild cheering and banging on the panelled walls. I and others around me were more circumspect and took the view that a great mistake had been made. As it turned out, David Cameron was right, and we were wrong.

With a guile that I had not been aware of, he had negotiated a coalition agreement which most of us could live with. More importantly, he had calculated that at the next election it would be the Lib Dems who would take the political hit. In retrospect, it was this decision which paved the way for the formation of the first majority Conservative Government since 1992. Either way, after 13 grim Labour years, whereby the country had been marched to the top of the precipice only to find that the expectations of the Promised Land and hopes of prosperity had been dashed as a result of a disastrous war with Iraq and a cataclysmic economic crisis, the Conservatives were back in power.

There was much excitement in Westminster. Who could forget the first joint press conference that was given in the Rose Garden of Number 10 Downing Street? Who would have believed it? Hand in hand, the governing partners jauntily strove up to the rostrums, seemingly joined at the hip. The eyes of the British media were glued on the Happy Couple. The question that no doubt was in their minds was: 'Is this a marriage made in heaven or hell?' Together they laid out the contents of the Coalition agreement.

The headline of the deal was that an emergency budget would be agreed within 50 days as part of an aim to significantly reduce the structural deficit over the Parliament. The banking system would undergo various reforms, the personal income tax allowance would increase alongside NHS funding in real terms, fixed-term Parliaments were created and a referendum would be held on the electoral system. There were also various other pledges concerning no more runways in London, reversing the erosion of civil liberties by scrapping the idea of

National Identity Cards and a larger funding premium for the poorest children to incentivise them to go to school.

It was obvious that there had to be compromise in the programme and the Liberal Party immediately began briefing that they would restrain, and even neutralise, what they saw as an extreme Conservative programme. When the Cabinet was announced later, a number of key positions were given to Nick Clegg's party. I found this particularly difficult to stomach. They had been our political enemies, sitting opposite us, berating us from the time I was first elected.

My early experiences in Southend West had coloured my views of them. Usually Labour candidates fought a straightforward campaign against the Conservative incumbent. The Liberal Party however was infamous for its pavement politics and had a reputation for being duplicitous on the doorstep. They would produce endless leaflets which would invariably contain personal attacks against me and my colleagues. So, I wondered, how would this arrangement work in practice once the door to the Cabinet Room had been closed? Would the two parties really trust one another?

When David set about forming the rest of his Government, he was left in a real conundrum. Many colleagues had been terribly loyal, worked very hard for the party and had undoubtedly been promised office. How could the PM deal with any number of people's disappointments at not being offered a job for the simple reason that a number of his Ministers had to be Liberal Democrats? As the various announcements were made, I could sense the disappointment amongst any number of my colleagues. I sensed that the newly formed administration would have its work cut out keeping colleagues onside when tough decisions had to be taken – but only time would tell.

Money could not have been tighter, so the first thing that they announced was an increase in tuition fees for Higher Education in England and Wales. Well, Hell have no fury. The Liberal voters felt scorned. The immediate reversal of their manifesto pledge caused outrage among the millions who had supported them. This was to be the first of many crises that the Government faced with student protests being organised and violence ensuing.

I don't know for sure, but I imagine the Liberals had taken this gamble as it would allow them to hold a referendum on electoral reform. They felt very strongly about the supposed inherent unfairness of First Past the Post voting. As it turned out, the public simply were not that interested, and the proposed change was roundly defeated. The gamble had not paid off.

For the party, it would prove a fatal mistake and one that they would never be allowed to forget. They paid the price in the 2015 general election by losing 49 of their 57 seats. A huge fall for a rising star. (I talk in more detail about David Cameron's resignation later on.)

So why does a fall in leadership happen? Well, perhaps vanity overtakes each and every one of us politicians. We believe we can walk on water; nothing could possibly go wrong. We actually begin to believe the endless flattery that we receive. But I am not sure that is necessarily the case. It is probably much to do with our parliamentary system, whereby our Ministers are also MPs who are subject to the maximum scrutiny not just at the despatch box, but by all the media outlets too. Any politician will only be as good as those who serve and support them – tiny pressures lead to mistakes, and increasingly through social media those mistakes are magnified.

Power certainly does corrupt. It can often be an aphrodisiac, after all it is rather wonderful being in a position to actually make a real difference to peoples' lives. But power comes at a cost and it is a truly remarkable politician who manages to survive the effect of power on one's own self esteem. I have no doubt that our country has been deprived of some potentially outstanding leaders as a result of their fall from grace when moving towards their peak. I am not sure that much can be done to avoid such calamities without fundamentally changing our political system and the way Parliament works.

That may well happen over the course of time and it could be that when Parliament leaves the Palace of Westminster our political system will also change fundamentally. That could be a good thing for the aspiring politician, but I am not so sure for the quality of our democracy. I suppose we should be proud and celebrate the fact that our political system, unlike so many others, does not allow corrupt politicians to stay in power. Ours is as brutal as can be, we do not just remove politicians because they are seemingly corrupt, which they are not, but we remove politicians because of their human frailties.

PART 3

Outside the House

UNTIL NOW THIS book has concentrated on procedure, personality and popularity. It is undoubtedly true that I have born witness to a fundamental paradigm shift in all three of these areas, and I suppose that is only to be expected when one occupies an office for 37 years in one of the most dynamic and highly charged professions in the whole of the United Kingdom.

What I have not yet discussed or attempted to tackle are the issues and policy areas that underlie these changes. In order to contextualise the shifts in the party-political spectrum and understand the fluctuating nature of who makes a good leader and why there are calls for Parliament to modernise, you must strive to understand the issues of the day. As Harold Macmillan neatly summarised in response to being asked about his greatest fear as Prime Minister, 'events, dear boy, events'; all politicians are subject to them. No matter how ideologically driven or issue-based your politics may be, the simple reality is that you tend not to be given the luxury to choose what to do. Most of your time will be spent extinguishing the multiple fires around you, with the small and constantly fading hope that eventually you will be able to implement your own agenda.

No matter how well you fight them, these events seem to continually appear and therefore shape the careers of the majority of leaders. However it is not just the individuals that they shape but the very institutions that are created to deal with them too. It would be quite possible to have a limitless range of issues to discuss, but for the purposes of this book I want to highlight the following areas where we have seen real change and which have contributed significantly to the differences previously described between being an MP in 1983 and entering the Commons for the first time in 2019.

War and terror

I have never claimed to be, or tried to be, an expert in defence and security. I have far too many colleagues with military backgrounds to make it worthwhile for myself to make this an area of personal priority. Having said that, it is an issue with which any responsible MP ought to keep up to date. Some of the greatest responsibilities of any Prime Minister and Parliament itself are to know when to go to war, how to protect our democracy against violent ideology and to speak responsibly regarding life and death decisions.

Just because war is not an area of expertise it does not mean that it hasn't played a pivotal role in my political career. In my time as MP for Basildon, I was very involved in the defence industry because I had a number of specific interests in the constituency – GEC Avionics for one. I vividly recall Alan Clark, who was in charge of procurement, arriving in a helicopter to look around our factory. Local residents, many of whose jobs depended on the outcome of defence procurement, wanted us to be tough in terms of our defence policy, and in Margaret they got their Churchillian leader.

Moreover, I'm under no illusion that I was a huge beneficiary of the afterglow of our successful campaign in the Falklands. Before the whole episode, the popularity ratings for the party were not so good, largely as a result of the difficult decisions that Margaret and Geoffrey Howe had to take over the country's finances. The initial impact of some of Margaret's key policies had adversely impacted on people's disposable incomes, but the Falklands victory changed the political landscape in a significant way. Britannia ruled the waves again. Margaret had proved herself to be fiercely loyal to her country and had shown to the rest of the world that she would ensure

Declaration of General Election
result, 1987.

Mother Theresa visits Parliament
in 1988.

Margaret Thatcher meets the whole
Amess family on a visit to Basildon
in 1992.

Princess Anne on a visit to Basildon.

Margaret Thatcher visits Basildon on the campaign trail in 1992.

David with his predecessor Rt Hon Paul Channon MP.

Katherine Amess with Pope John Paul II in Rome.

John Major with 'Essex Girl' Alexandra Amess.

David with Andy Stewart MP & David Hunt MP following a trip down a mine during the Miners' Strike.

Basildon count 1992 with Barbara Allen MBE, the Election Agent.

David with Michael Portillo. David was Michael's PPS between 1987 and 1997.

1922 Committee Executive dinner with Baroness Thatcher.

Ponies in Westminster for the passing of the Protection Against Cruel Tethering Act 1988.

Visit from William Hague for the 2001 General Election.

David always celebrates election victories with an open topped bus tour of the constituency to thank the voters.

David with Baroness Thatcher at an event at Canary Wharf.

Foreign delegation trip to Japan in 1992.

Investiture at Windsor Castle, 2015.

Stilt walkers arrive at Downing Street for the launch of Southend as Alternative City of Culture, 2017.

Maud Amess at the Cabinet Table in 10 Downing Street on the day she collected her Land Army Medal.

David with Lorraine Platt and Elise Dunweber. David is Patron of the Conservative Animal Welfare Foundation and has campaigned with Lorraine on many issues related to animal cruelty.

David celebrating his Knighthood in 2015.

David with Pope Francis. © Vatican Official Photographer

A final pre-Brexit visit to the European Parliament in Brussels in January 2020.

Brexit Day in Westminster, 31 March 2020.

As a senior member of the Speaker's Panel, David was asked to help chair the House of Commons until the election of Deputy Speakers following the 2017 General Election.
© Parliament TV

David asking Boris Johnson to make Southend a city during PMQs.
© Parliament TV

David with Margaret Thatcher in the Leader of the Opposition's Room before his election to Parliament.

Official portrait with John Major.

With David Cameron, 2010.

Official campign photo for 2017 General Election with Theresa May. © CCHQ

David with the new Conservative Party Leader Boris Johnson following his victory in the leadership contest in 2019.

our brave and magnificent troops defended our territory to the end. This played very well on the pavements of Basildon.

The Falklands War

I was elected to Parliament after the Falklands War had been successfully concluded by British forces. I remember only too well the feeling throughout the country when the Falklands were suddenly invaded by Argentinian forces. Many people did not have a clue where the Falklands actually were or know the history of the territory. By the time the conflict was over, everyone knew and equally understood why it was so important, symbolically, that they remain British.

When you look at a map, they are a very long way from the UK. As a result, when the islands were invaded on Friday 2 April 1982, an incredibly difficult decision needed to be taken. How could we get a force halfway across the world by sea, which was also capable of reclaiming British Territory? Well, as they (almost) say, 'cometh the hour, cometh the woman' and so it was that Margaret Thatcher rose to the threat of combatting the Argentine invasion.

The late Lord Carrington, Foreign Secretary at the time, felt the honourable thing to do was resign. Margaret was reluctant to accept but she did, and he was replaced by Francis Pym. She summoned a war cabinet, who met daily. On the contrary to her public image, she was no war monger like Tony Blair, but rather meticulously cautious in her approach. She was not only aware of the toll it could take on our already stretched forces, but was quite rightly very concerned about any possible loss of life. For any successful engagement to take place she felt she needed the support of the United States of America. Much has been written about her special relationship with Ronald Reagan. In this regard she used all her astuteness to enlist his support, which was crucial in order to ensure that the US not only supported her efforts but that support also included possible air strikes.

On 14 June 1982 Margaret addressed the House reporting the words of General Moore: 'The Falkland Islands are once more under the Government desired by their inhabitants. God Save the Queen.' Much controversy mired the sinking of the *Belgrano*, led by the veteran Labour Member Tam Dalyell. He would endlessly raise the issue in Parliament, but overall the British people's reaction to reclaiming the Falklands was one of pride and delight. Through Margaret's determination to stand up to a foreign aggressor, she was now seen as a formidable world leader. She had shown a depth of strength and courage which had not been seen since Winston Churchill's heroic leadership in World War II. The Victory Parade that took place in London was undoubtedly a historic moment in rejuvenating the patriotism of the British people. The return of our warships was a moving moment and Margaret's delight in the victory was clear when she stood on the balcony of the Guildhall as jet fighters flew over. For too long the British people had been loath to wave their Union Jacks. Now, it was once again respectable to be patriotic, wave the red, white and blue flag and sing the national anthem. There is no doubt that this restoration of national pride made a significant contribution to the General Election results of 1983.

From the IRA to ISIS

The security threats faced by the public and members locally, nationally and internationally are completely unrecognisable today from 1983. You only have to consider how the Westminster estate has changed so dramatically. Gaining access to Downing Street was once a straightforward matter. There were no high gates, no motor car barriers and no airport-style searches. Likewise, Palace Yard was very easily accessible. Now it is absolutely impossible for any member of the public to get in, thanks to the railings, barriers and 24/7 guarded turnstiles via which staff can enter and exit.

The IRA and the Brighton bombing in particular, precipitated this period of real change. Without going into detail of the IRA's justification for injuring and maiming innocent people, it was the death of Airey Neave that triggered it. Neave was a remarkable individual. He will always be remembered as the first British officer to successfully escape from the German prisoner of war camp at Colditz Castle, and he had been influential in persuading Margaret to run for leader of the party. He was one of her closest allies, but was blown to bits by a magnetic bomb that had been planted underneath his car. As he was driving up the ramp to leave the underground carpark in Palace Yard it went off. Whenever I use that carpark, I can't help but think of that horrendous event. Since then, all members' vehicles have been checked when driving onto the estate.

I have always tried to attend the annual Conservative Party conference. It used to alternate between Brighton and Blackpool. I very rarely stay for the leader's speech on the last day. It is commonly thought that the leader's speech is the showpiece of any party conference. There may be a role for members of the cabinet to be seen seated and looking on adoringly, but for ordinary MPs such as myself there is no such requirement. Seeing as there are more than enough people to pack out the hall, I think party members ought to have the opportunity to watch it in the flesh, so I give up my seat.

When the Brighton bomb exploded in October 1984, I had already returned home. The shocking images broadcast on TV showed the rather splendid Grand Hotel torn apart. Margaret and Dennis Thatcher had survived the attack, but cameras caught an unrecognisable Norman Tebbit, covered in dust, being brought out on a stretcher. As news filtered through, we learnt that five people had been killed. One was Anthony Berry, the member for Southgate, another was the wife of my Essex colleague, John Wakeham, Parliamentary Secretary to the Treasury at the time. Norman Tebbit's wife was left paralysed from the waist down and 34 others were injured in the blast.

Like most fair-minded members of our nation, I was absolutely shocked, numbed and horrified at this terrorist attack. Instinctively, I thought, 'I could have been there, it could have been me,' before concentrating on the reality of those who were actually killed and permanently maimed. I also felt disgusted. I could not understand how supposedly fellow Catholics could kill members of the human race for engaging in the democratic process. There is no question it made many of us Parliamentarians very anxious indeed.

Margaret, as ever, was heroic in adversity and immediately made a defiant speech as she walked to the Conference Hall to deliver her remarks. Against the advice of the police, she strolled through the front entrance of the hall in the full glare of the media. The words she spoke pay testimony to the remarkable woman she is:

> The fact that we are gathered here now – shocked, but composed, and determined – is a sign that not only this attack has failed, but that all attempts to destroy democracy by terrorism will fail.

It was many months later that I was in the Chamber when John Wakeham re-entered the House for the first time on crutches. The House rose to greet him. I am so pleased that the member's family room was named after his late wife, Roberta Wakeham, and also that he eventually found happiness again. The list of atrocities which the IRA were responsible for is endless. But to summarise them, they can all be described as heinous, cruel and wicked beyond belief.

The general public were advised to be more vigilant than ever and one immediate effect was that litter bins, being obvious targets of aggression, were no longer available in key locations. While security was most certainly transformed as a result of the Brighton bombing, Margaret made it very clear that we would never bow to the terrorists.

Today, a different type of terror exists. It can be argued that we politicians have in many senses been responsible for the way that threat has grown. By this I have in mind the disastrous vote that Parliament took, and I supported, to invade Iraq and remove Saddam Hussein.

It is a real challenge for our security forces to deter people who are prepared to take their own life in order to destroy others. I find it a little similar to the Kamikaze pilots of old. In recent years, these tactics have become even more savage. I never thought that I would live to see the day when on social media you can actually see people dressed in orange boiler suits being burnt alive, decapitated and thrown off the top of buildings. This really is turning back the clock to medieval times. Nevertheless, it is real no matter how impossible it may seem. Our security forces have to devise a strategy to combat it all, something which we are still struggling to do.

Who will ever forget the shocking sight of the Twin Towers collapsing? The most powerful nation in the world was publicly humiliated by being unprepared to combat the unthinkable action of aeroplanes being directed at world renowned landmarks. When the news first broke, my wife and I happened to be looking at the television. I did not think the images were real. I thought it was some production of an action movie. Fortunately, for those who had time to escape, there was some delay before the iconic buildings collapsed. Further horror was to come as people jumped to their deaths from the upper floors. It was heart-breaking to listen to the last telephone calls made from inside the structures. Nobody who was alive that day will ever forget those images.

President Bush somewhat excelled himself in terms of his statesmanlike reaction to the national disaster. It was of course during the time of the next Presidency that Osama Bin Laden's compound in Pakistan was shown live on TV, being entered by US forces and the perpetrator of the crime being killed. The effect of the 9/11 atrocities was that, if they were not already, the United States were fully engaged in the wars against Al-Qaeda. The objectives of these terrorist organisations are complex and difficult to comprehend but there is little doubt that underlying them is a perversion of Islam and pursuit of world domination.

Strategies to defeat these groups have been met with mixed success. Strong and wise world leaders are perhaps the key to an effective response and for that the world is wanting. We do not have, at the moment, men and women of the stature of Margaret Thatcher, Ronald Reagan or Mikael Gorbachev.

I find it hard to compare the two menaces discussed. Both the IRA and ISIS found themselves in the news on a daily basis for all the wrong reasons. Both organisations were unbelievably cruel. I would argue that knocking on a door and dragging a mother away from her family is wickedness beyond belief. I would also say I can't imagine anything much worse than being trapped in a vehicle and quite literally torn apart. One is not necessarily worse than the other, but they have undoubtedly posed different challenges to our security services, who continually have to adapt and stay ahead to keep the population safe.

Domestic attacks

The Twin Towers were symbolic to the rest of the Western world. The atrocity would mark the beginning of a new type of threat, one that we have since seen in all too much detail and far too regularly.

A group of foreign diplomats were visiting me in Westminster three years ago. I have a rather splendid room with a balcony overlooking Palace Yard and Parliament Square which provides a very good view of the estate. Visitors to my office are often complimentary of the quirky fixtures and fittings as well as the view from my balcony.

As the group were leaving my office, they asked if they could be shown to St Stephen's Crypt. As it turned out, that was a very fortunate request. It meant that we exited the building from a different exit from the one I had originally intended to leave from. I took my guests to the crypt – completely oblivious to what was happening above us. About half an hour into the visit, there was a knock on the door. We were advised not to leave, which I immediately thought bizarre. My secretary rang telling me that the whole estate was in lockdown because of a terrorist attack. My office had witnessed from their windows a 4x4 crashing into the railings surrounding Palace Yard before the assailant ran from his vehicle and through the gates where he murdered a police officer, PC Keith Palmer. I, together with my team, attended a very moving service in the crypt to mark the year anniversary of this tragedy. While I didn't know the relatives and friends of Keith Palmer, I thought it was important that we showed our support and respect for the fallen officer who was doing his duty on that fateful day. These were truly horrendous events and, as we now know, the terrorist had been deliberately mowing down passers-by on Westminster Bridge and had already killed four people before entering the estate.

Proceedings were suspended and Members locked in the Chamber. Security procedures were immediately set in motion which meant that people were kept where they found themselves. As the day unfolded, the diplomats and I got to know one another extremely well. We spent three hours in the crypt and a further four hours in Westminster Hall before being escorted over to Westminster Abbey. The British have a reputation for being stoical and calm in the face of adversity. This day was no exception.

Ever since the death of Neave, members of parliament have been given advice about personal security. As the MP for Basildon with a young family I had been informed of a death threat which was being made against me – apparently by the IRA. It was to coincide with the visit of Princess Diana to our hospice St Luke's.

We lived in a cul-de-sac with a lovely green in the centre. The police informed me of this threat and gave me appropriate suggestion of how to combat it. This consisted of having an emergency button next to our bed. I was instructed to press it in the event of an attack. Mercifully nothing happened. In the same manner that we were told to be careful at home Members were asked to be vigilant of the general public visiting constituency surgeries. This advice was triggered as a result of someone with a machete bursting into the surgery of Nigel Jones and killing one of his assistants. A traumatic event. His attacker had been a constituent that he had met many times before and was clearly frustrated by the progress being made on his behalf. It is appalling to think that his next logical move was to stab Mr Jones and his assistant repeatedly. We all make ourselves readily available to our constituents and are often dealing with members of the public who have mental health problems, it could happen to any of us.

The murder of Jo Cox was still totally unexpected. She had been an MP for a very short time, having been elected in May 2015. She was approaching the library where her constituency surgery was to be held, when she was attacked and killed in the most barbaric fashion imaginable. This event took place during the 2016 EU Referendum Campaign and had a galvanising effect on the campaign, the general public and Members themselves. My colleague Mark Francois alerted me to the attack, at which time he was unaware that Jo had actually died. She was a young woman with a family going about her duties as we all do, completely unaware of the threat that she faced. While it is often said that good can come out of someone's death, it is difficult to see what good can come from this senseless murder. Nevertheless, it is to be commended that the Jo Cox Foundation has been established to combat loneliness.

There can be no doubt that as a result of these heightened security concerns most Members have modified or changed the way they interact with the general public. The Commons authorities have taken threats very seriously and have issued guidance for the safety and security of not only Members, but their families. This includes security in their own home. I myself have over the years experienced nuisance from the odd member of the general public at my own property. We regularly check our locks and many others have CCTV cameras installed but probably the most significant change has been with constituency surgeries.

The British tradition has always been that Members of Parliament regularly make themselves available for constituents to meet them face to face at their surgeries. Now advice has been given to be more careful when accepting appointments. We are advised to never see people alone, we must be extra careful when opening post and we must ensure that our offices are properly safe and secure. In short, these increasing attacks have rather spoilt the great British tradition of the people openly meeting their elected politicians.

An equally worrying development has been the fallout from social media. Many MPs find themselves regularly being abused and bullied online. The police have enough to do without patrolling social media, but members are advised that they should always alert the police whenever threats to their safety are made. I myself have frequently received online abuse. My frustration is with the law governing social media generally. I think it is ridiculous that media sites host abusive comments in reaction to stories about an individual without there being any requirement for the abuser to leave their name and address. It means that these ignorant cowards are allowed to get away with, quite frankly, appalling behaviour and there is no means to find out who is abusing. The law in this regard needs to be changed and updated as a matter of urgency.

Iraq

I personally never really cared for Tony Blair. I used to get particularly annoyed when some of my supporters would suggest that he was actually a Conservative. He was hardly that, but was rather the biggest egotistical maniac I've ever met.

As a Prime Minister's unpopularity at home grows, they seem to spend more time abroad lauding it on the world stage. Like others before him, Blair very much took that path and if you analyse the number of conflicts that he allowed our country to be engaged in – Iraq twice, Kosovo, Sierra Leone and Afghanistan – it is truly shocking. The worst example would be his advice to join forces with the Americans and go to war in Iraq.

The Middle East is a very complicated and difficult region. Not that many commentators can produce a proper analysis of it, or explain it in a way in which politicians truly understand. Tony Blair certainly did not, but he still had plenty of unelected advisers that should have known better. We will never know the truth of what lead him to advise the Commons to vote for the war, and we certainly didn't learn the truth from the public enquiry and the rather pathetic evidence that he gave.

To me, it was absolutely typical of the man that he could 'be in bed with Bill Clinton' when he was President and then move seamlessly into the pocket of his Republican successor George W Bush Jr. I've always believed that the UK, with our history, produces governments who far better understand world affairs than most American Presidents do. That in itself is entirely understandable, given the nature of the American democracy and their relatively short history, not to mention their physical distance from Europe.

Saddam Hussein was undoubtedly a wicked, evil tyrant who had no conception of the word democracy and ruled his people with an iron fist. The world, however, is sadly full of such people and it shouldn't be the role of either the US or the UK to act unilaterally as world policemen, engaging in wars and enforcing regime change. I find this even harder to swallow when I read the huge number of documents which prove that this tragic episode amounted to the misleading of Parliament, the body that ultimately sanctioned its leader's irresponsible proposal.

Iain Duncan Smith (then Conservative leader) had a military background. I believed that he would have the correct expertise to ask the right questions and get to the bottom of the matter. Maybe I was wrong. As leader of Her Majesty's opposition, he was invited to Number 10 Downing Street to receive a private briefing on why we should join the Americans and overthrow Saddam Hussein. I recall Iain addressing the Parliamentary party in Committee Room 14 when he told us of the security risks that we would face as a country if Saddam Hussein stayed in power. Privately, I was of the view that we should not get involved in the conflict. I couldn't see what the British interest was in this whole matter. I further couldn't understand what the plan was once Saddam Hussein was overthrown, but I would have expected the leader of Her Majesty's opposition to be briefed properly.

The debate held in parliament on Tuesday 18 March was electric, and I went to the chamber being resolved to vote against the conflict. This was against the advice of my own party leader. However, Tony Blair stood at the despatch box and told the House that if we did not join forces with the Americans, our survival as a nation was in peril. He told us that weapons of mass destruction were aimed at the UK and could reach us within 45 minutes. I was shocked by this revelation and thought how could I possibly let my country down now? No matter how grave the consequences for our brave soldiers might be, it would be irresponsible to allow this dangerous madman to continue. I simply did not believe that a PM could lie or mislead the House to that extent.

So when I heard Tony Blair's evidence I changed my mind as to what I would do. I was so shaken by what I had heard, that when Robin Cook made a magnificent speech in which he explained his reasons for resigning from the government, and advising colleagues to vote against getting involved in the war, I simply was not listening. How I regret that now. The atmosphere in the Commons was absolutely charged as we took the decision to go to war. I had no idea how calamitous that decision would be. As we now know, we were all misled, best summed up by the dodgy dossier. The ease with which a report by Ibrahim al-Marashi, an assistant professor at California State University, entitled 'Iraq – Its Infrastructure of Concealment, Deception and Intimidation' was plagiarised by the Foreign Office and used by Colin Powell at the United Nations, pointed to at best a flawed system and at worst deliberate misrepresentation of an academic's work. In light of the Chilcot Inquiry, I believe the latter to be true.

There can be no argument that this act of folly, which came about as a direct result of Tony Blair misleading Parliament, has destabilised the world order and brought terrorism to our shores much sooner than would otherwise have been the case. I firmly believe that the action of taking us into war, with no plan as to what should be done other than regime change, holds a large proportion of the responsibility for the developments of various terror groups like ISIS and Al-Qaeda. Parliament must never allow the same mistakes to be made again and in the years since 2003, in terms of Libya and Syria, there has been a clear reluctance to repeat the debacle. Whether this has led to an overly cautious approach, I don't think we can yet be sure, but the memories of Iraq have most certainly ensured that a similarly reckless move will be avoided, in the short-term at least. That does not mean the 'War on Terror' has stopped but it has moved online, back behind our borders and into the most isolated of our own communities. Across the pond, a similar process has taken place but only time will tell if our joint efforts in the Middle East will draw us closer together or irrevocably harm the status quo and as a result the Special Relationship between our two countries.

The Special Relationship

Like many people, I have a love affair with the United States of America. I never expected to have two daughters living across the pond, but I'm sure every parent understands, you can't always control your children! One lives in Hollywood, which is a dump, and the other in Charleston which is rather wonderful.

One of the first parliamentary trips I ever went on was arranged by Christian Solidarity. The party was made up of British and American politicians visiting the Soviet Union.

It turned out to be a memorable experience. This wasn't only because of the people that I travelled with, but because the USSR was still under the auspices of the Secret Service. We queued up to see Lenin's body and the homage being paid to him was quite extraordinary. I did wonder whether it really was him or a wax work?! Today, of course, his place in Soviet history has been completely rewritten.

It was on this trip that my friendship with Robert Pittenger, until recently a Congressman representing North Carolina's 9th district, began. We struck up an immediate rapport and I'm so pleased that he successfully progressed on his political journey to Washington. He has a wonderful family and a lovely wife, Suzie. He's also godfather to our youngest daughter Florence. I was born a Catholic and I will die a Catholic, and we certainly share a common faith that what we are experiencing now is not the end. Visiting Robert and Suzie in their native town of Charlotte, I observed first-hand what a huge following their religion has. So vast was one of the churches that there were actually escalators to take you up to one of the viewing levels of the altar. They taught me much about America and why most Americans love the UK and our royalty. You would think America was glamorous, but like most countries they don't do the style, the glamour and the ceremonies in quite the way that us Brits can. They haven't always had glamorous Presidents and I get the impression that they envy our monarchy for that reason. Underlying all of their intrigue is the fact that America is a relatively young country and its citizens love the history of the UK and our wonderful old buildings.

You would think that there are some similarities between our two political systems. There are none. Even the colours of the two parties, Republican and Democrat, are the reverse of Labour and Conservative. I am biased, but I am convinced that the British system gives far greater clarity in terms of power than its American equivalent and I much prefer the fact that our Head of State is above party politics. Equally, there is a chasm between the contact and connection of the general public with American elected representatives and their British counterparts. When American interns come to work at my office each year, they are always shocked at just how closely I correspond with my constituents. Much of this, of course, is determined by the geography; by which I mean, America is vast and the UK is tiny.

I was a young man when I visited America for the first time, doing all the usual studenty things, Greyhound buses and the like. I have now visited many times, been to many states – each like another country – and have often been treated like a lord! I never get tired of the escapism that Disney and Universal Studios provide. While I can't say that I adore American cuisine, I do envy the availability of exotic food and just how cheap it is. I equally love its geography. All the states are so unique, filled with stunning landscapes, challenging accents and different traditions. I love their slightly over the top patriotism and their infective enthusiasm for razzmatazz, not to mention their ambition to be the best at whatever they try, not a bad trait at all.

That said, there is no getting away from the rather unhealthy lifestyle that a vast amount of their citizens indulge in. This was hammered home to me when I was on the Health Select Committee. We visited the country and met all sorts of important food and drink outlets. They were in complete denial as to what their products' effects were on the rising obesity epidemic, which is what our enquiry was all about. The two biggest companies that we visited were Coca-Cola and McDonalds – two huge corporations entrenched in the global psyche. I was mildly amused that no expense was spared in entertaining the Health Select Committee at their headquarters. I found it hilarious that they tried to convince us that their products – which were invariably full of calories, fat, salt and sugar – were not the problem but a lack of physical exercise held complete responsibility.

I thought this was absolute rubbish. After all, you don't die if you don't run but you most certainly will die if you don't eat. The idea that the whole British nation should get kitted out in lycra and run around the park a dozen times is one for the birds. People dip in and out of exercise because of human frailty. If companies like McDonalds and Coca-Cola could develop products that could satisfy the taste buds but without the calorie overload there wouldn't be such a problem. To me, both our countries pay lip service to the issues and have not really taken enough action to deal with a very serious problem. I am afraid that it is a tick box exercise because of vested interests. If that brilliant Committee report had been adopted by the UK and the world, we simply would not have the problems that we do today.

In my judgement, America is a better place to visit than to live in. When it boils down to it, my biggest problem with the US is the large social divide between the haves and the have nots. That said, I am so thankful for the wonderful American friends which I have. I just wish that there had been a different outcome to the War of Independence, how wealthy we would have been today!

I have always marvelled about how our tiny little island has enjoyed influence and control over so many parts of the world. I think it is something that we should be immensely proud of. Our critics would suggest that we have much to answer for, but I think that on balance, this is a harsh verdict. If you were to see a map of the world for the first time today and found that the tiny little land mass labelled the United Kingdom was the key ally of the United States of America, I believe you would marvel at how that island had managed to achieve that level of importance.

Funnily enough, politically there are not too many similarities. Maybe this is because of the way their democracy evolved out of colonial rule and the War of Independence. In most people's minds, America conjures up an image of wealth, power and huge expanse of lands. Politically, in spite of the somewhat unusual positioning of the current President, there is most certainly a special relationship between our two countries. Churchill first coined the phrase during World War II and there has been an ever-present military alliance during the 20th century which has been clear for all to see. More traditionally though, the common language, flows of migration, evangelical Protestantism, liberal traditions and the extensive trade of the 19th century created the foundations for our rapport to flourish. It is a partnership that I have watched with much interest during my time in Parliament.

Margaret Thatcher and Ronald Reagan provided me with my first and fondest memories of the US-UK rapport in action. I suppose you could look back today and think that it was rather an unlikely friendship, but no one should be surprised that the two world leaders got on so well. I believe mutual attraction was at the heart of it. Although elements of the media portrayed Margaret as a 'macho man', she used her feminine charms to great effect. She was also very much enamoured with what she perceived to be handsome men. So the Iron Lady was attracted to the dapper and suave former Hollywood film star. Their relationship can best be summed up by the accurate reporting of the telephone conversations that took place between the leaders. The Falklands Crisis had broken out and Ronald Reagan's staff informed him that Margaret was on the line from Downing Street. He said 'put her through' knowing only too well what would follow. Margaret left Ronald in no doubt at all that when the Americans needed help, the British would give it. Now the British needed his support in terms of allowing aircraft to take off from American bases.

As Margaret ranted on, Ronald held the telephone receiver aloft and said to his assembled team, 'Isn't she magnificent!' He had no problem dealing with a forceful woman, he rather enjoyed it. Both leaders believed in the market and free enterprise, they both abhorred communism and viewed the aims of socialism as somewhat perverse. They had a very firm view of the potential threat that the Soviet Union posed to the world. So when Mikhail Gorbachev became the new Russian Leader, his new approach led Margaret to say, 'This is a man I can do business with.' The combination of Gorbachev, Reagan and

Thatcher dominated the world scene and made it a better and safer place in which to live.

The same cannot be said of Blair and Bush. They were a total disaster. I had always admired George Bush Snr and felt he was unfairly rejected by the American people when he failed to secure a second term. He had been very supportive of Margaret's views on world affairs and if the two of them had been together longer, the debacle of Saddam Hussein's removal, in terms of outcomes, would never have happened. His son George though had secured the Presidency in extraordinary circumstances. The election was so tight that it came down to whoever would win the state of Florida, a situation that is not entirely unusual in Presidential elections. This time though it was rather incredible. The then Vice-President, Al Gore, who seemed a fairly sensible, well-intentioned candidate, was expected to win. He probably wasn't the strongest of campaigners, but it was nevertheless a shock when the vote was practically tied and it came down to the final state, where one of George Bush's brothers, Jeb, was Governor. There seemed to be paralysis for weeks while there was an argument about the ballot papers.

On election day itself, all the commentators were calling it wrong. In the morning, Gore had been declared the winner. Come the afternoon, Bush was told he had won, as he held a healthy lead in Florida. The hitch came when the media realised the final three counties to be counted in Florida were all expected to be strongly Democrat. At this point, and despite Gore having already privately conceded to Bush, the vote in the Sunshine State was split by around 100 votes. Eventually George Bush Jnr was declared the winner, in bizarre and extraordinary circumstances. Throughout his Presidency he was perceived not to have the same intellectual depth as his father.

In light of this controversy, when Tony Blair moved effortlessly from having a close friendship with Bill Clinton, someone who I never cared for, to a close friendship with George Bush, it appeared that he had been presented with an opportunity to have real influence. That he did, with disastrous effect. If he had shown real metal, and been honest, he could have persuaded Bush from his disastrous course of action in Iraq. I am sure of it.

As part of my degree, I studied International Relations and in particular the US political system. It is light years away from our own. I do understand why the three parts of government have been constructed to be a check and a balance on each other, I just don't particularly think it works very well. Their system was the result of the colonial experience, however bizarre it seems today, of the United Kingdom. Congress, the Senate and the President share power. When all three elements are run by the same party then there is real power and direction but that does not happen so often. Through my contact with students from the Catholic University of America, who I receive each year for an internship in my office via my friend Patrick Cormack, I have learnt first-hand how many American people do not understand Westminster. They think the Queen is like the President, Members of the Commons are like the Congress and Members of the Lords are like the Senate. I swiftly disabuse them of that misconception.

Since Herbert Hoover (31st President, 1929–33), Presidential libraries have been established in each President's home state in which documents, artefacts, gifts of state and exhibits are maintained that relate to their life. I have always thought it is a great shame that when British Prime Ministers die, however successful or unsuccessful they have been, there isn't a permanent memorial to their life's work. I am not saying that we have to copy the exact tradition of a library, and I understand that we do have the Churchill Museum and Margaret Thatcher's documents have gone to Cambridge, but in comparison this is very poor. I would have thought that future generations would appreciate a record of the former Prime Minister's achievements and controversies in their hometown. I have had the pleasure of visiting many of these in the US and thought Ronald Reagan's was particularly wonderful. The setting is iconic, and they've designed the library in such a way that you can sit on a static horse as if you are riding with the man himself just as the Queen once did. The newsreels of historic events during his Presidency were fascinating.

I have been fortunate to meet two Presidents. George Bush Snr happened to arrive in The White House when I was being shown around. More recently, when Barack Obama addressed both Houses in Westminster Hall on 25 May 2011 the Speaker introduced me as he was leaving. I should say I got very good eye contact and as he was looking around the Hall, I said I bet you'd like to hire it, which of course you can do now! There is little doubt that the Obamas are a delightful couple. Who can ever forget Barack's stunning Presidential campaign, 'Yes we can.' But what did he do? I can fully understand the celebration of his ethnicity, but a successful Presidency has to be about something more than that. I simply do not understand how it can be claimed that he left America or the world in a better state than when he had become President eight years previously. I do not feel that there were any big ideas in his domestic and national agenda. I am also somewhat puzzled by Steve Hilton's claim that David Cameron and Barack Obama did not hit it off behind closed doors. Publicly, the impression was given quite to the contrary. You would have thought they were best buddies in their causal dress, which I didn't really approve of, even down to having barbecues at Number 10. That's not to mention the most damaging folly of all, getting an American President to intervene in domestic politics. I would certainly love to know the truth of the relationship.

The current climate has produced the most unusual set of world leaders I have ever known. One of these is obviously Donald Trump. The Special Relationship between him and Theresa was a work in progress. You couldn't imagine two people with such conflicting personalities. Theresa is a relatively shy and reserved individual. Before she became Prime Minister, she was never known for socialising heavily. Trump is as brash an individual as you are ever likely to meet and, dare I say, rather uncouth. His fortune comes from (other than the family money) fancy hotels, 24/7 casinos and luxury items. I cannot imagine Theresa taking much pleasure in any of these.

Looking back on how Trump became President in the first place, it is likely that almost any candidate could have beaten him other than Hillary Clinton. She really was the worst candidate that could have possibly run. Either way, he got elected. No sooner had that happened than there was a race to be the first leader to meet him in order to curry favour. With hindsight, it was unwise for Theresa to win that race, but she wasn't to know that at the time. The footage of the pair of them meeting was toe-curling. Our leader was dressed in Republican red, finding her hand held by The Donald, supposedly to help her balance as they walked along the path by the Rose Garden. God Help Us All!

Without any regard for the welfare and well-being of the Queen and the Duke of Edinburgh, the American President was offered a State Visit. It felt like a rather rash move to me. This elderly couple can of course cope with anything, but why inflict on them the agony of having to entertain Donald and Melania? The reaction to the visit being announced was quite unprecedented. I chaired a debate in Westminster Hall after a petition was launched demanding that Trump be banned from the UK. The Speaker spoke out against having to preside over a Presidential address in Westminster Hall; and plans for Trump to open the new American Embassy were shelved as he labelled the new building as 'lousy' and 'horrible', a description with which I rather agree. It was clear that his visit would be tricky.

When he did arrive in July 2018, the Americans had received the message that it would be best to keep it short and sweet. The scaled down visit did take place but without the traditional pomp of previous State Visits. There were large protests particularly in London and Scotland, but I am not entirely convinced that much was achieved by them in terms of influencing the American President to change his style. He seems to rather enjoy and court such controversy. Moreover, I must admit being rather embarrassed by the Mayor of London's blimp which was absolutely pathetic, and I think even he realised that the stunt was a great mistake. As ever though, the Queen was brilliant and did her duties at Windsor Castle. There were some cringe worthy moments as The Donald had no idea how to walk with a 92-year-old and Melania could not shake her blank and robotic expression, but the ordeal was short-lived, just a cup of tea before Trump jetted off.

I suspect that it would be quite difficult for any British Prime Minister to enjoy the traditional special relationship with this US President, particularly as a woman. In contrast, the new and very young French President who clearly sees himself as Napoleon, albeit married to his grandmother, jumped in with both feet and treated the Trumps to a lavish State Visit. This was reciprocated. I found the whole spectacle both bizarre and sickening. The two First Ladies dressed in white (hardly fitting) and the two Presidents, God forbid, kissing one another. Then the French President was accorded the honour of addressing both Houses of Congress while bizarrely sticking the boot into his new ally's politics. Republican legislators must have been somewhat confused as to whether they ought to stand up or sit down. The lasting memories of the visit will be the humiliation of Donald flicking dandruff from Emmanuel's shoulder and the French being called 'perfect'. I think not.

Our Special Relationship seems to have stalled in as much as this American President seems to have far closer ties with everyone, even the dodgy North Koreans. The American President seems to meet world leaders and, while the meeting is taking place, heaps praise on them as if he was their best buddy before belittling them again. He made a fool of Macron, a fool of Trudeau, didn't manage to strong-arm Xi Jinping and made Merkel look even more awkward and dour than she actually is. As for our own then PM, Theresa May, the images of her meeting and dealing with Donald Trump were dire beyond belief. So, the traditional relationship that we revere does seem to be shaped and moulded by the personalities, the characters and the politics of whoever hold the two respective offices. In my time, it has been at its strongest and most effective when Thatcher and Reagan worked together so effectively. In the long run I don't think we should worry too much as things will change with the advent of the next incumbent of The White House. That said, we do need to be careful to not look ridiculous, to keep our dignity and in terms of trade, to get the best agreement that we can.

Uniting the Union?

We live in extraordinary times. The unthinkable seems to be happening. The unimaginable seems to be elected. Despite all of my positivity, there is no escaping that we are not immune from this turbulence and on this basis, I fear for the potential break up of our beloved Union. I never thought that I would live to see its possible demise, but I also never thought devolution would happen.

As far as I am concerned, it would be heresy if history were thrown out of the window and the UK broken up. Our kingdom is best when we are united, we are stronger when we are together, our economies grow faster and our security is better protected. At the risk of upsetting its most fervent supporters, I am not entirely convinced that devolution has been the great success that it was supposed to be. In reality, it was a response to the loss of political support for Conservative Party MPs in Wales and Scotland. There has always been the view among some that the government of our country was too London centric. My view is that all countries must have a capital and ours happens to be London.

London has changed dramatically from when I grew up in the East End. In many ways, this has been rather poorly handled. I say this because of my family's direct experiences in the East End. The original settlers and their families have all moved out. I think that is a great shame for many reasons. I'm not saying that government and councils shouldn't embrace modernisation, fashion and all of that, but I'm very puzzled that no government seems to have addressed what can be described as the mass exodus of original residents from various parts of the United Kingdom, most importantly our capital. Is it that with different nationalities moving in these original residents felt challenged or intimidated? I don't know. What I am completely sure of is that it is troubling and somewhat unhealthy to see the polarisation of the London Borough of Newham. Communal divides mean the style of housing, public services and buildings have taken on their own dramatic personalities. Rather than all come together and integrate, quite the reverse has happened. The East End community spirit that I knew growing up no longer exists in the same way. London is the greatest capital in the world but at the moment I do not see it as the triumph of multiculturalism like many others do.

I suppose the point I am making is that London is not all it is made out to be and there are fundamental flaws in the way it is developing as a city. I haven't even mentioned the worrying spike in crime. I am not sure if those in the devolved territories have picked up on this or not, but I do know they are fed up of hearing about Westminster and the capital.

Northern Ireland

The history of Ireland is well reported and there are those who will always hark back to the potato famine, rule by the monarchy and other flash points. Those individuals have long campaigned for a United Ireland. I believe that recent times have exemplified the value of its membership to the United Kingdom. Nationalism is on the rise again in Northern Ireland.

The expression of nationalist sentiments gained force in the most wicked of ways through the actions of the Irish Republican Army. That is not to excuse the terrible atrocities on the Unionist side, but when the division between the North and South of Ireland was made, the IRA seemed to be intent on killing their way to achieving their ultimate goal. This senseless approach resulted in the murder of countless people, including members of the Royal Family, the clergy, the military and politicians. Another tactic used was that of hunger strikes which took place in HM Prison Maze. Perhaps the best-known suicide was that of Bobby Sands. He was chosen as the Commanding Officer of the Provisional IRA Prisoners in the Maze and was striking to raise awareness of political prisoner's lack of rights. He wanted a Special Category Status that would free IRA members from ordinary prison regulations. He died aged 27 after 66 days on strike. His death sparked worldwide reactions both for and against the nationalist cause.

Margaret was Prime Minister at the time, and she issued a stern rebuke: 'Mr Sands was a convicted criminal. He chose to take his own life. It was a choice that his organisation did not allow to many of its victims.' Papers have since been released that displayed Margaret's human reaction, praising the efforts of the strikers and painstakingly ruing the unnecessary loss of human life. 'You have to hand it to some of these IRA boys. If they didn't go on strike they'd be shot by their own side. What a waste! What a terrible waste of human life!' However, she was also very nearly killed in the Brighton bombing and had always insisted that she would never negotiate with terrorists. True to her word, she never did. But there was undoubtedly a great price to pay with that steadfast approach.

John Major took a very different view. It was he, not Tony Blair, who started the peace process. I was extremely sceptical and never thought that the strategy would work. I was proved wrong and it undoubtedly has and still does, for the moment at least. Pundits have invariably been cruel to John, but I am confident his role in the whole peace process will be viewed with admiration when the history books are finally written. In the course of time, when government records are released, we will be in a much better position to judge how the talks came about. What undoubtedly was the case was that to initiate the conversations in the first place and make contact with terrorists was a huge gamble and one taken with considerable risk.

Blair, being the showman that he is, produced the Good Friday Agreement in the early days of his leadership. His then Northern Irish Secretary of State, the late Mo Mowlam, was famously parodied as having been side-lined to the role of making cups of tea while 'the important politicians spoke'. This was quite unfair. She played a considerable role in moving the process forward. Whenever I read about her life, I never cease to be amazed by the powerful personality she possessed. Known for her hyperbolic enthusiasm, she would be taking her wig off one day, hugging shoppers in Belfast the next, before responding to the Prime Minister with remarks such as 'I would rather be having vigorous sexual intercourse.' Tragically, she didn't live long enough to enjoy the fruits of her endeavours as a result of her fatal brain tumour. But her rather quirky way was absolutely instrumental in moving the dialogue forward.

Sinn Féin, led by the late Martin McGuinness and recently retired Gerry Adams, were never straight nor direct in condemning the violence which they had undoubtedly perpetrated. I never thought I would live to see a Northern Irish Assembly with the late, great Ian Paisley Senior on one side and Gerry Adams perched on the other. Her Majesty the Queen, who in anyone's fair judgement is a simply outstanding monarch, showed great generosity of spirit given the murder of members of her own family when she and her husband visited the Republic of Ireland for three days in May 2011. It marked 100 years since the last visit by a British monarch, which had taken place when the entire island was still part of the UK. The Queen, being the Queen, dazzled, speaking some Irish during her speech, striking a tone of sorrow and marking an important symbolic occasion by formally normalising relations following the 1998 Good Friday Agreement. She is a truly remarkable woman and has been an absolute stalwart of our country throughout my time in Westminster.

While both sides have a chequered history, I do see the situation as relatively stable despite all the noise being made about Brexit. No government will allow a situation where a hard border comes into play between Ireland and Northern Ireland.

Wales and Scotland

In my opinion, two issues drove the creation of the Scottish Nationalist Party and Plaid Cymru. First, citizens felt that London dominated Westminster politics too much. Second, those same individuals believe that their respective nations would benefit economically from being completely independent. I fundamentally disagree with those views. A fully independent Wales and/or Scotland would be in neither regions interest – I think they would struggle to survive, economically at least. For instance, the oil price crash is not good for the UK as a whole, but if Scotland were to go it alone, it would be a significant obstacle for them to overcome. I suppose that is the Scottish people's prerogative to decide upon, but it would be a great shame to narrow our British identity. One benefit of the current climate is that we are being reminded of the dangers of nationalism. It can be fashionable as well as very emotive, but I am hopeful that we experienced the peak of its popularity in the 2015 general election.

There are fundamental differences in support for Scottish and Welsh Nationalism. This was clearly exemplified during the 1997 referendum which asked the Welsh electorate if they supported the creation of an assembly for Wales with devolved powers. Despite not having any Conservative MPs in Wales after the 1997 election and a Labour whip enforcing Labour support for the assembly, there was only a 50 per cent turnout and of those that did vote, 50.3 per cent were in favour. A tiny margin.

The Scottish vote was held a week earlier and produced a far more decisive result. Again, my party were the only opponents of the creation of an assembly and the transfer of jurisdiction over tax-raising powers. There a 60 per cent turnout produced 74 per cent of the votes in favour of a parliament and 63 per cent supporting tax-raising powers.

Successive Conservative Prime Ministers have always supported the Union. They have always acted in the best interests
of all four countries. Not everyone would be supportive of
my view however, and Margaret was viewed with suspicion
by Wales and Scotland in particular. The Welsh were particularly opposed to Margaret's policies towards the trade unions.
During the Miners' Strike, 25,000 Welsh mineworkers lost
their jobs thanks to the subsequent pit closures. These closures
were inevitably going to happen anyway, but that doesn't hide
the fact that they left numerous communities struggling to fill
the void. North of the border, the decision to introduce the
community charge in Scotland in 1989 but only to the rest
of the country in 1990 provoked anger amongst the Scottish
populace and led to the arguments that Scottish voters were
being treated as guinea pigs for laws and projects in England.
In terms of a public relations exercise, it was an absolute disaster. Where the advice to do this came from I do not know, but
it was a very poor recommendation. As well as being incredibly inflammatory, it made it look as if it did not matter to the
government whether the policy went wrong for the people of
Scotland or not.

One issue that I have never been able to get my head around
is the strong relationship between the Scots and the Royal
Family. I find it somewhat puzzling that there is such a strong
independence movement in spite of this. It is no secret that the
Royal Family loves Scotland and Balmoral in particular, yet
the monarchy's closeness has never effectively dampened the
independence cause.

As set out in the devolution agreements, the Scottish Government has power to legislate on unreserved matters within
Scotland. The 2007 administration found hostility towards
their plans to hold an independence referendum in 2010. However, when the SNP won 69 of the 129 seats in Holyrood in
2011, they now had a majority of four and a fresh mandate to
call a referendum. Cameron did not really have any choice but
to agree yet he was still able to secure commitments and ensure

that the question was fair, legal and decisive. The referendum date was set for Thursday 18 September 2014.

The campaign saw all the main British Parties come together to make the case against Scottish independence and for maintaining the United Kingdom. I must admit that this tactic did not necessarily fill me with hope. After all, the Conservatives had been reduced to just one Member of Parliament in Scotland, the brave David Mundell, after 2010 but with Labour still going strong, I did not see too many reasons to worry.

Alex Salmond, the leader of the SNP, was a seasoned campaigner and an astute politician who gambled on the 'Aye' vote winning. The main party politicians who made the case against independence were Alistair Darling for Labour, Alistair Carmichael for the Liberals and Ruth Davidson and David Mundell for the Conservatives. None of these individuals had previously struck much of a chord in the rest of the UK, but maybe this made them more relatable in the eyes of voters. I recall the leader of the Labour Party in Scotland, Jim Murphy, telling me how unpleasant the campaign had been. He told me how aggressive many gatherings became and of the general tension throughout the whole of the nation. It remains a complete mystery today why Gordon Brown seemed so reluctant to play a major role in the campaign. After all, he had represented a Scottish constituency for many years and had a strong following among many Scottish people. He was noticeable by his absence and it was only towards the end of the campaign that he appeared at a rally and powerfully made the case for a No vote. Parliament, which was hardly sitting during those weeks, was as partisan as ever. Although judging by the noise made by the SNP members, you would have thought that the vote for independence was a foregone conclusion.

I must confess that I felt somewhat frustrated during the referendum campaign. For a while, there was the cry that the whole of the United Kingdom should have a vote. Logically, I certainly agree with that point. Many people I sensed were sick to death of what they saw as certain politicians endlessly whingeing about a lack of resources. They argued that if you looked at the ratio of people to land mass, Scotland had received more than their fair share of finances, yet some sectors like healthcare still had extremely poor outcomes. All this meant that I encountered numerous people who would, if they had had a vote in the referendum, have voted to get shot of Scotland!

The plea for everyone to be included in the referendum never gained traction and so it was very difficult to see how an English MP could possibly campaign in Scotland without getting a great deal of negativity. They would rightly question who we were and what right we had to stick our nose into what they regarded as an essentially Scottish matter. Notwithstanding those arguments, Scotland was a long way away and that didn't make it very easy for any southern MP to travel and help campaign on either side while continuing with their normal duties. So English MPs, other than those in the north, were left twiddling their thumbs while the argument was made about the future of the United Kingdom. You would have expected the referendum campaign to dominate Parliamentary business in the way that Brexit has, but it didn't and that was due in no small measure to the relatively few elected SNP members. I know most of those members quite well and would ask them how they felt the campaign was going. They always seemed very confident of a YES victory.

As it turned out, despite the Scottish people displaying clear reservations about London centric politics, they definitively rejected calls for independence. 84 per cent of the electorate voted and 55 per cent of them voted no to Scotland becoming an independent country. It would be an exaggeration to say that the Scottish independence referendum gripped the nation. That it most certainly did not. However, amongst English voters there was huge resentment at the fact that they themselves were not given a voice. After all, logically, they should have had a vote but were denied that opportunity.

Salmond must have been devastated by the result, but the 2015 General Election would have provided him with plenty of solace. The Nationalist vote had been buoyed up and the Conservatives, Labour and the Liberals were all reduced to one seat each in Scotland. It was absolutely remarkable. The Liberal Democrats had gone from a party in government to the fourth largest party in Parliament.

The SNP made an immediate impact, were terribly well-disciplined and all supported each other quite unlike the more traditional parties. Not only that but SNP members came from a diverse range of backgrounds and they would rail against London centric politics while clearly enjoying the Westminster experience. They know how to play to their audience at home. They were vocal, courteous and quite traditional in their Westminster activities.

Salmond used his vast experience and shrewd judgement to make sure that the SNP group were not 'contaminated' by the Westminster bubble. He, with one or two of his experienced colleagues, made sure that the group's voices were heard but that they were courteous and also observed the traditions of the House. He recognised that they would be most unwise to fall foul of the Speaker. They did for a while get involved in a tussle for Dennis Skinner's bench and on one or two occasions even tried to occupy the front bench. Furthermore, they attempted to continue with the Holyrood tradition of applauding speeches. That was against all convention and was eventually stopped. They made sure that they always had a representative to speak in Westminster Hall and rather enjoyed their promotion to the third party, leapfrogging the Liberals.

What struck me immediately was not so much the antipathy of the SNP towards us but the bad blood between them and Labour. That was quite understandable given that many long-serving Labour MPs had lost their Scottish seats. So the 2015 election resulted in a significant shift in the Parliamentary dynamics of Westminster. The Liberal Democrats must have felt humiliated as they struggled to have their voice heard. I can't imagine how frustrating that would have been for individuals like Nick Clegg and Vince Cable. They had recently occupied seats around the Cabinet table but were now treated as being totally irrelevant. This repositioning could best be seen at Prime Minister's Question Time when the SNP leader in the House of Commons, first Angus Robertson and now Ian Blackford, has their own slot to challenge the PM.

2017's snap election stopped their dramatic rise in its tracks. I am not entirely sure how Nicola Sturgeon (Mrs Krankie) is perceived in Scotland but in the area I represent, her hectoring went down like a lead balloon. I would go as far as to say she is hated in Southend West. I could only speculate as to why that is but if I were to hazard a guess I would put it down to her pushy nature and the lack of any obvious humility. Her party paid the price for ignoring other domestic issues at the election by losing half their seats to the three more traditional UK parties. You would have thought that would have changed her style permanently and for a while she appeared chastened. More recently however she seems determined to press on with her ill thought out plan. She has been particularly outspoken over our exit from the EU. She sees it as an opportunity to bash the government over its negotiating plans. Below the border, Brand Sturgeon has undoubtedly become toxic. There can be little doubt that the SNP leader, who had in part been overshadowed by Alex Salmond, was really enjoying her time in the spotlight. I recall being at the reception after Margaret Thatcher's funeral at The Guildhall. I found myself talking to the person who I found out to be her husband, a very pleasant gentleman who seemed to be more or less running the SNP.

He was then called over to join a conversation his wife seemed to be having with more important people than myself, which didn't impress me so much. The SNP leader has become terribly grand but unless she can deliver on achieving independence for Scotland her leadership is doomed to end in failure.

The whole question of the breakup of the United Kingdom and Scottish independence in particular, is not a new
issue. The future of the United Kingdom, devolution and
other related matters, was often raised in Parliament by a
Scottish member, Tam Dalyell, throughout his time in Parliament. It became known as the West Lothian Question, aptly
named after his constituency. He suggested that there should
be Scottish Votes in Parliament on specifically Scottish matters
and likewise English votes on just English matters. Following
devolution and its settlement we now have a procedure called
EVEL – 'English Votes for English Laws' – which critics, the
SNP in particular, perceive to be of no value at all and rather
meaningless. We will have to see how in the long-term this
matter is dealt with but for now I see the future of the United
Kingdom as being secure.

Banging on about Europe – Maastricht vs Brexit

Our membership of the European Union has long been con-
tentious. That is perfectly understandable. We face the unique
dilemma of being an island and thus not being geographically
connected to the Continent while at the same time sharing a
common history and residing only a stone's throw away from
the port of Calais. Considering this, the tensions between those
who want closer integration and those who want to rediscover
our independence should come as no surprise.

Ever since we were taken into the European Community by
Ted Heath, my party in particular has been split on the issue.
Despite all that has happened between then and now, the for-
mation of the European Union, the signing of the Maastricht
Treaty, its enlargement to 28 countries and the creation of the
Euro, to name a few, opinion has remained largely divided.
This most recently manifested itself in the 2016 referendum
and the subsequent fallout which I hope, once and for all, will
solve the question of whether Britain should be a part of the
European Union.

Referendum No. 1: 1975

This referendum happened years before I would become a Member of Parliament but that did not stop me from joining with 18 elected members led by Ronald Bell, Member for Beaconsfield, for the duration of the campaign. My view on the whole issue was pretty straightforward. If we had been a founding member then things might have been different but Charles de Gaulle's treatment of Harold Macmillan when he made the move to join was pretty insulting. On an emotional level, it felt like he had forgotten the British people's efforts to liberate Continental Europe and France, in particular from Nazi Germany. From a more democratic perspective, I could never forgive Ted Heath for not holding a referendum when he first took us in to the EU.

In the modern era, it would be unthinkable that such a fundamental and serious change in the way we are governed would not be directly put to the people. Consequently, it took the election of Harold Wilson's government to finally give the British people a say. In my opinion, the impact of a referendum as to whether or not to stay in the EU was quite different to the impact had it been held to consider our joining the Union in the first place.

Those of us who were old enough to vote in the first referendum will recall what a different atmosphere there was. Political engagement now would be largely unrecognisable to that generation of the '70s. In 1975 letters were written, newspapers were an important source of information and public meetings were still popular. In 2016, it was fought in a completely different way, heavily dominated by the use of social media. While public meetings were held, unless some hugely engaging politician (of which there are no longer many) was the speaker, people were not persuaded to leave their homes and listen to arguments made in a public place.

There has been an extraordinary turnaround since that 1975 referendum in terms of the positions of the main parties regarding our membership. The Conservative Party was seen as primarily being pro-EU. The governing Labour Party were led by the likes of Tony Benn and Michael Foot in opposing membership. That said, it could hardly be described as a unified cabinet position. In the 1970s there were also key government figures who wanted to remain.

The campaign was robust rather than ruthless and after much foot stamping by politicians the result confirmed the conservative nature of the British people and they overwhelmingly voted to stay. The result could not have been more damning. A 64 per cent turnout produced 17.3 million votes to stay in the European Community which was 67 per cent of the vote.

From what I recall of events those who were on the losing side accepted the result with seemingly good grace. Indeed, my view was that as long as we were members, we should make the most of whatever benefits there were to being 'in the club'. In general, I had always supported ties with Europe, whether that be in trade of goods and services, cultural and educational links or common defence issues. However, I was totally opposed to a United States of Europe with one government and one currency. Moreover, and this is crucial when thinking of today's circumstances, I don't once remember anyone suggesting we should have another vote to overturn the result.

Maastricht and Major

Having been elected in 1983, I was inspired and reassured that Margaret would fight and get the best deal possible when negotiating with any of our European partners. She was not going to let us be walked all over. In fact, she did the opposite and secured a rebate on what we were paying to the fund. This made perfect sense considering that we were the second biggest financial contributors behind Germany. Despite her dominance, I would still find myself far too often frustrated by the injustice of sticking to the rules while many of our partners did not. When Margaret did go, the John Major years that followed were overshadowed by internal party disputes regarding Maastricht and the single currency.

There is, I think, a very interesting comparison to be made between Major's Maastricht rebels and today's Brexit rebels. I suppose when you have the top job you need an iron constitution and a thick skin, and I am not sure that John Major did. Margaret survived not least because she didn't read all the awful things said about her in the media. On the contrary, John read far too much, and it wasn't always flattering, in fact it was rather bruising. For that reason, he increasingly showed his frustration, if not anger, at those who became known as the Maastricht rebels. The rebels felt that signing up to the Maastricht Treaty was a step too far and was the beginning of a journey taking us towards a United States of Europe with one government. Tensions between those who were loyal to the Prime Minister and those who felt he was betraying British interests grew in intensity. I well remember the press conference held by rebels in which they were portrayed as being potty. The group picture of Tony Marlow, Teresa Gorman, Dick Body and Teddy Taylor gave an impression of a rather wild group of people, not considered wholly sane or mainstream. This was quite unfair.

In those days, the Whips Office put huge pressure on colleagues to step into line. While I never saw it myself, one of the whips, David Lightbown, a physically substantial figure, was accused of using threatening behaviour. It is not the only allegation I had heard of throughout that period. The same office is a relatively genteel place these days, so the Brexit rebels like Anna Soubry, Nicky Morgan and Dominic Grieve did not face the same pressures. The Maastricht rebels did not have the benefit of social media, if you can call it a benefit. The sharing of news was a much slower process. The Brexit rebels were remorselessly given a platform, totally out of kilter with the number they represented in Parliament. The Whips were helpless to silence or restrain colleagues, for the simple reason that they no longer possess the patronage that they once had to make or break careers.

In the end Boris Johnson expelled 21 MPs from the Conservative Party. Anna Soubry and a number of Labour politicians defected to the Independent Group and some of the expelled Conservatives joined them. Most of them were not selected by their local Associations to fight the 2019 election and although some of them stood as independent candidates in their old seats they were rejected by the electorate.

Another fundamental difference between the Maastricht rebels and the Brexit rebels is obviously concerning the substance of what they were protesting about. The Maastricht rebels were dealing specifically with the direction of travel of our membership of the European Union. The Brexit rebels were not really complaining about the direction of travel, despite maintaining they were. They fundamentally disagreed with the result of the referendum and wanted a rerun to take place.

One day in particular highlighted the difficulties faced by our government. I remember Black Wednesday only too well, 16 September 1992.

The Chancellor of the Exchequer Norman Lamont had William Hague as his PPS. Michael Portillo was Chief Secretary to the Treasury and I was his PPS. As a sort of reward for our work we were chosen to go on a delegation to Japan led by the late Peter Viggers, MP for Gosport. Peter would later become notorious for allegedly claiming for the expense of a floating duck house for his Hampshire home. I remember my excitement as we left Heathrow, I had never been to Japan before. Although I should confess, when we did arrive there, I was a little disappointed as the bullet train didn't stop where it was supposed to, the capital city was bathed in smog and our visit to Hiroshima was somewhat eerie. I had arranged with a friend who lived in Hawaii to fly on to see him after the trip was over, so in essence I would be flying literally around the world. What a wonderful opportunity!

The policy of shadowing the Deutschmark and then entering the Exchange Rate Mechanism was one which Margaret Thatcher had not been happy with at all. John took a different view having been Chancellor of the Exchequer before being Prime Minister. From my discussions with Michael Portillo I don't think Norman was that enthusiastic about joining but had little option than to do his master's bidding. Joining was a disaster. The pound plummeted and there was a financial crisis. I will never forget watching from Japan in horror as Norman was harassed coming out of Number 11 Downing Street. He swiftly brushed his hair to one side and with one fell swoop announced that a turbulent day on the markets had led to the government withdrawing from the ERM (the European Exchange Rate Mechanism). It was a catastrophic day for the money markets and such a contrast to 1992 when so many people told me following my re-election as MP for Basildon they had made money on the market. On Black Wednesday, as it became known, those same individuals lost a huge amount of money. An emergency debate was called which the government couldn't prevent. Parliament was recalled and all MPs were needed. I was mortified. We duly returned home and there weren't even any votes! Thanks to the cut and thrust of politics, I never got to go to Hawaii.

Major and Lamont fell out badly which eventually resulted in the latter's removal from office. Many thought this was grossly unfair as Norman had been very vocal in his support of the PM. What had been a wonderful surprise and a dramatic election victory turned irrevocably sour and triggered the damning defeat we suffered at the '97 election.

From that moment onwards, the issue of our membership of the EU was to be at the forefront of Tory divisions and so it was that David Cameron went into the 2015 General Election promising the British people that if the Conservatives were re-elected, a referendum would be held on our membership of the EU.

Referendum No. 2: 2016

David Cameron, who I had not supported as a candidate for leadership of the Conservative Party, proved to be a brilliant

Prime Minister and Westminster performer. He dominated the House of Commons and led the coalition government with great effect. It is a cruel matter of history that quite unfairly, this very successful PM will perhaps always be remembered for calling a referendum on a subject which he turned out to be on the losing side of. The political pressure had begun in 2011 when 81 Conservative MPs, of which I was one, revolted against the party line and called for a referendum on Britain's European Union membership. A five-hour Commons debate was triggered by an e-petition which called for a referendum on whether the UK should stay in the EU, leave it or renegotiate its membership. We were defeated 483 to 111 but made our mark on Parliament.

In 2013, Cameron made the Bloomberg speech, in which he set out his reasons for calling for a change in the way the EU worked. On 7 May 2015, he was returned to Downing Street having achieved the first Conservative majority government for 23 years and with that committed to holding a referendum on our membership of the European Union. It is no exaggeration to say that his actions electrified the media and those in the House of Commons who had long campaigned for us to leave. I was absolutely delighted, as I never thought we would be given such an opportunity again within my lifetime.

When the draft EU deal was published, Eurosceptic MPs like myself were not at all happy with it. The so-called deal was meaningless, and made us all the more determined to argue the case for leaving. The main sticking points were in essence about the deal not securing that which we all wanted, taking back control of the future direction of our country in terms of immigration and reciprocal rights. The deal was formally announced and the referendum date set. I was excited and inspired by the opportunity that was now presented. However, I felt in the back of my mind that the British people, being conservative with a small c, would vote to remain.

It was pretty well-known on which side most Members of Parliament were, most had told their electorate in the previous campaign. What wasn't quite so obvious, given the long vaunted collective cabinet responsibility, was how individual members of the cabinet would vote. There was much speculation, including the position of the then Prime Minister Theresa May. The leading 'thought-to-be' Brexiteers in the Cabinet were John Whittingdale, Theresa Villiers, Chris Grayling, Iain Duncan Smith and Priti Patel. What was not so obvious were the voting intentions of Michael Gove, Boris Johnson and Sajid Javid. While it was thought they had Brexit leanings, they had not yet declared their position.

Gove was the first to break cover, emphatically outlining the arguments for us leaving the European Union, declaring 'our country would be freer, fairer and better off outside the EU'. Others preferred to keep their heads in the sand. Sajid Javid had incorrectly been assumed to be enthusiastic about us leaving, but as it turned out he backed Remain, which if he had long-term ambitions was somewhat damaging in terms of the support that he might eventually expect from Brexiteers.

The one senior figure who everyone wanted to hear from was Boris Johnson. He was often described as a close friend of David Cameron. That might well have been the case and they were certainly together at university. There is also plenty of pictorial evidence that they mingled in the same social spheres. Cameron was two years younger than Boris at Eton, before following him to Oxford, where they were both members of the famous Bullingdon Club. It was known that they hadn't always seen eye to eye and most certainly had completely contrasting approaches. One was smooth and hard-working, the other charming and likeable but reliant on wit. I will let you decide which one is which! Either way, due to their mutual background, Boris's decision was seen as particularly important in relation to Cameron's future and as an indicator of the strength of the Prime Minister.

The atmosphere was feverish when Boris was surrounded in the street outside his home by the media. It was time to declare his intentions. 'I would like to see a new relationship based more on trade, on cooperation, with much less of this supranational element.' Boris would be voting and campaigning for us to leave the European Union. The shock waves felt from this announcement resonated most strongly in Number 10, where his actions were seen as a betrayal of his friend. I was delighted, as he was certainly a well-known public figure who, however bizarrely he behaved and acted, was an acclaimed character with a very large following. I personally liked Boris a lot, but then who doesn't? He is a very unusual politician and when I first met him I really had no idea that he would eventually hold enough gravitas to become first Mayor of London, then Foreign Secretary, never mind Prime Minster. Sometimes, you just can't tell. The Leave campaign were thrilled, and the media lapped it up. Things had just got a lot more interesting. I had already booked to have Boris to speak at my Dining Club fundraiser at the Union Jack Club. He received the sort of reception for a Conservative politician I had not seen for many years. Unorthodox he might have been, but my supporters really engaged with him. The Brexiteers now had more than one big hitter and Cameron had been publicly wrong-footed.

In spite of my privately held pessimistic views, I entered the campaign on a positive note, wanting to give this unexpected opportunity my best shot. In recent years I hadn't really been involved with the various groups on my side of the argument. As a result, I wasn't up to speed with the split in terms of who might become the organisation promoting the official Leave campaign. In the red corner was Vote Leave and in the green corner Grassroots Out. The choice of who would be the official campaign was crucial, as they would be the ones to benefit from public funding. Vote Leave seemed to have the heavy guns backing it whereas Grassroots Out struggled other than with two colleagues, Tom Pursglove and Peter Bone.

Peter came to see me in my office to explain what was happening, he was a doughty campaigner who had once been a resident of, and former Councillor in, Southend. I agreed to take piles of literature and campaign material from him and try and get it delivered in our town. I also agreed to appear at a rally in the Circus Tavern, Purfleet. This I duly did with a number of speakers, the main attraction of whom was Nigel Farage. I rocked up at the Circus Tavern and was led into the arena, which was a bit like appearing at a slightly seedy working men's club as the B-list entertainer. My speech was fairly well received by those assembled, who I subsequently learnt were mainly UKIP supporters. Needless to say, when their leader climbed into the room he was welcomed in a manner not far removed from a revivalist Billy Graham meeting, they absolutely loved him. He didn't pull any punches and was very forthright in how and why he thought we should leave the European Union. He got a rapturous ovation and I had a brief chat with him as he left, surrounded by his 'heavies'. As I drove back to Southend I decided that I wouldn't repeat the experience as I had effectively, I felt, legitimised some of the damage that UKIP had done to my own party. As it turned out Vote Leave comfortably got the support it needed. The battle lines were now drawn. The fight would be between Vote Leave and Britain Stronger in Europe.

It certainly was a good start to the campaign, as people like myself no longer felt isolated as members of the Cabinet were now prepared to put their heads above the parapet. Parliament adjourned for the recess and campaigning started with vigour. Locally, I decided to have a public launch on Ridgway Green with my guest speakers Patrick O'Flynn of UKIP and Brendan Chilton of Labour Leave. We drew an excellent crowd. I gathered together a group of people who would help me campaign in Southend West. It couldn't be done through the Conservative Association as, although we were overwhelmingly of the view we should leave the EU, the Conservative Party had to be seen to remain neutral. We did doorstep knocking as I always do and received a pretty positive response. At weekends I worked with some UKIP members at stalls in various shopping centres in the constituency, giving out the bog-standard leaflets and balloons. I asked a parliamentary friend, Bernard Jenkin, the erudite MP for Harwich and North Essex, to come and address a public meeting. It was very well attended, and he got a good reception from the audience, who were overwhelmingly in agreement with him. As he left the meeting, he shared with me the intelligence that the campaign seemed to be going well but like me, he suspected that we wouldn't quite do it.

On the other side of the argument, things seemed to be progressing with a little less speed. On 14 April, the Labour leader Jeremy Corbyn made his first Remain speech. This was bizarre seeing as he had always wanted to leave the EU. Since we had been elected on the same day my view of the EU hadn't changed and as far as I could tell Jeremy's hadn't either. I could not understand this change of heart and privately wondered how it would play in the Labour heartlands which as far as I understood would vote heavily to leave.

I cannot say I was impressed with the Government's antics either. In spite of their denials, the government machine was used to remorselessly frighten the electorate into voting to remain in the European Union. A so-called factual and impartial booklet was even produced. Stamped with the 'HM Government' logo, the leaflet was entitled 'Why the Government believes that voting to remain in the European Union is the best decision for the UK'. I was outraged by the production of the leaflet. Taxpayers had paid £8.9 million for the privilege. I am not sure such a propaganda tool should ever be used again. It wasn't just the leaflet but the fact that individuals, who I was of the opinion should have remained neutral, were getting involved. The Governor of the Bank of England, quite inappropriately, pointed out what he perceived to be the risks of us leaving but the most bizarre intervention of all was that of Barack Obama. What on earth possessed the Remain side to think it would be helpful for an American President to tell the British people that in any future trade deals they would go to the back of the queue. Hearing this from the leader of a former ally went down like a lead balloon. The nation felt insulted. Surely President Obama knew it was a cardinal sin for foreign leaders to interfere in other nation's elections. If anything, he bolstered the resolve of those already determined to vote to leave the EU and those who might be tempted to do so. It might sound crude but British people do not take kindly to foreigners telling them what to do.

Not only was the government machine against Brexit, but the BBC were too. The anti-Brexit propaganda was remorseless. I rather take the Denis Thatcher view of the broadcaster and I find it very annoying that the publicly-funded organisation should, whoever the government is, be less than even-handed in its analysis. We should nonetheless be very proud of the broadcaster – they have some wonderful journalists and the reporting can be of the highest calibre – but during the Brexit debate they were (for once) pro-Government. They emphasised Cameron's views and portrayed the leave campaigners as being somewhat swivel-eyed.

The general consensus among people like myself was that the PM and others had run an extremely negative campaign, not pointing out what positive merits there were from being a member but suggesting to the British people that the sky would literally fall in if we left. There would supposedly be dire consequences from our departure. The pound would crash, investment would stop, huge numbers of jobs would be lost, taxes would go up, there would be an economic crash the like of which we have never seen before. Most sensible people saw through what was happening and far from boosting the Remain campaign, damage was being done to their cause.

The campaign was completely overshadowed by the horrendous death of Jo Cox. My parliamentary friend, Mark Francois, first alerted me to the breaking news that an MP had been seriously injured. Like everyone else I was stunned. A young and successful woman was cut down in the prime of her life, torn from the family who loved her. This sort of thing just was not supposed to happen in the UK. It appeared that a supporter of some far right organisation had been responsible for her murder, and although no one spelled it out in plain language, the clear impression was given that the campaign to leave the EU might in some part have fuelled the mind of Jo's murderer. I privately wondered how this would play with the campaign and came to the conclusion that it might well cause some people to have second thoughts about our leaving. Campaigning was suspended over that weekend and heartfelt tributes paid to our fallen colleague. The mood had turned very sombre. It was this chilling feeling that we would relive a year later after the Westminster and Manchester attacks. No one really had the stomach to resume the battle for hearts and minds.

Nevertheless, the campaign did restart and perhaps the most unedifying public debate by national politicians was held on 21 June at Wembley. Quite how the participants were selected I do not know, but it ended up as one man against five women. Normally when a man debates against a woman, if the man is too aggressive, he will not receive a sympathetic hearing. On this occasion the man was Boris and he found himself up against five forthright women, two of which were from his own side. Ruth Davidson, the leader of the Scottish Conservatives immediately laid into him, not only interrupting him but berating him. Worse still, the Home Secretary Amber Rudd made the classic remark that Boris was not the man you wanted driving you home at the end of the evening. In hindsight the Remain campaign got this last public spectacle very wrong. To the viewers, it came across as four bullying women against one hapless man. All the opinion polls indicated that while the vote would be close, Remain would prevail.

I still woke up on the morning of 23 June feeling extremely excited because I would at last be given the chance to express my displeasure at the way our relationship with the EU had developed over recent years. Essex was long known to be sceptical of our membership, so it was no surprise to me that the polling stations were busy, some with queues of people wanting to vote before they went to work. Was it too much to hope that people like myself who had long wanted us to leave the EU would be more determined to vote than those wishing to remain?

As the day wore on my excitement continued to grow, although I kept telling myself not to be too optimistic. I decided not to go to the count: there didn't seem much point as it wasn't a party matter, so I watched from the comfort of my home. The first results showed that the leave vote was holding up well and there had been a high turnout. It took some while for the first declarations to come in but as they did my optimism grew too. The results in the north of the country in particular showed very substantial majorities for Vote Leave, whereas in London the reverse was true, which confirmed my suspicions that the demographics of London were changing. After all, as many second and third generation Europeans lived in our capital city, it was hardly going to be in their interests to support a move to end freedom of movement for themselves and their families. David Dimbleby had a host of guests in his studio, one of whom was Lord Ashdown. He famously made the remark that he would eat his hat if the British people voted to leave the EU. I suspect he has suffered terrible indigestion ever since.

I stayed glued to the TV until the point was reached where, quite incredibly, it was plain to see that the vote to leave the European Union was edging ahead. Just before breakfast, Dimbleby made the historic announcement that the British people had voted by a margin of over one million and by 52 per cent to 48 per cent to leave the EU. I was shocked, exhilarated and delighted. The result and the turnout were beyond my wildest dreams. My first thought was if only Margaret had been alive to witness it. I had no doubt that wherever she was then, she would be celebrating with other similar minded spirits. At last she had had the final word on Ted Heath's experiment. The British people had spoken, and we would be taking back control of our government, our future and our lives.

There is no doubt at all that the result was a devastating blow for David Cameron. It was also a huge disappointment to a number of Cabinet Members, but particularly the Chancellor of the Exchequer, George Osborne. He was in every sense David's right-hand man and in many respects actually ran the Government. He had obviously been so confident of the result that he had thrown caution to the wind and instructed the Treasury civil servants to issue studies before polling day suggesting all manner of dire economic consequences if the country voted to leave. Interestingly, the Foreign Secretary Philip Hammond and the Home Secretary Theresa May had been very quiet during the campaign. They had let it be known that, on balance, they were against the UK leaving the EU but had not voiced this forcefully. This stance was to prove very telling in terms of the subsequent leadership campaign.

The fallout

Cameron appeared outside Number 10, conceding defeat on the issue. It must have been an incredibly difficult speech to make. He argued that, because of his stance over our member-ship of the European Union, he felt that the country and the Conservative Party needed fresh leadership. For my part, I had been one of the MPs who had signed a letter to the Prime Minister, before the result was known, urging him to stay in post in the event of a defeat and steer our passage through the choppy waters of departure. I must confess that I had never imagined that the letter would have to be sent.

As far as I was concerned, he had been a first-class leader of the party and a very effective Prime Minister. He had also been at the centre of all our dealings with the bloc and had reassured everyone that, in the event of Brexit, the Civil Service would have a plan from which to work. It is now clear that they did not. I felt that with all his skills he would be the best person to deal with the situation and once we had actually left the European Union, we could take a fresh look at the leadership of the party. It was not to be, and so David Cameron set in motion the Party's arrangements for the election of a new leader. I was desperately sad for David and George.

Having been involved in far too many Conservative Party Leadership campaigns before, I was both cynical and sceptical as to what would happen next. The Westminster bubble nearly exploded with excitement as the battle for the heart of the Conservative Party and the leadership of our country began. There was intense speculation as to who the candidates would be. Conservative Party rules provided for elected MPs to give the membership a choice of two candidates. The question was, who would be the chosen two.

Because David Cameron was so young, he hadn't really set up any colleagues to campaign for him. In any case, somewhat like the Blair/Brown partnership, it was always perceived that when the time came for Cameron to retire then George would be his successor. Cameron seemed to rely on him for so much, not least to choose Ministers when reshuffles took place. It was a standing joke in Westminster, that if you were a friend of George's, you would get a place in Government. That was invariably how it seemed to be. George must have been in a state of shock at the referendum result. In different circumstances, he would have quickly announced his campaign and been the frontrunner, but it was not to be.

Much attention turned to the eccentric Boris. Who will ever forget his bouncing appearance with the President of China at the Beijing Olympic Games as he accepted the flag being handed to him for the 2012 Olympics? He had become a cult figure and that, as well as many of his other mayoral responsibilities, such as organising the London Olympics, had shaped his image. His magnificent and unusual bouffant seemed incapable of being tamed. His appearance was often as if he had arrived at an event fresh from rolling in a haystack or walking through a wind tunnel. His voice was extraordinary. It was staccato, posh and riveting. When he spoke, one never was quite sure what to expect. Was he really serious or was it all a clever act? Yet if you wanted to fill a hall or a stadium as a politician, Boris was your man. He was recognised wherever he went, and it wasn't just the Japanese who would take endless photos of him.

Others began to emerge. David Davis had been the front-runner when Cameron was elected leader and many thought that in spite of his age, he was planning a campaign. It never materialised. Liam Fox however had been a candidate before and it would appear that he still had leadership ambitions even though he his star had waned in some people's eyes. Extraordinarily, Stephen Crabb and Sajid Javid – both of whom I liked very much – decided to run on a joint leadership ticket. If only they had asked my advice first, I would have categorically counselled them against making such a rash decision. Whether Ruth Davidson, the leader of the Scottish Conservatives, had encouraged Stephen I am not quite sure but no sooner had his campaign been launched than it ended in tears. I felt desperately sorry for him and his family. Such is the brutality of Parliament.

It had been speculated that Michael Gove might be a candidate. He was a substantial figure in the party, an intellectual and a real radical. However, he said that he would be supporting Boris Johnson. They had worked together in the referendum campaign and, as far as the outside world knew, got on extremely well and trusted one another.

Finally, two ladies threw their hats into the ring. Andrea Leadsom, a really lovely woman, had done much to detoxify the Conservative brand which wanted to leave the European Union. She was the brains behind Fresh Start. This was the organisation supported by a lot of Conservative MPs which had put the flesh on policy to leave the EU. The other was Theresa May. Theresa was the dark horse. She was aided and abetted by Chris Grayling, someone she obviously trusted, as her manager. I had observed Theresa with puzzlement since her arrival in Westminster. I was sitting in the Commons one day with Ann Widdecombe to my left and Theresa May to my right. Ann lent across me and said to her 'I'm glad you're letting the grey grow through.' I could not believe what I had just heard from my forthright friend. I had thought it was a streak but then what do I know? Theresa very calmly did not bite. She had been a long-serving Home Secretary but throughout her time in Parliament had been seen as a bit of a loner. She had not courted popularity amongst colleagues or nurtured support for a leadership bid, but she had been seen as a very steady pair of hands. She was well-known for her love of vibrant shoes and certainly, in her early days, which most present members would be unaware of, her somewhat racy clothes. She certainly was not a clubbable person spending time in the tea or smoking rooms but more of a no-nonsense and serious politician

The media enjoyed trawling over the merits and flaws of each candidate. It seemed as if Boris Johnson would be the favourite, not only with colleagues but also when it came to the party membership. I decided not to publicly align myself with anyone, having done so too often in previous campaigns. I did a rare thing by keeping my own counsel and meeting all the candidates in person.

A real media event and piece of political drama was Boris Johnson's speech on 30 June. Live TV cameras showed a large room full of parliamentary colleagues anxiously waiting for their hero to arrive and announce his candidacy. In a dramatic announcement he declared that he would not run in the election. The look on my colleagues' faces was an absolute picture. I won't embarrass any of them by mentioning their names, but my observation was that some were genuinely shocked. Nonetheless, there were others thinking that they had backed the wrong horse and already wondering how they could shamelessly join another team.

After this electric press conference, which had been billed as Boris' coronation, the real reasons behind his decision broke. Michael Gove, his 'friend', had decided to run himself. We can only speculate about the precise truth behind what happened. In all the circumstances, Boris was most gracious. It appeared, according to Michael Gove, that discussions between the two the previous evening had convinced Boris that he was the wrong person to lead the party for numerous reasons. The banner headlines the following day read: 'Boris Betrayed by Friend'. For some, it was truly shocking; to others, it seemed that Michael was standing for entirely selfish reasons.

For my part, I agreed to go and have a chat with Michael as someone who I greatly admired. I was curious to know the real reasons for his actions. His response to my direct question was not completely convincing. It is true that when I met Michael the atmosphere was febrile and, as one would expect, he was probably distracted thinking about the next person he was seeing. So he did give me an answer to the Boris situation but it was perhaps one that he thought I wanted to hear. Nevertheless, I liked and respected him, and he genuinely wanted us to leave the European Union. I knew Theresa best and so there was no great need for me to see her. I made arrangements to have a chat with Andrea. She hugged me, as is her wont, and was reassuring as to her vision. The voting then took place. It should be understood that the most duplicitous untruthful electorate in the world is none other than Members of Parliament. They would say to your face that they were going to vote for you and then do the exact opposite. No doubt the remaining candidates were fully aware of the electorate's unreliability and of the possible outcome.

Graham Brady, the Chairman of the 1922 Committee, in Committee Room 14 confirmed that the two candidates who would go forward to the membership were Theresa and Andrea. While there had been some movement in support from Boris to Michael it was not enough to get him into the final two. And so history was made. What we knew for certain was that whoever was to become leader, it would definitely be a woman. A second female Prime Minister would follow the late Baroness Thatcher and as David Cameron observed 'no Pink Bus' was required in reference to Harriet Harman's pink vehicle that toured 70 constituencies in 2015 to talk to disenchanted female voters. I had my own private thoughts; neither candidate was quite like Margaret. Both were strong candidates though and had many qualities that would make either an excellent Prime Minister.

The extraordinary election then took another remarkable twist. Andrea, who was somewhat inexperienced as a parliamentarian having only been elected in 2010, gave an interview which implied that, as Theresa May has no children, she would not understand the nation's problems that, as a mother, Andrea would. The effect was cataclysmic. In a very short space of time her campaign fell apart and she appeared outside her home, alongside her supporters and bravely announced that she would be withdrawing. So there it was. There would not be a contest for the leadership of the Conservative Party. Instead there would be a coronation. For me, although I felt desperately sorry for Andrea, I was somewhat relieved that there would not be a protracted contest for the leadership over the summer months. It was time for decisive leadership.

On the date that Theresa was duly elected, I found myself congratulating the PM in a way that I had not done since the 1980s, by planting a kiss on either cheek. While not by nature a touchy-feely person, and there's nothing wrong with that, being kissed on either cheek was something that she would have to get used to as she met some of her ghastly European counterparts who would attempt to foil her negotiating position.

That night, as I drove home to Southend, I reflected on what had been a truly remarkable few weeks. When I first became an MP, an experienced member said to me that all political careers end in tears. I began to realise how correct those words had been and I just hoped it didn't happen to me!

Brexit hopes

Although I voted and campaigned for us to leave the European Union, I didn't feel in my bones that the referendum result would go the way it did. I thought that the conservative nature of the British people would result in a vote to stay. The fact that they didn't continues to surprise me today and I often pinch myself to check that I'm not still dreaming. Without question, it is possibly the most profound and serious political event to have happened in my time in Parliament. Yes, throughout those years there had been continual discussion and unrest on the

Conservative benches about our membership, but I just didn't expect events to unfold in the way that they did under David Cameron's leadership. That is what makes politics so exciting, that the unexpected can and does happen. It is a truly extraordinary time to be involved both domestically and internationally.

As an Essex MP, I was in a county which was overwhelmingly Eurosceptic but I had no appreciation of what was happening in the Labour heartlands of the Midlands and in the North. The fact that a number of those constituencies should have voted in such large numbers to leave came as quite a shock.

My hopes for Brexit are the same as most people. We should get on with the process as quickly as possible and secure the best outcome for our country. The reality is that Conservative MPs had been given the impression that the machinery of the Civil Service had been geared up for both eventualities – to remain a member and to leave. That obviously was not the case, no serious work had been done and certainly no details of how we would implement the result planned for. I much regret that wasn't done, it should have been. It is quite wrong that it wasn't, and we are all paying the price for that now. I am a born optimist so my dream is not reliving the past glories (if they can be described as that) of the Empire, but of a strong, United Kingdom re-establishing itself as a beacon of light throughout the world. A government espousing and delivering decent values, based on the rule of law. Working with the rest of the world for peaceful coexistence and the defeat of terrorism but fundamentally re-establishing ourselves as a sovereign nation, restoring power to the democratically elected House of Commons so that people once again when asked to cast their vote in a General Election do so in full confidence that their vote matters and that we are once again an independent nation with the freedom to choose our own destiny.

PART 4

The Future

I HAVE NEVER wanted to be seen as a dinosaur or reactionary, but my children enjoy reminding me that that is how I come across. Life passes by so quickly and it's easy to forget how you saw the world when you were young. Nevertheless, we're talking about a thousand years of history in the place where I work and, (dare I say), a place I love. I'm recounting a relatively brief timescale within that period and it really is the pace of change that I don't like. Things are generally happening far too quickly, without enough careful thought and rigorous scrutiny. Much of that has come about through the advent of technology, but I think at the heart of it, enormous damage was done as a result of the very large number of Members who left the House some years ago. It's not been about evolution, more like a revolution, and that makes me uncomfortable. We have lost too much experience, much of our connection with the past, and I feel that wiser and experienced voices just have not been there to say, 'hang on, let's think again'.

I have never been one to make predictions, especially when discussing my own political prospects. In that regard, I have always left the guessing to others and allowed the actual results to do the talking for me. Nevertheless, it is fun, even if sometimes mildly depressing, to look into the future regarding Parliament, Parliamentarians and political parties.

Restoration and renewal

As far as the Palace of Westminster is concerned, we now know that by 2025 we will have moved out of the building.

That very action is bound to generate a completely different atmosphere. I simply do not believe that it will be possible to recreate the uniqueness of the Chamber in a new building. In a less than subtle way, this process is already well underway and the customs and proceedings that I have heralded in this book are coming under siege on an almost daily basis. The British Parliament is the mother of all Parliaments. We are an unquestionably old democracy with an unwritten constitution evolved over centuries. While it is not always widely understood why we do things as we do, they often become quite clear when the 'method behind the madness' is explained.

There is no doubt that the fabric of the building itself is decaying. It only takes a detailed tour of the basement to discover that for yourself – the need for restoration is not in question. But what worries me is how external bodies have been asked to manage the whole process. This is indicative of the current trend in parliamentary procedure, where all of these technocratic bodies tend to make decisions on how Parliament should operate. Equally, the House has become more and more commercial. Some of this is part of the outreach programme and some of it is about raising money to maintain the buildings. Ironically, these commercial events and the increased footfall has meant that without the required maintenance work, more damage has been done to the fabric of the building. When this reached its peak, a grim report was produced giving us options regarding how to restore and renew the building.

I and a significant number of MPs feel that it was a huge mistake to agree to move out of the building for ten years. One Parliament cannot bind another, so ten years is a very long time. I hold a genuine fear that we may never return to the much-loved building and that a so-called modern legislature will be built with the old one remaining open solely as a tourist attraction.

The party system

For much of my life there have been two main UK political parties, the Conservative Party and the Labour Party. While there are a number of examples of the emergence of a third, they have never really taken off to become any more than that. The Liberals for instance have never returned to their high point, in terms of the number of parliamentary seats they enjoyed at the start of the last century. It could be that on this occasion, left-wing Conservatives might just possibly join with Liberal Democrats and form some sort of new organisation, but I'm not convinced. Starting any new party is always fraught with difficulties and we no longer even have influential figures to kick-start such a development.

The Referendum Party and then the United Kingdom Independence Party have attracted a very considerable number of votes, but this has never been translated into Members of Parliament. Are UKIP dead and buried? It seemed as if they were, but if those supporting Brexit are not satisfied with the current negotiations, some of them may well desert the Conservatives and indeed Labour, leading to UKIP rising like a phoenix from the flames. The SNP did send shock waves through Westminster when they won all but three of the seats in Scotland. However, there are simply not enough Scottish seats for parity with the big two. So, while they can wield significant influence, there will always be a ceiling for the nationalist parties of the home nations. There will always be the prospect of the emergence of a third party, but I am confident that the traditional split of government and opposition will hold out in the longer term.

What has happened is that the Conservative and Labour parties have reinvented themselves in terms of political beliefs. There was once a straight divide between them: Capitalism vs Socialism. From a political point of view, one of the unfortunate consequences of Margaret Thatcher's success was the complete defeat of socialism, which is how we got Tony Blair and New Labour. Despite tailoring the Labour Party philosophy to attract middle England, the combination of the Iraq War and the Financial Crisis put an end to this idea. At that point in time, the wisdom of having two basically capitalist, pro-enterprise political parties seems to have become defunct. Ed Miliband acted as a bridge towards the era of the left-wing Jeremy Corbyn, while David Cameron paved the way for compassionate Conservatism. Oh, how different this would have been had David Miliband been elected leader of the Labour Party. Just as New Labour had taken over the old Labour Party, Momentum has now begun to pull it in the opposite direction. They are promoting an unashamedly left-wing agenda, something that most people thought had long been dead and buried. Renationalisation, anti-capitalist, anti-business, anti-nuclear weapons, anti-America and (in reality) anti-European Union. There was much that they were against. What was less comprehensible for most centrist and right-wing Labour members was how they could possibly deliver a prosperous economy?

I have a feeling that against this background and with our decision to leave the European Union, the two main political parties will actually re-establish the old fault lines of their long held political philosophies. This will again close the playing field and narrow the opportunities for a third party to really develop. It is far more likely that the Labour Party will reinvent itself again, but this time with a primarily capitalist and enterprise-driven policy agenda. In contrast, I see the Conservative Party again reinventing itself on the global stage and championing all that has made Britain great in the past. The globally recognised and revered ideas of small state, people power and individualism need to be recreated in the modern world. The dragon of socialism was slain, but it has reappeared in a newer format. The Conservative Party must renew itself with some fresh ideas too.

Internationally, the Brexit decision will shape foreign policy and Conservatives have always been strong on defence. We will have to reinvent a strategy to tackle not just terrorism but the whole spectre of cybersecurity. Domestically, we have always been seen as pro-monarchy. None of us know how the Royals will evolve once Queen Elizabeth II is no longer our monarch. We need a proper strategy in terms of tackling crime generally. There will be huge issues concerning an ageing population which no one has been prepared to face up to. However, for our party to flourish, it will need to find a solution to how to properly finance care and provide pensions for future generations. The Conservatives need an innovative scheme, but with a different outcome from reducing the housing stock as Right-to-Buy, if we are to ever resolve the current housing crisis. There are so many issues for my party to tackle and we will need a very special person to meet those challenges.

Career politicians

Some might say that there have always been career politicians and that probably is the case. The main difference, I believe, is that politicians of the past were better at disguising their ambitions. To be frank, there is no such thing as a modest politician. The idea that any of us are dragged screaming and shouting to the House of Commons to serve our constituents is absolute fantasy. We have all wanted the job and have fought hard to get it.

When I started, I wasn't as aware of the strength of desire for office as I now am. In Margaret Thatcher's day I became used to the annual reshuffles. For my own part, I never had any great ambitions for Ministerial office and was just delighted to serve as an MP. With time however, you can't help but be vexed when more and more of your colleagues get preferment and you don't. It may never be said directly to your face, but the implication is very much that you are simply not up to the job. Well, I say with no bitterness at all that I have known a huge number of Ministers throughout my time. Some have been absolutely brilliant, while others have been a complete and utter disaster, so you can never quite fathom how one becomes a Minister in the first place. We all like to think that latent talent will be noticed, but unfortunately that is not always the case. A far more reasonable assessment of how this happens can be made by watching the corridors and finding the aspiring and ambitious new member who has latched onto someone who can give their career a boost. The first stage up the greasy ladder.

When I say career politician, this is what I mean – someone who does not necessarily have principles or strong convictions. I do not mean this in a nasty way, but they may cut their cloth according to which way the wind is prevailing. While this sort of person would not necessarily go as far as to support another party, they are most certainly capable of changing their views on a whole variety of issues. One of the most stupid things my own Party ever did was to have open primaries. You would think that it was obvious that opening selections to the general public would mean that the candidate chosen would not necessarily be a strong Conservative.

There are various members of the House that I find very difficult to place within a political party at all! Underlying this has been the increase in the number of MPs who have only ever worked in politics and have absolutely no real experience of life and all its ups and downs. They seem to have worked for public relations companies, run parliamentary offices, been Ministerial advisers or worked for the party's central organisation. These people may well be splendid, and they might be what modern politics needs, but from my perspective there are far too many of them and the judgements they make are not always for the good of the country.

Long gone are the days when someone was content to be just a backbench MP. A number of MPs have ambitions way beyond their own capabilities and when they are given a chance of office, are doomed to failure. They are invariably promoted too soon and lack experience, not only of life, but of the way that Parliament works. Some people have a terribly high opinion of themselves thanks to a pre-ordained vision of what they would like to become. He or she will invariably curry favour with 'the king or queen maker of the day' and while there are some wonderful people in the Commons, there are also some who are frankly ghastly – pompous, arrogant and self-serving. This type will often be having a conversation with you, but their eyes are all over the place seeing whether there is someone more important than yourself around.

The career politician just wants more and more power. Ironically, during my 37 years, that power has gradually slipped away from elected politicians. It often seems that we are powerless and just exist to be blamed when things go wrong. I find this development very, very galling. Everyone knows what MPs earn and how they do their job, there is no mystery about any of these things. In contrast the roles of the management of so many unelected quangos are often shrouded in mystery, their salaries and benefits are often way beyond what they deliver. I think this situation is intolerable and without any question is damaging to the organisation for which they work. However, invariably their incompetence only damages the standing of the Government, rather than the organisation.

The slow death of Parliament?

It seems to me that at the moment we are living through a period which can best be described as the slow death of Parliament. Up until now I have felt this was the direction in terms of loss of power, but it has now spread to the building.

We unquestionably used to hold more power than we have now. Our standing with the general public was much higher and respect for the institution was much greater. It could be that as I age, I see things through rose-tinted lenses, the violin comes out and I drone and on and on and on about how much better everything used to be. I think not. We are a much more affluent country than we were when I was first elected, prosperity has spread even though our population has grown considerably.

In my early years representing Basildon, I managed to persuade the then Minister and his Civil Servants to repurchase 10,000 properties, which had been sold off under the

Right- to-Buy but had now become uninsurable as a result of clay heave. I stopped two school closures, I prevented a silver birch forest being razed to the ground to make way for another useless bank and with two days left I stopped the closure and relocation of Basildon A&E Unit. These are things which I would have great difficulty in achieving again today.

Over the years Ministers' power has drained away. Inevitably lost partly to the EU, but under the Blair years there was an inexorable push towards the development of unelected quangos in every facet of our lives. Wherever you look it is no longer the Minister who has the power. Yes, he is there to blame if things go wrong but seldom does he have REAL power. This is fundamentally wrong. Politicians are elected, governments are elected, and the country can get rid of them if they don't perform in the way it wishes. In contrast, those who run these quangos are extremely difficult to fire. A really galling development has been having to pay these people vast sums of money to leave early. No one is sacked for incompetence anymore, but instead they 'step down'. When David Cameron's coalition took office in 2010, they genuinely made an effort to change this powerless situation and get back control for Parliament. I, indeed, chaired the Bill that brought in the legislation to make this happen, but in reality, the success has been very mixed and has been on the margin. I think it will take a very strong government, who by definition will have a good majority, to change the present situation. On an optimistic note however, the decision that the British people took to leave the

European Union should at least restore some powers back to Westminster. If that doesn't happen it will have been absolutely pointless voting to leave the EU in the first place.

There are other aspects of course, ones that I have discussed throughout this book. the change in sitting hours; only having proper votes on Tuesdays and Wednesdays; commercial tours of the Palace of Westminster; lobbyists going to advisers and not Ministers; the emptiness of the Chamber since it has been televised; and the lack of proper coverage and scrutiny of the debates that take place in good quality written press.

I think there used to be an aura around someone who was an MP, they were seen as a terribly important person and people would be very deferential to them. They weren't exactly seen as 'gods' but were nevertheless highly regarded. That esteem is no more. Some of this has been self-inflicted, but it is not all down to the MPs. Voter turnout has been steadily falling, despite governments of the day making it ever easier to actually vote. There is no doubt that there is a certain amount of voter apathy (in spite of the recent Brexit induced spike in interest), I happen to think it is about time we got a grip on the situation. We need to convince the general public that their vote really does count, and it will make an important difference to their lives. We need to make Parliament relevant again, it is not just about the magnificent and wonderful state opening with all the glamour that entails, it is rather more about the unglamorous work that MPs undertake; scrutinising a bill in some Committee Room or interrogating people who appear before Select Committee meetings. It is also about the MPs holding their regular surgeries, listening to people's problems and helping to fix them. It is about Members immersing themselves into community activities, ranging from church services to dog shows, from school visits to hospital visits and the openings of organisations and events. This is what an MP does, and it is important to the lives of constituents. The overwhelming majority of MPs are decent, hard-working people who really have gone into public service to try and make a difference to people's lives, but I would say that wouldn't I! It's just such a shame that MPs have been denigrated and are often so defensive about what they do. My experience has been that they are invariably good women and men who have quite possibly been misunderstood.

Postscript

I WRITE THIS book whilst I am still a serving Member of Parliament. I also write it without any thoughts of retiring just yet. I realise that many Members only write books about their experiences when they have decided to leave the place, but I wanted, without upsetting too many people, to write something whilst still being in a position to speak with knowledge of how the place in which I work continues to change.

I feel as if I'm on a journey and I'm not entirely sure when it's going to end. I certainly never expected it to last so long when I was first elected in 1983. I am aware of my good fortune to have experienced all manner of extraordinary events. I have travelled to most parts of the world meeting kings, queens, Prime Ministers, Presidents and Popes with the blessings and support of my family and the electorate.

It has been frustrating and at times sad to be watching the place I work slowly diminish, but my work is not yet complete. I want to achieve more for the town of Southend. I want to still be able to make a difference, to change people's lives for the better. After so many years of wanting us to leave the European Union, I'd like to be around at least for a while to ensure that the benefits of our departure are felt by everyone in the country and particularly by my constituents.

Whilst I am most unhappy that the decision has been made to leave the building whilst it is restored and renewed, I want to ensure that when the work is completed, Parliament returns to its historic home.

Brexit is the most significant political event of my career. What follows is my diary of the unprecedented Brexit events of 2019.

Countdown to Brexit

20 December 2018

MPs broke for the Christmas recess already absolutely sick to death of the endless arguments and bad feeling over Brexit.

7 January 2019

The House returns. I drove to Westminster feeling very pessimistic. It seems that, in spite of all the rhetoric from the Prime Minister and her inner Cabinet, we are nowhere near striking a sensible deal with the European Union. I certainly enjoyed Christmas and the New Year and, now that I am back, I have the feeling that every other MP also enjoyed spending time away from the Palace of Westminster and the seemingly endless machinations to do with the UK leaving the European Union.

9 January

Usual uninspiring exchanges between the party leaders. As ever, Brexit has re-emerged. The start of the much-vaunted debate on the EU Withdrawal Agreement. I stayed for the opening exchanges between the party leaders, no real surprises in anything they said.

10 January

Arrived in Westminster late this afternoon. The Withdrawal Bill debate was over-subscribed and contributions were time limited.

11 January

These days, with the way that Parliament has changed, I am not in on a Friday very often, but I was today to make my contribution to the Withdrawal Bill debate. I had originally intended to speak on Monday 14 January, but the debate was abandoned as no agreement had been reached. I was called early and followed a speech, which I agreed with, given by Emma Lewell-Buck. I set out, in very stark terms, my own life-long opposition to our membership of the European Union. The House was reasonably well-attended, and I felt better for getting my views off my chest, as it would be easier from now on to just send the speech to interested constituents. I had been waiting a long time to have my say on this issue. Had dinner this evening with my friend Mark Francois, we had a good old gossip about colleagues generally, their ears were not just singed they must have been burning.

14 January

I've driven back to Westminster. Had very serious meeting with the excellent James Brokenshire, Secretary of State at DHCLG, re fire safety matters generally and the Grenfell Tower disaster in particular. I signed the book of commitment for Holocaust Memorial Day. Couldn't help thinking how Labour Members doing likewise must have been feeling, given their own party's difficulties with claims of anti-Semitic views and positions taken by the leadership.

15 January

Final day of debate for the Withdrawal Bill. There has been much media speculation on the result.

I was taking my guidance from the ERG Group and would be voting no. There was certainly a tense atmosphere when the division bell went for the first vote. As ever, there weren't as many votes as were planned, some weren't actually moved at all. As advised by the ERG Group, I voted no except for John Baron's amendment where I voted aye. Sadly, the numbers were relatively small supporting it. When the last vote came and the House had to take a view on the Government's position, I could tell immediately by the huge numbers going through the no lobby that the government were in for a massive defeat. The Government was defeated 432–202. Really bad. The front bench looked shattered, the PM and Chief Whip in particular looked chastened. There were immediate points of order, which was predictable and the Leader of the Opposition, who had apparently been prevaricating on the issue, said he would table a motion of No Confidence in HM Government.

16 January

Once again, the exchanges between the party leaders were a non-event in terms of the country and the world at large. Just grandstanding.

I was preoccupied with various meetings and only caught the end of the wind-up debates. Solid performance from the Conservative Minister, particularly competent performance from Tom Watson. He undoubtedly resonates with sensible moderate voters. Michael Gove gave a typically theatrical, barn-storming performance, didn't hear the end of it because I went into the division lobby early. When voting started there were rave reviews of his speech.

I was very confident that the No Confidence vote would be lost, and it duly was. Conservatives fell in line with the DUP to defeat it, and there were certainly a few Labour Members missing.

22 January

Ended the evening with drinks in the Smoking Room, although nobody smokes anymore! Essex colleague, John Baron, showing his gratitude for support of one of his Brexit amendments.

23 January

PMQs again. No surprise, Brexit was the main issue. Nothing further gleaned on the issue. Chair piece of Delegated Legislation. Everyone seems very amicable, no big row. Various meetings in the afternoon. Meet in Peers Lobby with Ann Widdecombe and Lord Alton. Just like old times with only one member of the Gang of Four now missing, our great friend the late Ken Hargreaves, MP for Hyndburn, we really do miss him.

24 January

DEXEU question: I think it is about the first time I have had an oral DEXEU Question. It gives me an opportunity to repeat my desire that Southend become a city. Business Questions: I raised the issue of animal welfare and linked it to us leaving the European Union.

29 January

In the afternoon hosted and opened a Turkish Ceftus meeting, then had to leave for umpteen divisions.

Caroline Spelman and others had their motion carried by a very small majority, but in practical terms it was meaningless. As ever there were points of order but the PM didn't stay for them, she looked furious with the outcome but really she demonstrated poor judgement or was given bad advice in terms of the defeat inflicted on the government. I returned home that night feeling jubilant, a good job done at the office in telling my party that we had to leave the EU with a proper arrangement that meant we wouldn't still be in the EU for a further two years. All the really important motions were soundly defeated.

11 February

Drive to Westminster, attend Admin Committee meeting and chair Programming Sub-Committee for Immigration and Social Security Co-ordination (EU Withdrawal) Bill.

14 February

Anniversary of my father's birthday and Valentine's Day. Love was everywhere, particularly at Business Questions. Love even broke out between the Speaker and the Leader of the Commons

18 February

Before I leave Southend the news breaks, at last a group of Labour MPs quit their party. Well, this comes as no surprise.

However, the list of seven is not entirely as one would have expected. Ann Coffey was perhaps a surprise. Watched video of the press conference, really nice people, obviously very sad to be leaving their political home, some of them after many years. Very brave and tough decision, may all be a damp squib or could really take off and be the nucleus of a new party. Only time will tell.

19 February

The media is full of the Labour split but now turns to possible defections from other parties, primarily my own, the Conservatives. All the usual suspects are mentioned, repeated by colleagues I bumped into, who rather naughtily didn't seem fazed by their expected departure but were rather looking forward to it. Indeed, they were somewhat disappointed, as I found out when I attended the 1922 Committee reception on the Terrace, that the defections hadn't happened. Perhaps they are waiting for PMQs the next day. Can't imagine why the February recess was cancelled. I attended the meeting of the ERG, where we were given a summary of the latest developments. No surprise in the general mood that the Withdrawal Agreement was pretty awful. Just seen two Conservative MPs who are rumoured to be jumping ship. The body language and eye contact told me they would, and I expect a third female MP will join them

20 February

Staying in London overnight, drove into Westminster resolved to go to PMQs. I had looked on the Order Paper and there were only two Conservatives with questions, which meant lots of free hits. Driving in there were all sorts of rumours about Conservative defections. Arrived in office at 11.00am, the news breaks that three female members of the Conservative Party were going to sit as Independents, absolutely no surprise. Going to Chamber for PMQs. A very strange atmosphere and the Chamber not particularly full. Certainly, no sense of excitement, as when the Gang of Four broke loose from the Labour Party. I spotted the 11 Independents sitting on the opposition benches with the other minor parties. I got called, decided to ask a fundamentally serious question rather than light-hearted, I think it was the right call. As I left the Chamber I looked across at the Independents, I sense the enormity of their decision, particularly for the Conservatives, is already dawning on them. They will soon tire of talking to each other in the Chamber. Huge decision for them all personally, it may or may not be the start of a realignment of politics, it doesn't feel like that at the moment.

21 February

Stayed in London again overnight. Travelled in to ask a Business Question as per usual. The House was sparsely populated, so no real reaction to the defections from both parties from colleagues. The Independent Group, for whatever reason, missed the opportunity to occupy the green benches. I have no doubt at all that the enormity of what they have done will now be dawning on them. They may well have ploughed a very lonely furrow. I can see trouble ahead for the group in terms of clashes of the egos of some of the members.

25 February

Arrive at Westminster, for a Monday relatively early, but suffering from a heavy dose of Brexit fatigue. My God, what a mess the Prime Minister seems to be making of it all. More delays, more meaningless votes, what on earth is she playing at? Later in the day news breaks that Labour will support another referendum. So much for democracy, and how patronising and arrogant. Not sure how their decision will play out.

26 February

God help us all, because only he can. The Prime Minister is making yet another statement about Brexit. Didn't bother to go to the Chamber, I am so fed up with it all, just watched a little bit on TV. More capitulation, Labour sell-out wanting a second referendum and now my own party treacherously delaying Brexit and ruling out a no deal. Truly shocking. Spent the whole day attending various drop-in events – hold up a plaque, smile, press release done, constituents think you have been terribly busy. Oh, how Parliament has changed. Did have, however, a really good meeting with a Home Office Minister about how to protect exotic pets. Loved the way he dealt with officials, basically told them to do something.

27 February

Yet again, the media has built this up as crunch day for Brexit, which it never is. Spent the day at meetings and various drop-in events, also chaired a DL. Had snatched conversations with various colleagues, stood by the Speaker's Chair for a short while at PMQs. As ever, not that full, strange atmosphere, can't help thinking how it has all been dumbed down since the PMQs that I experienced when I first joined the House. Chaired DL, competent Minister and opposition spokesman, sensible exchanges, lasted 20 minutes. 7.00pm division bells ring, go across for the first vote. See the Prime Minister talking to a colleague who has just lost their mother. Bump into another colleague who has got some difficulties and is not being well-supported by my party. Labour amendment defeated by a substantial majority. SNP vote defeated by a large majority. No clarity with whipping, rather unusual on this occasion, by the group coordinating like-minded people such as myself. Had hoped that the Cooper amendment wouldn't be pressed, but it was. Stood with a number of colleagues by the division lobbies, not sure whether to vote against or abstain. Eventually got the message we should abstain and that is what most of us did. Not at all happy that no deal seems to have been lost as a negotiating lever, very fed up that there could be talk of delaying our withdrawal from the EU, given that the PM has said at least 109 times that it was going to happen on 29 March. Had a word with my whip in passing at the appalling actions of the Cabinet that morning. Many colleagues outraged by the behaviour of some in holding us to ransom with threats of resignation. All Party discipline seems to have been lost – very, very depressing. The anger was real. Mood seems to be changing among like-minded colleagues to do everything we can to support an agreement, so we do leave the EU on 29 March. Returned to Southend tonight thoroughly fed up.

4 March

Usual statements and UQs but as seems to be increasingly the practice, no Parliamentary business in terms of a debate. Finance Bill pulled at the last minute. Points of Order raised. House in sombre mood, yet more stabbings, something really needs to be done to stop the slaughter but what? Politicians don't seem to have the answers. Transport Secretary under the cosh yet again, bailed out by Health Secretary, this really is so bizarre. Mixed messages re next week's vote on our departure from the EU, I am beginning to lose the will to live. If only we had firm leadership and someone to get a grip on the situation. More insults for our country from the ghastly, juvenile Macron.

6 March

Underwhelmed at the prospect of another PMQs, all very uninspiring as ever. Waffle and prevarication on our negotiations with Brussels and a poor response to the horrendous growth of knife crime.

Went off to 10 Downing Street to present a petition to stop puppy smuggling – interesting group of members. Return to the main building and berate Network Rail and c2c on their pathetic excuses for poor communications, unreliability and, in short, a poor service.

8/9/10 March

Attended a gathering of various organisations involved in supporting people with physical and mental health issues. Later canvassed in local by election for a Council seat. Amazingly, Brexit was not mentioned on the doorstep. Weekend, attended various local events, Brexit constantly mentioned, with everyone gloomy and not understanding Westminster at all.

11 March

Drove to Westminster with the certainty that Brexit would dominate all of our proceedings. Besides usual drop-in functions, attended the Admin Committee where colleagues took, rightfully, a tough stance on the allocation of passes.

12 March

Attend extraordinary meeting in the Attlee Suite addressed by Prime Minister. Find myself sitting with two Essex Brexit colleagues, either side of which sat dour Remainers. There was a surreal atmosphere at the meeting. Prime Minister who, to make matters worse, is now losing her voice, shades of the Party Conference, made an ineffectual speech, regurgitating the same old answers. Sycophantic loyalists everywhere, much more noticeable those who were silent and not clapping. I have seen it so many times before, this leader is a busted flush and all the power of the office that she holds has drained away. Managed to fit in a great meeting with the Lions Club of Great Britain in Committee Room 14, they liked my joke that Brexit does not mean Brexit and we will make a complete mess of it. Attended the ERG meeting, this time in Jubilee Room. Got there early to nab a seat. General mood was grim, I found my conscience genuinely torn as I am beginning to panic that time is running out and we will end up losing Brexit completely. Find myself changing my mind as to whether or not to support the so-called rotten deal. Suella Braverman and Theresa Villiers made some good points when they spoke, I am drawn to oppose the Bill. On leaving however, I hitch up with Fiona Bruce, a thoroughly good egg – can you believe it I changed my mind again and find I am not the only one. The division bells go, I am still torn, but on the verge of supporting the PMs deal. Reluctantly I go through the aye lobby, tell my whip who is waiting that I am hating supporting this – she hugs me. Notice PM surrounded by colleagues, not sure what is going on. The result is announced, catastrophe, defeated by 149, although a fair number of us switched our vote. Couldn't bear to remain in the Chamber, go back to my office and watch it on the monitor.

Endless points of order, very strange atmosphere in the House, just like the stillness before a hurricane.

13 March

Whole day dominated by what will happen with the next vote.

Spring Statement today, usually a huge event and the Chamber packed. My goodness, how support is disappearing for the PM and her Chancellor. Conservative benches very empty, statement a complete non-event. Again, attend the ERG meeting, this time in Portcullis House. Well-attended and well-organised. Unlike Remainers, those who voted for the deal are warmly welcomed back, no unpleasantness, no reprisals. My goodness, Rees-Mogg, Steve Barclay and Mark Francois are working their socks off. I sit next to Dominic Raab, definitely one to watch. Division Bell goes, I join the lobby to oppose taking no deal off the table. Tragically, motion lost by 4, how on earth is this happening? Join aye lobby to protect no deal and support the PM, sit next to a very dejected Kate Hoey – where is everyone, we are losing Brexit. This time numbers dropped to 278.

14 March

As the enormity of what happened dawns on everyone, anger sets in. On the Conservative benches party discipline has completely evaporated. Absolute disgrace, Minister and members of Cabinet no longer support the Government. This cannot continue. Text message from PM's Parliamentary aide, would like to see me for half an hour before the vote. I decline, as I had a much-needed hair appointment!

15 March

Drove to surgery expecting increased numbers as a result of Brexit, as it turned out bizarrely it was relatively small and the one person who did come to see me about Brexit couldn't wait, most strange.

18 March

Drive to Westminster in a reflective mood.

Most odd day at Westminster, the place awash with rumours. Speaker's announcement and the bombshell delivered, ruling against the Government having the same Meaningful Vote this week. Brexit has temporarily been scuppered, lots of anger in all parts and the Speaker's authority challenged. Government doesn't seem to have a Plan B. All the news is about the Meaningful Vote and the Speaker's interpretation of precedent, the country is now in crisis.

19 March

Paralysis at Westminster as PM tries to decide what to do. Usual drop-in events to attend. To make matters worse, supposed to be a security strike in the Commons the next day.

20 March

PMQs really flat, strange atmosphere. We now know that Theresa May will be asking for an extension, albeit short. This goes down like a lead balloon. I stand and look at her from behind the Speaker's Chair, all her authority has now definitely gone. Later, wherever you go colleagues are plotting. Text message, the PM would like to see me briefly at 7.00pm, I decline, the situation is hopeless. Announcement made she will broadcast to the nation at 8.00pm. Bet the excitement is unwarranted, bet it will be regurgitating what we have heard before, could be wrong. Bump into a number of my DUP colleagues, they are standing firm unless she says something different. I wonder, perhaps Brexit might just happen next week.

25 March

D-Day in Westminster with Brexit. First job was to chair DL. All seems straightforward until a very experienced Labour hand decided to give the Minister a tough time – quite right too.

All very amicable though. Brexit fever reaches a pitch. Missed ERG meeting but already had decided how I would vote. High drama when vote declared, government lose control of the business, real turmoil, this is getting very serious. Endless points of order which I couldn't bear listening to. Media awash with what happens next.

26 March

My birthday, complete non-event. Not sure much to celebrate but I am still alive, another year older and cards get fewer.

Anyway, meeting with a close American friend and his son, who treat me to a lovely birthday lunch.

All helps to take my mind off Brexit. Resolve to attend ERG meeting, completely ruined by endless votes. Meeting descended into a farce, much confusion about tabling of amendments. Unanimity among the group seems to be on the slide, not good. People rushing past me to get to the Table Office, managed to sign some of the amendments, but resolved to go myself to the Table Office. I eventually signed all the amendments I wanted to.

27 March

Did interview with Dutch TV, to what end I am not sure, but I really do like Dutch people. And then the big one, the Conservative Leader/Prime Minister addresses the '22. Get to Committee Room 14 to be greeted by the media amassed outside. When I get into the room it is jam-packed with people, many of whom were unelected, absolutely ridiculous, badly organised. Many MPs could not get into the room. Hardly as momentous as when Margaret was brought down, but in those days there were not as many Peers. I began to steam at the poor organisation and decided to stand on a seat at the back next to two Peers I had never seen before. Meeting starts, could hardly hear what was being said, colleagues don't know how to project their voices or use a microphone. Theresa stalks in, as ever inappropriate banging on the wooden façade as if she is a hero, sickening really, hypocrisy all around. Room awash with planted questions, surreal atmosphere as if disaster wasn't happening, which it certainly is. At the start of the meeting the chair told us not to repeat outside what took place. Completely ignored by some people attending, who spoke to the media and to make matters worse misrepresented what had been said. The reality is nothing new came from Theresa's mouth, same old line about her deal or no deal. Story spun that she was going to be leaving the job as Leader of the Party and PM. Ridiculous, we knew that already as she would be challenged and would lose in November.

28 March

Attend Business Questions, more people than usual as there was likely to be a vote later in the day. At least no serious spat between Speaker and Leader of the House this time.

29 March

Whips telling us to stand ready for votes throughout the day. I ignored that message and kept my appointments at two schools before making my way to Westminster. Took part in bizarre vote triggered not by the Government, who have lost control, but by other MPs. As ever, no majority for anything, what a waste of time.

Had a meeting with the new Chief Clerk of the House, excellent appointment, sensible and wise. I now know the reality of the situation that the House is facing re Brexit, which is grim. Praying now for a miracle.

Returned to Southend to address my AGM. Sombre mood among the assembled – in my speech I tell it like it is. Readopted again as Conservative candidate for the constituency, I must be mad. Who would want to be a Conservative MP at the moment?

1 April

Attend reception for Parliamentary Party on the Terrace. Awash with runners and riders for the leadership of our Party.

Any number of them simply not up to the job. Mediocrity rules the day. Attend indicative votes, every proposition defeated, the crisis gets worse.

2 April

Business fizzles out. PM makes broadcast to the nation after marathon Cabinet meeting. Announces she wants to work with the Leader of the Opposition. Fury and confusion everywhere. Does this mean we are now being sold out?

3 April

It's PMQs today and I am the only Conservative on the Order Paper. Thought long and hard about what I should ask, settled on a mixture of irony, humour and local populism. Had to be right as called just before spat between PM and Leader of the Opposition. On this occasion I seem to have judged the mood right, question seemed to go down well and put a smile on otherwise sombre faces. Strange atmosphere in the Chamber, anger all around on the Conservative benches. Theresa May and Jeremy Corbyn have exchanges on poverty, not on Brexit. However, many Conservative colleagues vent their anger towards the PM as a result of her resolve to deliver a Brexit plan with the Labour Leader. Leave Chamber to lots of nice remarks from colleagues. Usual meetings, have lunch in Members Dining Room. As I test the mood among colleagues (gloomy), everyone counsels against a General Election, believing if there were one it would be Armageddon for the Conservative Party. Attend 1922 meeting, what a contrast to the previous week. Relatively sparsely attended, Liam Fox does not appear to be the big draw he once was. He trashes the Labour policy on joining a customs union. Parliamentary neighbour for Rochford & SE opens questions by asking about arrangements for another leadership ballot. Rules don't allow one to officially take place until the end of the year, but sense if enough letters are sent in (50 per cent plus one) then an election for a new leader will take place. Division bells sound for the first of a number of votes – drama as there is a tie 310–310. Speaker follows the precedent of voting with the status quo. No more indicative votes thank goodness. Next vote government lose by 312–313, can't understand where the three extra votes come from. Backbench emergency Bill rushed through Parliament to howls of protest. Measure designed to tie PMs hands not to leave the EU without a deal.

4 April

Attend Business Questions. Talks at Number 10 continue between party leaders, look as if the Easter recess has been lost. High stakes, everyone is now waiting to see what happens next. Contenders for leadership of the Conservative Party are working overtime to garner support for their bids. Not sure yet who the final two to be put to the membership will be.

5 April

A busy surgery, nearly everyone mentioned Brexit in passing, and a man and woman were frustrated by the way the Conservative PM and Leader is handling the issue. I can't say that I disagree.

8 April

Should not have been at Westminster, supposed to be Easter recess but because of the Brexit fiasco Parliament is sitting. Arrived late at Westminster, nothing much happening, still waiting for PM to let Parliament know what her intentions are re Brexit. As it stands, supposed to be leaving on Friday with no deal. Obviously not now going to happen. Colleagues, I see, are demoralised and fed up, having been back to their constituencies campaigning for the local elections and finding the mood grim.

9 April

Various votes on EU matters, feel liberated voting against the Government each time. More in the no lobby than I had expected, colleagues in surprisingly buoyant mood. It was a

Parliamentary first, it was a colleague's birthday and the strains of happy birthday could clearly be heard in the Chamber. Go into the Library to digest the situation. Attend ERG meeting, not quite the force it was, leadership seems somewhat weakened and slightly downcast. Meeting held in Committee Room 14, lots of space this time, which I am pleased about. Look around the room and see many former colleagues from the Commons, they received applause when their spokesman Lord Hunt gave an account of their efforts in the Lords. In contrast, I could sense the frustration that we didn't seem to be doing much in the Commons as a group to make Brexit happen. As ever, seem in the dark. For the first time I realise there is a real lack of experience in these particularly complex and challenging circumstances. News breaks that the no vote was 110, but 80 colleagues, many of them Ministers, abstained. Over two-thirds of the Conservative Party is obviously opposed to Theresa May's approach to Brexit and her negotiations with Labour. Go in the Tea Room with one of my mates, something I haven't done too much recently, given the changed sitting hours. What an eye opener, saw more friendly and smiley faces at the Labour end than the Conservative end. It looks now that contenders for Theresa May's job are in double figures and they are all in the Tea Room, you couldn't make it up. Some of them are not up to the job they occupy as Minister, let alone becoming PM.

Return to Southend that night slightly buoyant.

10 April

Drive in from Southend, another pointless day. Decide to miss PMQs, I had my moment of glory the previous week. Right decision, nothing much happened. Arrive in office to find computers all down, just what I didn't want. Decide to attend '22 meeting, no speaker booked because House wasn't expected to sit. Room not as full as I would have expected. Meeting started with the usual sycophantic planted loyalists. Why they bother I do not know, makes absolutely no impact. Not many incisive points made. Following a question from one prominent Brexiteer, Minister got up in a fit of pique, threw his chair down and said, 'I have had enough of this, vote for the deal' and stormed out. Another colleague, who is well-known for his military expertise, raised a point warning the Committee of the Labour trap as a result of the talks which are being held. Said our Party was in great peril, that must be the understatement of the year. Stayed in mother's home that night and waited up for the result of the European Council meeting. Just as expected, there is a further delay to Brexit but not the longest one that some countries wanted or the shortest one that the ghastly French President was jumping up and down about. Instead they have gone for Halloween, very appropriate.

11 April

Travelled to Westminster, as ever to attend Business Questions. House pretty full because of expected statement by PM after lunch. I decide to go on animal welfare issues again. As a result of various meetings, only in Chamber for a short while to listen to PMs statement. PM dressed in black, very appropriate. Sombre mood on Conservative benches, various loyalists still giving support but Brexiteers desperately unhappy. First Brexiteer question calls on her to resign. Given all the stress and the long hours thought she looked remarkably well and dealt with questions quite ably. Come to the view she is demob happy and perversely relishing the situation. My thoughts are that her resignation will be precipitated by the '22 Committee and its executive, following the local elections. My hunch is however that she will be the PM who will see that we leave the EU whilst the leadership contest continues. New leader and PM probably be in place in time for autumn party conference, when they may seek to exploit their honeymoon period with a General Election. Will just have to see how it all pans out. If ever the House was delighted for a belated Eater recess it was now. Just annoyed that there is not the usual Easter recess adjournment debate!

13/14 April

Canvassed for local elections, absolutely dreadful response. Issue on the doorstep is Brexit and the PM. If I took the advice of many respondents on the doorstep in terms of what they would like to do to the PM, she would have to be a contortionist to survive. Really cheesed off that although I am doing what the majority of my constituents wanted, we are all seemingly being tarred with the same brush, disgraceful. Sunday – day of rest and family matters.

16/17 April

Canvass with local candidates, trying to raise morale. Imploring residents who have always been Conservative not to take it out on our local candidates. Meet with mixed success.

18 April

Visit Southend Hospital to distribute Easter eggs. Gratefully received by children and staff. More canvassing even though candidates have gone on strike. Response better than had been expected.

19 April

Small surgery, suspect most people thought I wouldn't hold one on Good Friday. Convinced myself that is what God would have wanted. More canvassing, mixed responses but the week without Parliament sitting clearly beneficial to the candidates.

20 April

Invited to bowl first wood for local bowling club. Big turnout, greens looked wonderful, very happy occasion. More canvassing, response surprisingly good with our wonderful candidate who has been left virtually on her own. Attend yet another bowls club event elsewhere, everyone in good humour including local councillors. More canvassing in most challenging part of the constituency. Great local candidate, as he is not already the incumbent has nothing much to lose.

23 April

Oh dear, back to Westminster after short recess. I am filled with foreboding at what might happen. Whilst Parliament has not been sitting a terrible atrocity in Sri Lanka. So many innocent lives destroyed by suicide bombers. Young woman in Northern Ireland loses her life, victim of stray bullet as terrorism momentarily returns to the province of Northern Ireland. Please God no, it seems this time the warring factions are united in their condemnation of the murder.

London practically brought to a standstill by climate change protesters, huge disruption. Vast sums of money going on policing the event, quite to what end I do not know. Fine words spoken by politicians jumping on a bandwagon, whereas a solution to climate change requires determination and a commitment from world leaders – which doesn't much seem to be happening now. UK already signed up to many things which protesters are complaining about.

26 April

In the afternoon canvassed in local elections, residents only want to discuss one subject and that is Brexit – not good. The dissatisfaction with the PM continues to grow, I fear the worst.

29 April

Drive to Westminster. Endless talk about the PM, in short, she has no future and colleagues are getting angry and fed up with her, very depressing.

1 May

International Development Question to the impressive Secretary of State, got a great answer. Followed by question to the PM. These days not necessary, if you are a Conservative, to be on the Order Paper – you have a great chance to be called in any case. Chose the opportunity to raise the Music Man Project performance at the Royal Albert Hall and of course city status for Southend. I think even colleagues are getting frustrated that whilst nothing happens on Brexit, nothing happens on city status. I hear John Redwood shout, 'For goodness sake woman, just say yes!' Attend Admin Committee, always useful to pick up what is going on even if MPs seem to increasingly have less control over the running of the place in which we work.

2 May

D-Day, disaster day, local elections. As was my normal practice, spent the day touring polling stations. Strange, depressing atmosphere, which always does not bode well. Had to return to Commons for adjournment debate which would come on early due to poor attendance in the House. Subject: value of building New Towns. Spoke about my experience representing Basildon, seized opportunity to 'put the record straight'. Caught train back to Southend, arrived 5.00pm. Go to Party HQ and resume the tour of the constituency. Call into polling stations and use the car loudspeaker to encourage people to vote for our candidates. Never shared with any of the locals my feelings about likely outcome, but I knew it would not be good. Return home before polling stations have closed. Decided to get to my local count at midnight and enjoy or squirm as the political pundits dissected the likely results. Gloom soon descended as the Conservative losses got worse and worse. Turn up at the Southend count, worst premonitions were confirmed. Lose eight seats in total and control of the Council. Crying shame that some excellent councillors paid the price by losing their seats because of Westminster incompetence. Return home to continue watching as the results come in. Conservative losses grow worse and worse, mainly Lib Dem gains. Retire to bed having had my worst fears confirmed, my Party has been badly damaged.

3 May

Woke to do radio interview for my local station. I didn't pull any punches in attributing the blame for our shocking performance.

4/5 May

Turn on TV, endless speculation about who the next leader and PM would be. So glad to be leaving for my youngest daughter's wedding in Charleston, South Carolina. Never been so glad to leave England for a while albeit courtesy of British Airways.

Arrive in the US for a really joyful week, full of fun and happiness. Unconventional American wedding, held outside in the grounds of a tea plantation. As most fathers would say, my daughter looked stunning, radiant. She had married a really good man. Such a relief from the agony of Westminster.

13 May

Return to UK. Not looking forward to arriving back at Westminster, which I did this evening. As ever, by the time I got there, Parliament had adjourned, nothing happening other than the build-up to the European elections on 23 May.

17 May

Surgery again not as busy as usual. Must reflect general malaise. Visit local manufacturing business who had initially been supportive of Brexit, now finding delay has affected their business. Rather generously, he did not turn on me.

22 May

Little happening, as ever, at Westminster. All time low at PMQs, hardly a cheer raised on either side, everyone in the main parties fearing the worst in the European elections, which despite speculation went ahead. Where is everyone, they can't be campaigning for an election we were promised would never be held. Day rife with rumours of Theresa May announcing when she would be leaving Downing Street. Who is running the show? Bit like the tail wagging the dog. Arrive back in Southend to find Leader of the House has resigned. Very honourably took the view that she couldn't bring forward legislation she didn't believe in. Such a shame, really nice lady. I think it seals the fate of when the PM will resign.

23 May

Euro election day, God help us. The elections that were not supposed to happen, can't believe that they are. Get up early to vote at my local polling station. Smiles all round as I walk in. Voted Conservative, obviously, but with great disappointment that the election is happening. Travel to Westminster for Business Questions. Who will answer? As it turned out, a Government whip. In all the circumstances he did very well. Afternoon Whitsun adjournment debate. The few MPs who were around managed to use the time available to good effect. Tributes all round to former Leader of House and long serving clerk retiring. Atmosphere surreal, continued speculation about not if but when the PM will be leaving 10 Downing Street. How true the saying is, 'all if not most political careers end in tears'.

30 May

Cross over to St Margaret's for memorial service of a dear former colleague. Wonderful conviction politician, Toby Jessel. Last time I saw him was ironically a few weeks earlier at Lord Spicer's memorial service. He shook me by the hand and said you must get Brexit done – I am hanging on to his encouraging words. Later that day had my first meeting with one of the candidates wanting to become Conservative Leader/PM. The interview took place in his office, spent probably over half an hour listening to the candidate's plans not only to leave the EU but how they would govern the country. At the end of the presentation I not only asked some questions about what they had said but I made a number of personal criticisms, not only of the individual concerned, but of the Government and the way our party was being run. The candidate, as always, was a perfect gentleman and impressive and persuasive but possibly, like us all, flawed. That night I gave careful thought about what we had shared.

4 June

Parliament returns from its Whitsun break and the fun begins to elect a new leader of the Conservative Party and PM. I am increasingly sounding like Victor Meldrew wherever I go, I must stop it or so my wife says! Drive to Westminster for various events and have a meeting with another of the leadership candidates. Meeting takes place in the candidate's room in Norman Shaw North. A really lovely person who I gave support to in the last election campaign. They set out their well-thought through plans for us leaving the EU. Not only that, they have policies on everything. Very impressive. Obviously keen for my support, I said I would give it careful consideration as I was seeing everyone. My gut feeling is no real momentum or enthusiasm among colleagues for this candidate, sadly, this time around. Later meeting with next candidate cancelled.

5 June

Numerous summer events but only one topic being discussed. Go to Chamber for Cabinet Office Questions then meeting next of the leadership contenders. This meeting took place in the candidate's office, youngest of the contenders, tech savvy and doing a very impressive job in Cabinet. I held back from blaming them for what I felt was profound incompetence at the heart of government. Very impressed with the presentation, in my heart of hearts felt that this time the opportunity had come too soon for this candidate.

6 June

International Development Questions, answered by the most unusual candidate in terms of his campaign. Got a typically cerebral answer. As usual I ask a Business Question. Then go on for a meeting with my preferred leadership candidate in his room in Portcullis House. This is an individual, and I reminded him of the occasion, who came to see me when we had the last leadership contest for advice as to whether he should run as a candidate. I said no, it was too soon. Extraordinarily, he took my advice and perhaps that of others. If only all the candidates in this election were so savvy. He set out his plans on Brexit and his ambitions for the country. I was reassured that he had those unique qualities that you not only need in a leader, but you need in the highly stressful job of PM. At the end of the meeting I told him that whilst I would be seeing all the candidates, I would be supporting him as long as he was in the contest, he was genuinely pleased. I drove home that night to Southend with a weight off my shoulders about my decision, but told no one what it was.

10 June

Attend meeting with the bookies' favourite candidate for the leadership of the Conservative Party/PM. Have heart to heart in his office. He reaffirmed his resolve to leave the EU on 31 October and talked about his ambitions for the country. I observe his physical changes, presumably as a result of his new relationship. Slimmer, hair tamed and more subdued. I said I welcomed the fact that he had a sense of humour, as long as it was directed in the right way. He slightly bit back, I then told him straight what I thought of his performances thus far in office, the state of the party and what I thought he should do if he gets the top job. He subsequently ignored all of my advice! I left thinking that he was both a good and kind man who with the right support could just perhaps make a real success of the job of leader of the Conservative Party and PM of our country.

After attending various other events, I then have a further meeting with another of our leading contenders. He gave probably the most impressive presentation, had a real plan, very enthusiastic. When I started to give advice at the end of his presentation, he actually admitted he was already having a bit of a makeover, not to mention voice training, it has certainly worked. I left feeling I had been with a thoroughly decent colleague whose own life story was quite remarkable, and whatever happened in the contest should be at the heart of our government.

Attend Admin Committee meeting, very interesting as always, 6.00pm announcement of leadership candidates. Attend hustings held by the 92 Group. Even though there were many interruptions for votes, I return to the room on every occasion in order to listen to them all. Felt very sorry for those who had, drawn by ballot, entered the hustings after most colleagues had gone, very disappointing I thought. Absolutely fascinating watching them all perform. Some of them better than expected, some as I had expected and others quite disappointing.

12 June

Final leadership hustings organised by '22 Committee. Some interesting performances, one of the candidates is certainly the joker in pack, in every sense. Yet further events in Parliament.

13 June

Main focus of Parliament and media's attention is on today's first ballot for the Conservative Party leadership. After some who have withdrawn, we have a choice of nine. Ballot opens at 10.00am at which time I put up on my website that I would be voting for Dominic Raab. I thought I shouldn't show my hand until the contest started but then wanted everyone to know what my intentions were. Walk over to vote, extraordinary scenes. Corridor full of a mix of journalists and MPs. Both groups possibly talking absolute nonsense, nervous speculation on what the outcome would be. Very strange to see so many colleagues in on a Thursday. I am always here for Business Questions but so many others aren't. Asked my usual Business Question then went back to the office to wait for the result of the leadership ballot.

Colleagues, but not myself, gather in Committee Room 14 for the announcement. Executive of the '22 walks into the room like the Soviet Politburo, pathetic really. Thank goodness there were no spoilt ballot papers, so we at least know how to count.

As predicted, Boris came top comfortably, my candidate does reasonably well but not quite as well as I had hoped. Three candidates eliminated, couldn't make the threshold. Not surprised really, as too many candidates in the field. Go off to chair proceedings in Westminster Hall, my mind wanders as to what will happen in the next round, media have a field day. Pity three good candidates, two of whom were women, were all eliminated, but given the way things are at the moment I wasn't surprised. Indeed, I was surprised that four were not eliminated. Interesting to see where the momentum is and the lobbying.

17 June

Drive to Westminster with only one thing on my mind, the leadership. Afternoon, yet more hustings for the leadership candidates. I only caught the presentation by my candidate, lots of his supporters in the room, I thought it went well and he was greeted with warm applause.

Throughout day catch up with various Parliamentary friends to talk about the leadership contest.

18 June

Second round of voting for the leadership contest. Bit nervous about my candidate's chances, doesn't seem to have enough momentum to get the required 33 votes, just have a gut feeling about it. Such a pity as he really is such a great guy. Busied myself throughout the day by attending many Parliamentary functions. Phone messages and texts keep arriving from candidates and their supporters. One extraordinary meeting with someone who wasn't an MP, but said he could facilitate a meeting with the candidate he was supporting. I think he was a little bit embarrassed when I told him I had already had the meeting and had told his candidate what I would be doing. Coming back from House, walk past my candidate, wish him well with fingers crossed. He seemed excited and relaxed, also passed another candidate rushing to see the votes counted. Broad smile, again looking fairly relaxed. Spend rest of the time dictating letters to my secretary but distracted by the looming declaration at 6.00pm. Just as I thought, my candidate is eliminated, and I am very disappointed.

19 June

This is getting serious. Leadership ballot three. My iPhone is full of phone messages, text messages from the candidates still in the contest, all wanting my vote, am I reading too much into tactical voting I wonder. Boris is certain to be in the final, it is a question of who he will come up against. Agree to meet Jeremy Hunt today at 1.30pm. Jeremy's room is next to the PM, door locked so I knocked. In I went, sat opposite one another, he made his pitch which was rather impressive. I know he could do the job, looks very Prime Ministerial. I told him what I thought of the Cabinet and our Party generally and then I told him straightforwardly of my intentions, we left on very good terms. He is a good chap and a serious politician. I told him he wouldn't need much of a makeover. Traipse up to Committee Room 14, corridor awash with journalists. Not a patch really on leadership contests when Margaret Thatcher was challenged for PM, but there we are, how times have changed.

20 June

D-Day. Obvious now that no candidate is going to drop out of the contest. That meant for many colleagues who are not usually here on Thursdays two ballots for leadership. Ran over to Chamber for Business Questions as Urgent Question was withdrawn, and it didn't go up quickly enough on the annunciator. Speaker understanding but Conservative benches practically empty. Go up to vote in fourth leadership ballot. Not so many journalists outside, decide to go back, as I did last night, for the actual result. Home Secretary eliminated, not quite sure, with often duplicitous colleagues, where the votes will now go, who will be in the final two? Fifth leadership ballot, unless there is a tie this will really be the end of the matter.

Decide to take some staff members over to watch events, real sense of history. Go back to hear the result, glad I did, worth being there for. Agatha Christie couldn't have made up the story any better – Boris Johnson 160, Jeremy Hunt 77, Michael Gove 75 and yes, one disallowed ballot paper. Media very disappointed, as it will be a civilised and gentle contest, would have been much livelier if Michael Gove had seen it through to the final two. End of all the excitement, walk down with my team to Central Lobby, interviews are being given where colleagues momentarily can puff themselves up. As I know only too well, these moments don't last. Now over to the members, but thank goodness there is no coronation but a real choice for local membership. We will know the result by 23 July. All the talk in the evening on the news channels is about the contest between the Foreign Secretary and the former Foreign Secretary, we will see how it all plays out

21 June

Surgery, quite busy. Lots of comment about the Conservative leadership contest.

24 June

Late start for Westminster. What a relief, no more votes on who should lead the Conservative Party, it is now over to the membership. Disaster in the Boris camp but then he seems to thrive on it. Weekend revelations of a bust up with his girlfriend, hostile neighbours ensure media is informed. Difficult to tell what damage will be done, but Jeremy Hunt's camp seem to have their tails up.

26 June

A day packed with receptions, the summer avalanche of goodwill and chinking glasses is everywhere. Popped in briefly for PMQs, many more people there than I would have thought. Left feeling underwhelmed by the exchanges, although the Government side seemed to have their tails up, perhaps in part because of what is to come. Evening events, more summer parties.

29 June

Main activity Armed Forces Day. Without question one of the best ever. Blazing sunshine, parade extremely well done. All the news channels continue to obsess about the Conservative Party leadership contest. Money now being sprayed around like confetti, Chancellor of the Exchequer not amused, doesn't much matter as he is not going to be in post for much longer.

2 July

Summer has well and truly arrived. Lots of receptions to go to. Most important meeting of the day is with Education/Schools Minister and local teachers. We presented a united front and I made sure the civil servants were 'fingered'. In the evening the Tiffin Cup final. Our entry made it to the last 13 and became the regional winner. My heart was pounding as the results were announced. Oh dear, we were sixth, never mind the restaurant were pleased.

4 July

Brexit day for locals. Both candidates for leadership given opportunity for rally, which only one was able to take up – the Boris camp. Started day by asking Business Question, always worthwhile as raised the profile of an issue of importance to many people. Left by train for Southend to attend rally. Arrive at venue – packed, standing room only. Great job done by organisers. Star attraction was Jacob Rees-Mogg, spoke well to an audience who were always going to give him a good reception. After event, mortified that no picture taken with wonderful supporter, Rofique Ali, and his magnificent cake. Rescued situation later – cake went to St Albans. Follow up from meeting excellent. Rare occasion, actually swayed votes towards Boris.

10 July

PMQs dominate the day, demonstrates how power has slipped away from the PM. Whilst showing a bit of mettle, still nothing substantial or worthwhile in exchanges.

15 July

Drive to Westminster to ask Home Office question in support of a group who are dedicated to encouraging young people not to participate in violent crime. Rest of the day spent at receptions and gossiping about the outcome of the Conservative leadership contest.

16 July

Various drop-in and lobbying events at Westminster. Nothing of any import happening in Chamber. Everyone waiting to see who the next Prime Minister will be.

17 July

1912 lunch with guest of honour Priti Patel and spoke much common sense. Priti showed great empathy with the guests.

Decide to attend final hustings in Conservative Party leadership contest at Excel Centre. Meet with group of colleagues. Very well-attended. Real bustle of excitement. Shown to so-called 'VIP Room' for members. For once drinks and snacks decent. Then led out with a few others to the main hall. Pass one of my colleagues dressed dramatically in red, must have been borrowed from the PM. Sit in the front row on reserved seats. Why not? Determined to have a good view. Boris speaks first. Much better than I had expected. Quite tough interviewing from Iain Dale. Boris sat on the edge of the seat. Wondered if he was going to fall off. Huge support for him in audience. Jeremy then follows him. Oh, I do wish he'd wear a jacket. After all, it is a symbol of authority. Don't approve of dressing down. Unlike Boris who speaks from the podium, Jeremy wanders about the stage very distracting. Nevertheless, he performs quite well and has many supporters in audience. Left the session greatly cheered in the knowledge that my party and the country would be alright whoever wins.

22 July

Last week of Parliament before the summer recess. Make or break for the Conservative Party.

Drove to Westminster moderately inspired and excited by the prospect of a new government.

Walk with friends for reception at Number 10 Downing Street hosted by the PM to say thanks for our support. Bets taken which creep would pay tribute. As it turned out, no one really did other than three muted cheers. Very strange gathering. Actually arrived at the same time the PM and her husband were walking along the corridor. They gave my colleagues and I a summary glance. They did not look happy, but awkward as usual. Not so much a party as a wake. Hospitality echoed the premiership, somewhat frugal and disappointing. Grounds full of anxious colleagues wondering if they would lose their job or be offered something for the first time.

Unbelievably, although I shouldn't be surprised anymore, a couple of colleagues who are actually trying to bring the government down appear in the grounds. You just couldn't make it up. As I decide to leave the reception, I try to find the PM and say goodbye. There she was surrounded by well-wishers. I gently tapped her on the back, held either arm, kissed her on both cheeks and said, 'Where is your husband so I can say goodbye? Do look after yourself and take a rest.' As I looked into her eyes, she had a haunted look. Really didn't seem well and the enormity of the ending of her premiership was clearly hitting her hard.

23 July

The day that British politics changed direction, perhaps forever.

Catch train to Westminster and walk to the QE2 Centre to listen to the result of the ballot for Conservative Party leadership. Staggered to find most people not gone into the hall but standing around and engaging in pointless conjecture about the impact of the impending result. Enter hall, take seat in front row, number one. Not reserved for me but pretty confident no one would argue. Really nice lady came to join me, I want her as my Police and Crime Commissioner. Gossip with other like-minded colleagues as we wait for result.

Hush descends, nothing happens over a 15-minute period, and then the show begins. Rather impressive short film about the Conservative Party and its leaders since its formation, and then, oh dear, in walks the Chairman of the Conservative Party, who I am rather underwhelmed by in that job. Thank goodness he hands over to the joint acting chairmen of the 1922 Committee, who seizes the moment of history in a joint Oscar-type announcement, thankfully getting the names of the winner and loser correct. Cameras pan on the faces of the two contestants, who obviously knew the result a long time ago. They both smile at each other.

Rapturous reception for Boris as he goes to the podium to deliver an effective, commanding and amusing speech. What a relief compared to what has gone before. The dark clouds are disappearing. He leaves the venue quickly as the main participant in the day's historic events. Leave QE2 building for lunch with former MP friend. Enjoyed exciting gossip of what the future may hold.

24 July

Spotlight very much on the PM's last questions, which I decide to attend in my normal place. It lasted a record 53 minutes. Bobbed up and down for an hour without success. Tricky for the Speaker to keep everyone happy. Perhaps it was best that my voice wasn't heard. Predictably participants did not rise to the occasion. Inappropriate exchanges between PM, Leader of the Opposition and the SNP. With a few notable exceptions, enormity of the occasion was not grasped.

As PM sat down for the last time, Conservative benches rose to applaud, an innovation of which I thoroughly disapprove until we change the rules. I've seen six Prime Ministers leave office; this particular departure did not feel as historic as that of Margaret Thatcher. PM departs for 10 Downing Street.

TV covers the departure of the retiring PM outside Number 10. Husband joins her at podium, all very awkward and somewhat tragic. Camera follows car as she goes to the Palace.

Next shots show the new PM 'kissing hands' with the Queen. Cameras show new PM arriving at Downing Street. Makes real tour-de-force speech on the steps of Downing Street. Sceptics realising, perhaps for the first time, that there is much more to this man than meets the eye. Rod of steel re Brexit, really cheerful vision for the future of our country.

In the afternoon dash to Lords cricket ground with my secretary to watch Ireland-England Test Match. Weather boiling hot. Spent most of the game on social media looking for reshuffle announcements. England skittled out – not what was forecast but nevertheless great atmosphere and a wonderful venue.

25 July

Boris Day.

Arrive at Westminster to ask Defra question with already a new Secretary of State, a proper Brexiteer. Ask Business Question. House unusually packed. New Leader of the House a perfect shoo-in for his new role. Decide to stay in Chamber and await the arrival of the new Boris Johnson. Much excitement and we were not to be disappointed. Whole House captivated by the rhetorical skills of the new Prime Minister. Labour and opposition benches looking glum generally. Sets out a brilliant action plan for leaving the European Union and governing our country.

Bob up and down to catch the Speaker's eye which I did eventually. Yippee, unlike his predecessor, who I never really got anywhere with regarding making Southend a city, the new PM said yes. Alleluia! Alleluia! My party has been rescued and our country is on the road to recovery. Harold Macmillan's Night of the Long Knives put in total shade by the dramatic appointments which Boris Johnson now makes. Unfortunate to see some lose their jobs, for whatever reason, but by and large the new Cabinet and its team of Ministers should get Brexit done with a brighter future for us all.

Summer Recess

Usually, Summer is a very quiet time in terms of political speculation, not so this year. All the talk was of meeting Boris Johnson's avowed intention to make the Brexit deadline or die in a ditch. Parliament returns on 3 September to debate an emergency motion on the prorogation of Parliament. Twenty-one Conservatives have the whip removed when they supported the emergency motion. The speed of events is now breath-taking, and I simply cannot understand the motives of the 21 MPs. Yes, some of them by their own self-inflicted wounds have killed their career within the Conservative Party, but others were absolutely key to our future and now they have gone, absolutely bizarre.

At the end of the vote, Boris Johnson gets to the despatch box and announces his intention to hold an early General Election. The Labour benches look very sombre but of course for the election to be held two-thirds of Parliament would have to vote for it. The numbers are simply not there. Privately, I certainly don't want a winter election. The news is full of speculation, I just can't see a winter election happening.

4 September

BJ's first PMQs.

MPs vote on holding an early General Election. Those in favour 298, those against 56, but of course it doesn't pass as 434 votes are need (two-thirds) under the 2011 Fixed Term Parliaments Act. In recent years Parliament has always had a two-week recess for the conferences. Suddenly announced that Parliament will prorogue on 10 September, the pace quickens, dramatic scenes – Labour and SNP protesting and trying to stop the Speaker processing to the House of Lords. Bizarre in the extreme, I have certainly never seen anything like it before. Gina Miller, together with some politicians opposed to Brexit, mounts a campaign to get the Supreme Court to overturn the decision of Parliament to prorogue. Much debate as to whether or not the courts have the right to override Parliament, which has always been supreme.

17 September

The Supreme Court begins a three-day hearing. No real indication given as to how the hearing has gone, but on 24 September in pantomime proceedings, with the Supreme Court milking the spotlight for all it's worth. Lady Hale adorned with an awful spider brooch, announced to the world, or at least all those that were interested, that the view of the UK Supreme Court was unanimous that prorogation was unlawful.

24 September

Very dangerous territory. The elected against the unelected. The executive against the judiciary – not sure how this will end. Great confusion now among Parliamentarians as to what will happen. Some opposition members grandstanding and tweeting that they are already back at Westminster. The reality is that Parliament resumes the following week. Unclear what affect this will all have on the Party conferences, rather depressingly, it seems that they will go ahead. Pity, they are all a bit of a waste of time and in my view could easily be held over a weekend. Such a shame as they used to be wonderful occasions – but not anymore.

8 October

Parliament prorogued for second time before Queen's Speech. State Opening of Parliament will be held on 14 October. Bizarrely, opposition members complain about this, yet in the same breath they have been moaning that this was the longest session ever since the English Civil War. Indications given that the whole occasion will be greatly scaled down, and so it was.

14 October

State Opening of Parliament without all the usual trappings. As is my normal practise, I stand near the bar of the House of Lords having processed down to hear Her Majesty deliver a speech which in every sense appeared to be an election manifesto. Oh Dear! Perhaps they are serious about having this election before Christmas. Ministers and officials continue to travel back and forth to Brussels.

17 October

UK and EU negotiate a new Withdrawal Agreement. Plenty of speculation about how the vote on it would go.

19 October

House of Commons sits for the first time on a Saturday since April 1982.

24 October

Government win Queen's Speech vote by 310 to 294. Meaningless really, as they won't get the Withdrawal Bill through. Boris, admitting defeat with the Bill, recognising his inability to meet his deadline of 31 October, again lays a motion for an early General Election to be held on 12 December. By this time, I was getting really worried. An election two weeks before Christmas? Surely the government can't be serious. Enormous speculation in the build-up to the vote, with at one point, opposition parties rumoured to be against the election. Then all of a sudden, Labour table an amendment to the motion, which was never approved by Parliament, to hold the election on 9 December.

Can't believe this is happening. Nuclear button pressed. A General Election will be held on Thursday 12 December. Ironically, I happen to pass one long serving Labour member who I knew well who seemed very exercised about the vote. I told him that privately, I was less than enthusiastic about it. He criticised his own party for going along with it and said that many good colleagues will lose their seats as a result of it – 'it's all Corbyn's fault'. (When Parliament returned after the election, I happened to note that the same person had lost his own seat – how cruel is that!)

31 October – 12 December

Old Article 50 deadline passes. Nothing left now but to pre-pare for the election. Parliament dissolved on 6 November. I spoke to my team about the forthcoming campaign and how we would fight the election, which I felt would obviously be on one issue. I was privately less than confident that this enormous gamble would be successful, irrespective of how safe Electoral Calculus regarded my own seat.

With the new Speaker elected, all thoughts turned to the General Election. I however, immediately realised that there wasn't going to be any election to choose new Deputy Speakers. That, I felt, put me at a huge disadvantage, in that the support that I had quietly nurtured could not be guaranteed after the election, as a number of people who I knew I could truthfully rely on would not be standing again. Furthermore, there was no certainty as to who would be re-elected. My immediate thoughts were, having done it so many times before, to make sure that our decamping of the office to my constituency went smoothly.

I knew, or at least hoped, that however reluctant I was to have an election before Christmas, this time we would at least have a proper campaign with a manifesto that would not only keep our own supporters happy, but would attract new sup-port. I have never pretended to be tech savvy, but following conversations with colleagues I was now fully signed up to Twitter, but would not respond to the inevitable abuse. For the first time joined MPs WhatsApp groups, even though I had been warned that many of these groups, perhaps out of boredom, are full of trivia or colleagues talking drivel, 'Look at me'.

There was also much speculation about how one would canvass during the short hours of daylight. I perhaps stupid-ly decided that I would continue to canvass morning, after-noon and evening. I often have thought what would happen if I didn't knock on any doors, probably it would be a relief for constituents, but what a risk. In any case you have to do some-thing, you can't just sit and wait for the election itself.

The campaign began with my traditional launch on a local green. In order to try and be modern I decided, following again advice from colleagues, to have a wrap on my car. This was a decision that I am glad I took and was money very well-spent. Even in the dark the logo 'Get Brexit Done' and all the rest of it showed up.

Over the years the reporting of elections has changed dramatically. From my point of view the present set of commentators, with one or two exceptions, were not in the same league as those who reported on these matters when I was first elected. Perhaps the advent of the digital era meant that change was inevitable, but I did so enjoy the swingometer. Most colleagues, I learned, seemed glued to something called Electoral Calculus, which as it happened proved to be pretty accurate. It indicated that I had a 90 per cent prospect of holding my seat.

For me locally, I learned quite late in the day who my opponents would be. I had always welcomed a large number of opponents, it makes the hustings more interesting for a start. To my great disappointment, at the close of nominations there were only going to be three people standing against me, the smallest number ever. As usual, there was the one rather unusual candidate, called Joseph 77. To this day I still don't understand what he was talking about and was none the wiser after the hustings, but he was a jolly nice person.

My Liberal opponent, bizarrely, was the same person who stood against me 23 years ago, when I first became the MP for Southend West. All those years ago, although she had never met me, she inspired the worst negative campaign I have ever been involved in, which amounted to 'we don't want this man from Basildon'. The hypocrisy was that just four years later the Liberals put up a candidate living in the Isle of Man. The Labour candidate was an enthusiastic young man who had fought a local election seat earlier in the year in May.

Much had been said about what a great campaigner Boris was, particularly in his campaigns for Mayor of London. This was now going to be put to the test. All the speculation had been about the Brexit Party and where they would stand their candidates. The impression that I had been given, not least by my friend Ann Widdecombe, now a Brexit Party MEP, was that unless the Conservative Party agreed to a pact not to stand against each other in certain constituencies they would put candidates up everywhere. The Conservative Party organisation let it be known publicly that there would be no pact. Most of my colleagues thought that it was unfair to put up a Brexit Party candidate against a Conservative Member who had consistently supported Brexit and feared that their vote would be split. For my own part I could never quite understand the logic of splitting the vote, but had become accustomed to having UKIP Party candidates stand against me, none of which did particularly well.

Then came the announcement that the Brexit Party would not stand candidates against any sitting Conservative Member of Parliament. That, without question, was a game-changer. The big shock, however, was that the Brexit Party leader would not himself be a candidate That I felt was completely untenable and would in certain respects damage the Brexit Party's hopes of getting any of their candidates elected. It then became obvious that there was a serious falling out among key members, so much so that four of their MEPs left the Party and announced their support for the Conservatives.

My local association members were very pleased with the announcement and I think collectively heaved a sigh of relief. I decided to convene a meeting/meal at my home with my neighbouring Conservative colleagues at the start of the campaign rather than towards the end, as I had done previously. I am glad I did, it was a very useful sounding board to find out what other colleagues thought about the campaign thus far and whether or not locally we should ask for a change in strategy. By and large all of them thought we were set fair to be re-elected with a majority government. I had my own reservations, in as much as I don't like taking risks. Labour had done so well just two years earlier and I didn't know how the general public would react to an election being called so close to Christmas.

As it turned out I needn't have worried. Unlike previous elections, I didn't ask any notables to come and support me, I thought it was unfair to do so in the winter and in any case if they had any time they should concentrate their efforts in the target marginals. Ann Widdecombe, of course, could no longer campaign for me, not just because she was a Brexit Party member but was a candidate herself in the election. Watching the media coverage, I was less than inspired. Inevitably, there were the usual arguments about whether the PM would take part in interviews with all of the other party leaders. As it turned out, his reluctance to be interviewed by one interrogator did him no harm whatsoever. Privately I was increasingly annoyed by what I perceived to be the rudeness of interviewers, continually interrupting whoever the politician was before they had hardly got a word out of their mouth – totally unacceptable.

As the campaign wore on I checked with various colleagues how they thought things were going, after all I had no knowledge of the party's fortunes in the Midlands and the North, yet we were endlessly told we were taking down the 'Red Wall'. I had no idea at all whether or not there was a sea change in support for political parties in various regions about to take place. Nationally, the party leaders were zigzagging all over the country. The Labour Leader seemed to enjoy campaigning and had plenty of energy. Looking at the national reporting of Boris's campaigning you would have thought that he didn't display the energy he was said to possess. Reliable sources however tell me that he was everywhere, meeting and greeting real people. Perhaps the media had their own agenda.

One real shock to me was how the Liberal campaign, and their leader in particular, quickly imploded. I had always thought of Jo Swinson as a most able, capable lady and whilst I thought her policy of revoking Article 50 was utter madness, I did think that her message would resonate strongly with some Remain voters. Again, how wrong I was. My colleagues reported that the Conservative support in the Labour heartlands was real and that there was a seismic shift in support between the two major parties. I tuned in regularly to the MPs WhatsApp group; much of it was nonsense but I didn't seem to be the only crank canvassing in the pitch dark. Whilst others abandoned the evening slot I didn't.

I usually like General Election campaigns, but I hated this one. Yes, I was keen to get Brexit done, although I had begun to loathe the word, but it seemed so odd canvassing when it was cold and dark, and as the campaign wore on being overwhelmed by people's Christmas decorations. The evening canvass session came to be known as the graveyard slot, but I managed to inveigle enough of my volunteers to accompany me on these outings. As far as the opinion polls were concerned, there really didn't seem to be much change in them from when the election was first called, and in no time at all the talk was not of a Labour majority government but how forces against the Conservatives could join together to stop Boris Johnson returning to Number 10 Downing Street.

In terms of my social media coverage I began to embrace the immediacy of it all, and partly through boredom and frustration decided not just to continue with Central Office messaging but to post a 'Dog of the Day'. Even though I say it myself it proved to be a masterstroke. It is when you canvass that you realise just what a nation of animal lovers we are and how many people own dogs. You name it, I admired, cuddled and smooched with dogs of all shapes and sizes and, touch wood, none of them bit me. I developed this message further by deciding to do a video about animal welfare sitting on a horse. This later became an internet sensation for the simple reason that I, and not the horse, looked so ridiculous.

I only ever attend one husting during an election as, unfortunately, they invariably prove to be a waste of time in that nearly everyone arrives at them with their mind already made up who they will vote for. This time the hustings were to be held towards the end of the campaign whereas two years earlier the day of the husting coincided with the Westminster atrocity and the local church quite rightly decided not to go ahead with them. These hustings are well-organised. My heart sank when I turned up at the hustings, instead of being full of church worshipers it was full of Labour and Liberal Party activists, not looking particularly friendly.

I could more or less identify how everyone in the audience would be voting, not least of whom was a real snake in the grass who had inveigled his way into my office for work experience and had been spotted on the Labour campaign team – how bad is that? One of the more politically active Labour supporters was filming the whole proceeding, no doubt wishing to tweet anything which I said and making it inflammatory. All was going swimmingly for the opposition until one gentleman insisted on having his question about anti-Semitism addressed by the candidates. That undoubtedly was the highlight of the evening, but our doughty chairman made sure that the meeting wasn't abandoned when the questioner became insistent that he got an answer to his point about Labour being anti-Semitic. I left the church with my office team in the comforting knowledge that I had neither gained nor lost any votes.

Pity really, as up until now these hustings had always been of some real value. Just one week left to polling day. I still wasn't convinced that the Conservatives would get the majority they so desired but ploughed on with my door-knocking campaign. The only mutual aid I had been able to give, owing to my limited resources, was to my good friend in Thurrock. Jackie won the seat for the first time in 2010, it had been Labour before with an excellent moderate MP. She won the seat by 92 votes and miraculously retained it in both the 2015 and 2017 general elections with more or less the same three figure majority. Absolutely remarkable how she coped with the intense pressure she was under, which I had experienced myself when I was the MP far Basildon.

Nigel Farage had been testing the waters with a mailshot as to whether he might stand in Thurrock. That was now ancient history, Jackie had no Brexit Party candidate. Thurrock was a heavy Leave voting area so I couldn't see where the vote would go other than to Jackie. As it turned out my confidence was spot on, she was returned with a majority this time of over 11,000.

The night before polling day I did the final canvassing session with a small crowd of valiant supporters. I find canvasing infectious and often don't know when to call a halt. When it reached a point where all of us had had a positive response on the doors we were canvassing, I decided for superstitious reasons to stop. I went home that evening frankly relieved that the whole ghastly election was now over and that there was nothing more that I could do to affect the result.

The day of the election was like no other election day I had experienced before. It was the depth of winter – damp, cold and frosty. I went to vote myself first thing in the morning, arriving at the polling station in a church just around the corner from where I live. Even that seemed surreal, with Christmas decorations everywhere. The body language of those voting at the same time I did indicated that I had the support of the majority, but certainly not everyone. I then embarked on the tour of the constituency, having first gone to my HQ at Iveagh Hall.

It is my tradition to visit every polling station, not just to show my face and ensure that everything is being conducted in a proper manner, but to say thank you to those who were acting as tellers and to be seen by those voting when I arrive. Most of the polling station clerks reported to me that people had been queuing up early in the morning and there was a heavy turnout. I myself wasn't convinced that that was the case, as they may just have been making comparisons with the local and EU elections. Polling day always passes quickly, but on this occasion, it again felt strange, with it being dark at 4.00pm in the evening. I visited the three railway stations and did some loud hailer work, reminding commuters, if they need reminding, that there was a General Election on today and I would appreciate their support.

A friend drove me around the constituency and we eventually called it a day at 9.30pm in the evening and I headed home to wait for the dreaded exit poll. My wife was waiting for me, eager to know how the day had gone and what my thoughts were. We have always had great fun speculating about what will happen. I said to her that I wouldn't put it any stronger than it felt OK. No sooner had I sat down with my wife and we had poured ourselves a glass of wine each, than the countdown came for the 10.00pm exit poll. Just as the last bong sounded, the BBC, notorious for getting things wrong, as they certainly did when I was famously re-elected for the third time in 1992, predicted a Conservative majority of 86. My mouth dropped open, surely it couldn't be right. My wife, who hadn't knocked on one door gleefully said, 'I told you so, you were worrying about nothing!'. Well, true enough Labour had done all it possibly could with their disastrous policies to hand us a comfortable victory, but not with such a large majority, incredible.

I sat back to watch the unfolding drama. Although I have to say, in truth all the fun of predicting the actual result has gone out of the window. As it turned out, Electoral Calculus was right about my seat at the very start of the campaign. There had proved to be little movement whatsoever between the first opinion polls at the start of the election and the real result. Flicking between the TV channels, remembering that Sky is invariably quicker than the BBC, we had been told to expect the first result in well under an hour. That turned out to be a false promise. The TV cameras kept going backwards and forwards to tell us how the counting was going but obviously in these Labour heartland seats the votes were very close, or much closer than they would normally be.

Eventually the first result came in, and it indicated that the exit poll was pretty well spot on. As the night unfolded, traditional Labour seat after traditional Labour seat fell to the Conservatives, with some truly spectacular swings. No longer could it be said that Conservative Party support had overwhelmingly shrunk to just the South and the South East. Conservatives had been elected everywhere, throughout the whole of the UK.

I had arranged with my team at the count for them to let me know when I should leave for the declaration; it wouldn't take me long as the count was only ten minutes from where I live. I didn't get a phone call, so I made contact with the person who had been driving me round that day to ask how things were going. His response was pretty inconclusive, which I thought was odd. I then turned to my iPad to look at the live stream from our local newspaper. There was the grinning Labour candidate, who arrived at 10.30pm, suggesting that it was the best result ever for the Labour Party in that constituency and he was quietly confident. If he really believed that he must have felt mightily embarrassed/disappointed when the scale of the Labour defeat nationally and locally dawned on him later that evening.

I then spoke on the phone to two further supporters at the count; both, unlike the first, were very confident of the result. I had been told that the count would be concluded by 2.30am, so it was a great surprise to me when my agent phoned at 12.30am to say things are moving very quickly, you need to get here David, they are just verifying the bundles, you have scored a handsome victory. I drove to the count with one of my grown-up daughters, my wife had long since grown tired of what she perceived as the ritual of it all. This particular daughter is probably the most political of my children and somewhat to the right of the Party.

When I entered the hall, the counting had indeed stopped and there were smiling Conservative faces everywhere. They were naturally delighted by our result locally, the count for the two Southend seats taking place under the same roof, and my Parliamentary colleague, whilst having a larger constituency, had achieved a similar swing to which I had. The returning officer called for the candidates to come and look at the spoilt ballot papers, I left it to my agent. The local Liberals, who at every count I have ever been to, walk around the hall with their silly clipboards, giving the impression that they are running the show, were pathetic. The Labour Party looked very crestfallen.

No declaration of result could ever compare to the joy I felt when I was first elected in 1983, that was unique and very special. My 1992 declaration was of course the thing that very briefly propelled me onto the national stage and was a truly satisfying result. This time, I didn't really feel anything other than glad the whole wretched thing was over, and I ended by wishing everyone a very happy Christmas and New Year, which in itself seemed bizarre. I returned home to find my wife had not fallen asleep in front of the TV but was enjoying the unfolding events of what turned out to be a Conservative landslide.

My immediate thoughts turned to the upcoming contest for Deputy Speaker and my heart sank when I learned of the many Labour friends who I know would have supported me losing their seats, not to mention the whole swathe of newly elected Conservative members most of whom I didn't know. By the time the last result was declared the next morning the Conservative Party was elected with an overall majority of 80. To be precise the biggest Conservative majority since when I was first elected in 1983 when we had a majority of 144.

I remember thinking 'thank God, Parliament can function again'. However, there would be many idle hands on the Conservative benches now, I just hope the Whips have the skills they will need to maintain some sort of party discipline. Incredibly, the Whip came through letting us know that the State Opening of Parliament would happen the following Thursday – surely that couldn't be right, how could things be organised so quickly, but they were. I had the luxury of having removed hardly anything from my Parliamentary office and my wonderful team and friends transferred everything back to Parliament as if nothing had really changed.

For me, who had been cocooned in Southend for six weeks, it was a strange feeling to walk back into the office for the first time. If you are the candidate and haven't already got the job, fighting an election is normally such fun. The same is not true if you are already the member, the stakes are high, not only for oneself but for those who work for you and of course constituents very much expect you to continue working for them regardless of the General Election campaign. I quickly settled in and resolved as I always do, to speak on the very first day of the Gracious Speech. I let my friends in the Speaker's Office know that that was what I would be doing; I needn't have worried, they already had me down to speak.

I have seen so many gatherings at Westminster after a General Election. They are invariably a mixture of joy and sadness. The general public have little appreciation, and why should they, of the human side of the fall-out from elections, but regardless of party allegiances you cannot help feeling for those defeated candidates who face the distressing task of clearing their Parliamentary office and coping with their new non-status. I have often thought that more support should be given to defeated MPs, the whole process seems to be rather brutal and somewhat humiliating. I noticed on my own floor one young Scottish colleague, who had lost his seat, surrounded by well-wishers, but both mentally and physically not in the best of shape. I decided not to intrude, but just as with a bereavement, support at a later date would probably be more welcome.

Walking around the Estate I could hardly tell who was an MP and who wasn't, so I was reluctant to approach anyone to support me in my bid to become a Deputy Speaker until I knew exactly who was or wasn't in the electorate I needed to target. I then, however, did approach people who had been successfully returned and with one or two exceptions received a positive response. I had decided long ago really to make a proper attempt at this election, and even at my count I announced I would be a candidate for Deputy Speaker, besides having already announced it in the Chamber of the House of Commons. No one could be in any doubt that I was serious this time. Bitterly regretting that I bottled it when the 2017 Parliament was assembled, something I will always regret.

The swearing in process was a picture to behold, taking place over several days, supposedly done on the basis of seniority. Whilst queuing up to swear my Oath of Allegiance, I approached a number of colleagues as to whether they might support me in the Deputy Speaker contest. It really is the most horrible process to put oneself though, asking your own colleagues to support you in what is, in effect, an internal election. The huge contrast with that process and the one I had just been through is that when you are rejected on the doorstep, and rejection does hurt, you may never see that constituent again.

This is very much not the case with your own Parliamentary colleagues! Something which if you have a long memory and hold grudges as I do can make things a little awkward.

The State Opening of Parliament, the government had decided, should take place as quickly as possible and before Christmas, in order to ensure that the 31 January deadline for Brexit would be met. The poor Queen had, only a few weeks earlier, attended one State Opening of Parliament and now she was faced with another. Quite rightly it was decided that this one would be greatly scaled down, limousines used rather than carriages and no Household Cavalry.

There would be one further great difference to this particular State Opening of Parliament. No Dennis Skinner would be present. He had incredibly, lost his seat to the Conservatives. If he had been successful, he would have been Father of the House and over the years it had become a ritual when Black Rod entered the Commons Chamber and summoned us all to attend on Her Majesty, he would wisecrack that he wouldn't be going. There had been much speculation as what he would do as Father of the House, as with technically no Speaker, it falls on the Father of the House to start proceeding off and lead the Commons to process to the House of Lords in order to listen to the Gracious Speech. Whether he would have boycotted the ceremony we shall never know – it truly was the end of an era.

The newly elected Prime Minister addressed the House but not really in the triumphal way that some might have expected. When the Labour Leader got to his feet to reply there were none of the traditional 'hear, hears' instead he was greeted in silence.

Having made my speech quite early on that day, Parliament rose on Friday for the Christmas recess. As a returning MP there was much to be done in terms of fulfilling my usual Christmas duties, not to mention getting the Christmas cards out. My thoughts, somewhat belatedly, turned to Christmas with my family and mentally a period of quiet before the Deputy Speaker contest was held in the New Year.

It was a great joy, however, for me personally to still be a Member of the House of Commons when legislation was passed to ensure that we did leave the European Union on 31 January. I arranged celebrations for that day, starting in Parliament Square and then on to a wonderful party at my HQ, Iveagh Hall. A recording of Big Ben sounded 11.00pm, the precise moment at which we left. Southend's Town Crier read out the proclamation confirming our newly won free status and we raised the Union Flag. I am quite sure that together with the overwhelming majority of people in the UK, they also raised a glass to the end of a period in our history where, frankly, it felt as if we were being bullied by so many of those we had helped to liberate in the Second World War. All that remains for me now is to decide what to do with the next five years. I know, perhaps I will write a book.

Post-postscript

Bloody hell. Just recovered from the gruelling general election campaign, Brexit/leaving the European Union, flooding and now we have coronavirus/Covid-19 – the biggest and most frightening challenge of all. As I write and finish this book, what is happening now is surreal. We are all caught up in some sort of dreadful science fiction movie and I vividly recall one of my set books at school, *Day of the Triffids*. People speculate about how the world will end; I just hope this isn't it. Extraordinary scenes throughout the world and in our own country, the like of which I thought I would never see and scariest of all we really don't know how it is going to end. Every one of us is wondering if we might fall victim of the virus and worse still lose our lives. It is difficult to find reassurance whilst dealing with something that none of us have had to face before. Worries about the spread of Covid-19 being accelerated by the number of people working on the Parliamentary Estate. Some MPs and staff have now caught the virus.

* * *

Houses of Parliament closed to visitors from 17 March – that is really going to disappoint some people!

* * *

The PM announced lockdown measures on 23 March. Emergency legislation rushed through Parliament

* * *

Parliament has been dissolved on 25 March. It is really difficult to assess how well not only our Government, but the rest of the world are responding to this crisis.

* * *

Clap for Carers starts – it's my birthday, 26 March.

Leader of the House announces that Parliament will not reopen until 21 April. Goodness, can't believe this is happening. What an introduction for newly elected MPs. All our normal procedures abandoned. My office in Westminster closes, staff told to work from home except for one member living in Southend, who joins me in our Association office, Iveagh Hall, which becomes our centre of operation until further notice. The pattern of life has changed for everyone, it is amazing how quickly everything becomes like a ghost town; you can hear the birds singing again, the air seems to be clearer and there is hardly any noise from aircraft. There are now only occasional cars passing by and no more traffic jams – you make a journey and if you time it well, you don't have to stop but always catch the green lights.

The Government's daily press conferences are becoming slightly tedious and unenlightening. Each day three participants stand at the lecterns, make statements and try to respond to journalists' queries, in both regards the participants meet with mixed success. I suppose it brings it home to me how short we are these days of gifted natural communicators; politicians have certainly lost the skills. I don't know why the Government haven't prevailed upon Sir David Attenborough and Dame Judi Dench to do the main messaging. The Queen yet again has come up trumps (not in the nightmarish American sense of course), she somehow manages to get the tone right and even the most pro-Republicans do listen.

* * *

Oh dear, you couldn't make this up, now Boris Johnson has become ill, admitted to hospital on 5 April. Mind you I didn't think he looked too great the last time he was standing outside Number 10 clapping for carers. One or two of my colleagues think he is going to die; I am not so sure; I think the health professionals are sensibly being over cautious.

* * *

Yes, I was right – he recovers! Discussions between the Speaker of the House of Commons and officials how to restart Parliament safely. During the recess House of Commons Digital Services worked to implement technology allowing sittings to take place virtually.

On 16 April the House of Commons Commission announced that Parliament would move to hybrid proceedings, with provision for up to 50 MPs in the House of Commons Chamber and with up to 120 contributing remotely via Zoom.

* * *

Parliament resumed on 21 April. Oh how I miss being in Parliament. I make the journey to see what the building looks like. Stickers everywhere saying, 'Practice Social Distancing', telling everyone to stay two metres apart. On Wednesday 22 April the House of Commons sat virtually for the first time in its 750-year history. Incredible scenes, endless pictures captured of MPs, via Zoom, asking questions of the PM. What dreadful wallpaper some have, not to mention the poor taste in books.

* * *

On 29 April I return to Commons to make my first physical speech following lockdown on the Fire Safety Bill. So peculiar to speak in a sparsely populated Chamber, with red crosses where not to sit and very few green ticks where you could sit. All atmosphere and spontaneity has evaporated. Better than nothing I suppose, but not a proper Parliament. Many teething problems in developing a hybrid Parliament but given lack of experience of developing things for such a situation, pretty amazing what has been achieved.

* * *

Pressure builds for a return to physical proceedings, which resumed again on 2 June. Whew, great to be back. My team gradually return and the operation up and running by the end of the month. I even manage to resume physical surgeries with social distancing at the beginning of July.

* * *

Slowly but surely life in Parliament returns, but not as it once was. To me this is a sterile Parliament. Wherever I walk around the Estate there is hardly anyone, they must all be hiding in their offices. Really strange to have all the doors to the Chamber left open and now we have queue barriers everywhere – Portcullis House, Westminster Hall, even in the Lobbies.

The first time the bells sound for a division there were chaotic scenes as confused Members join long queues to vote. Goodness me, we are now having card readers introduced to vote. Don't the non-traditionalists love it all. Thank goodness the Leader of the House announces the summer break, but only to last for August.

* * *

Parliament returns beginning of September. Party Conferences abandoned, all to be held virtually. That's a relief – a complete waste of time and money. Lockdown restrictions gradually eased. Number of infections and deaths reduce. Daily press conferences stop, can it be that life is returning to normality again?

* * *

Oh no, prophets of a second spike prove right. Further restrictions, although not a complete national lockdown, now announced. Constituents and their Members of Parliament not happy. Total lack of scrutiny, government not really being held to account for its decisions. Worries about Christmas grow. Where is this all leading?

* * *

Goodness, now we have a tier system being introduced. Different tiers in different parts of the country. The four parts of the UK making uncoordinated announcements. Is this a race to the top or the bottom I ask myself? Disputes growing among colleagues as to who has got the most or least restrictions. Then local Mayors falling out with the government big time, and now the Speaker of the House of Commons advises we all wear masks moving around the Parliamentary Estate, including the lobbies when voting. A bit of a relief, you don't always have to talk to colleagues now. Told to reduce staffing levels on the Estate, cry goes up from some, let's revert to a virtual Parliament again. Brexit negotiations go down to the wire, where is this all going to end I ask myself?

In earlier chapters I bemoaned the quality of many of our world leaders, I just hope now that they are not found wanting. I do not want this to be my last book.

Glossary

1922 Committee

The 1922 Committee, formally known as the Conservative Private Members' Committee, is the parliamentary group of the Conservative Party. The committee, consisting of all Conservative backbencher MPs, meets weekly while parliament is in session and provides a way for backbenchers to co-ordinate and discuss their views independently of frontbenchers. Its executive membership and officers are by consensus limited to backbench MPs, although since 2010 frontbench Conservative MPs have an open invitation to attend meetings. The committee can also play an important role in choosing the party leader.

Adjournment debate

Adjournment debates are held on the motion 'that the House (or sitting) do now adjourn'. The term refers to the short, half-hour debate that takes place at the end of each day's sitting in the House of Commons.

Administration Committee

The Administration (Admin) Committee is a Select Committee that considers the services provided for Members, their staff and visitors by the House of Commons Service and makes recommendations to the House of Commons Commission, the Speaker and Officials on how those services are delivered.

Chairman of Ways and Means

The Chairman of Ways and Means is the principal Deputy Speaker in the House of Commons. As well as deputising for the Speaker they have specific responsibilities such as chairing Committees of the whole House, coordinating the sittings in Westminster Hall and oversight of all matters connected with Private Bills.

Chief Whip

The Chief Whip is a political office whose task is to administer the whipping system that tries to ensure that members of the party attend and vote as the party leadership desires.

Clerk of the House

The Clerk of the House is the most senior official of the Commons and advises the House on its practice and procedure. The Clerk is politically impartial and sits at the Table of the House between the Government and Opposition frontbenches.

Committee Stage

Committee stage is where a Bill is considered line-by-line and is normally the next stage after a Bill's second reading. It is an opportunity for changes to be made to the wording or for new clauses to be added. In the House of Commons this task is normally done by a small number of Members of Parliament in a Public Bill Committee. Occasionally it is done in the Chamber by a Committee of the whole House of Commons, as is usual in the House of Lords.

Delegated Legislation

A Delegated Legislation Committee is set up to debate a statutory instrument (or a group of related statutory instruments). The Committee membership is usually 17 MPs, plus an impartial Chair. The Selection Committee appoints the members. Under rules agreed in September 2017, the Government will have a majority on Delegated Legislation Committees with an odd number of members in the 2017 Parliament. The Speaker appoints the Chair from the Panel of Chairs (a group of MPs nominated for this purpose). The Committee includes at least one minister and at least one spokesperson from the official Opposition. Sometimes a spokesperson from the third largest party is a member as well.

Division

Divisions are used for counting those in favour or against a motion when there is a vote in the House of Commons or the House of Lords. The House literally divides, with members choosing to file through one of two lobbies on either side of the Chamber where they are counted and their names recorded.

Erskine May

Thomas Erskine May's guide to parliamentary practice is properly entitled 'A treatise on the law, privileges, proceedings and usage of Parliament' but it is commonly referred to as Erskine May (or simply 'May'). It is generally held to be the most authoritative reference book on parliamentary procedure. First published in 1844, when Thomas Erskine May was Assistant Librarian, it is now in its 25th edition.

European Economic Community

The European Economic Community was an organisation that aimed to bring about economic integration among its member states. It was created by the Treaty of Rome of 1957. Upon the formation of the European Union in 1993, the European Economic Community was incorporated and renamed the European Community. In 2009, the European Community's institutions were absorbed into the European Union's wider framework and the community ceased to exist.

European Research Group

The European Research Group (ERG) is a research support group for those of the United Kingdom's Conservative

Members of Parliament who choose to subscribe. Founded by Sir Michael Spencer (MP for West Worcestershire 1974–2010) in July 1993 in response to growing concern about Britain's continued integration into the European Community through the Maastricht Treaty.

Europhile

A Europhile is a person who admires Europe or is in favour of participation in the European Union.

Eurosceptic

A Eurosceptic is a person who is critical of the European Union and European integration. It ranges from those who oppose some EU institutions and policies and seek reform, to those who oppose EU membership outright and see the EU as un-reformable.

Father of the House

In the Commons, the title Father of the House is given to the MP who has the longest record of continuous service.

Filibustering

Filibustering is deliberately wasting time during a debate by making overlong speeches or raising unnecessary procedural points. In this way a Bill or a motion may be 'talked out': stopped from making progress within the time allowed.

Good Friday Agreement

The Good Friday Agreement, also known as the Belfast Agreement, was reached in multi-party negotiations and signed on 10 April 1998. This agreement helped to bring an end to the violence of the Troubles in Northern Ireland that had been ongoing since the 1960s.

Hansard

Hansard (the Official Report) is the edited verbatim report of proceedings of both the House of Commons and the House of Lords. It is published daily when Parliament is sitting and records what is said in the main Chambers of both Houses, as well as proceedings in Westminster Hall, Public Bill Committees and other general committees.

International Monetary Fund

The International Monetary Fund is an organization consisting of 189 countries working to foster global monetary cooperation, secure financial stability, facilitate international trade, promote high employment and sustainable economic growth, and reduce poverty around the world. Formed in 1944, it came into formal existence in 1945 with 29 member countries. It now plays a central role in the management of balance of payments difficulties and international financial crises.

'I spy strangers'

Stranger was the term used for anyone who was not a member of either the House of Commons or the House of Lords. It was replaced by 'Members of the Public' in 2004. 'I spy strangers' was the traditional request for members of the public to leave the galleries of the House of Commons so that the Chamber could sit in private. Following a request from the Modernisation Committee in 1998, the procedure has been abolished and replaced by a simpler one based on the motion 'that the House sit in private.

Inter-Parliamentary Union

The Inter-Parliamentary Union is an international organization of national parliaments. Its primary purpose is to promote democratic governance, accountability, and cooperation among its members. Other initiatives include advancing gender parity among legislatures, empowering youth participation in politics, and sustainable development. The organization was established in 1889 as the Inter-Parliamentary Congress.

Maiden speech

A maiden speech is the first speech made in the Chamber by a new member of the House of Commons or the House of Lords.

Manifesto

A manifesto is a publication issued by a political party before a General Election. It contains the set of policies that the party stands for and would wish to implement if elected to govern.

Motion

A motion is a proposal put forward for debate or decision in the House of Commons or House of Lords. A motion must be proposed (moved) before any debate or vote can take place in Parliament.

Oath of Allegiance

Members of both the House of Commons and the House of Lords are required to take an oath of allegiance to the Crown before they take their seats in Parliament after a general election or by-election and after the death of the monarch. Any MP or Member of the House of Lords who objects to swearing an oath can make a solemn affirmation, which omits the religious references, instead. This process is known as swearing in.

One-line/single-line whip

A single-line whip is a guide to what the party's policy would indicate, and notification of when the vote is expected to take place; this is non-binding for attendance or voting.

Pairing

Pairing is an arrangement between two MPs of opposing parties to not vote in a particular division. This enables an MP to be absent without affecting the result of the vote as they effectively cancel each other out. Pairing is an informal arrangement which is not recognised by the House of Commons but must be registered with the Whips. Pairing is not allowed in divisions of great political importance.

Parliamentary Private Secretary

A Parliamentary Private Secretary (PPS) is a Member of Parliament designated by a senior minister in government or shadow minister to act as that minister's contact with MPs. This role is junior to that of Parliamentary Under-Secretary of State, which is a ministerial post, salaried by one or more departments.

Party Chairman

The Chairman of the Conservative Party in the United Kingdom is responsible for party administration and overseeing the Conservative Campaign Headquarters, formerly Conservative Central Office. The role was created in 1911 in response to the Conservative party's defeat in the second 1910 general election. The position is not subject to election, as it is given by the party leader.

Party Political Broadcast

A party political broadcast (also known, in pre-election campaigning periods, as a party election broadcast) is a television or radio broadcast made by a political party. Parties are allocated broadcast slots (usually around five minutes long) free of charge on broadcast channels using a formula set by Parliament.

Points of order

A point of order is an appeal to the Chair or Speaker for clarification or for a ruling on a matter of procedure in the House of

Commons. The MP must explain their reasons for believing the rules of the House have been broken and the Speaker decides whether it is a valid point of order or not.

Prime Minister's Questions

The Prime Minister answers questions from Members of Parliament in the House of Commons every sitting Wednesday from 12.00pm until the end of Question Time at 12.30pm.

Private Members/ Backbench Bills

Private Members' Bills – or Backbench Bills – are introduced by individual MPs or members of the Lords rather than by the Government. As with other Public Bills their purpose is to change the law as it applies to the general population. Very few Private Members' Bills become law but, by creating publicity around an issue, they may affect legislation indirectly.

Private Secretaries

A Private Secretary (PS) is a civil servant in a governmental department or ministry, responsible to a secretary of state or minister. A Private Secretary is normally of middle management level; however, as the key official responsible for disseminating the decisions and policy steers of ministers and as their gatekeeper, the role is of considerably greater significance than their grade would suggest. Depending on the status of the political principal the official works for they will be aided by an Assistant Private Secretary (APS), or even head a private office.

Referendum

A referendum is when a question is decided by putting it to a public vote. Referendums are an example of direct democracy. In the UK, most decisions are made by Parliament on behalf of the public which is known as indirect or representative democracy. For example, the 2016 United Kingdom European Union membership referendum or the 2014 Scottish independence referendum.

Restoration and Renewal

The Palace of Westminster Restoration and Renewal Programme has been established to tackle the work that needs to be done to preserve the Palace's heritage and ensure it can continue to serve as the home of the UK Parliament in the 21st century and beyond. The House of Commons and House of Lords will temporarily move out of the building to allow the works to take place.

Returning Officer

A Returning Officer is responsible for overseeing elections in one or more constituencies. The role of the Returning Officer must be impartial and their role is to ensure that the conduct of an election is in accordance with the law.

Select Committees

Select committees are small groups of MPs or members of the House of Lords that are set up to investigate a specific issue in detail or to perform a specific scrutiny role. They may call in officials and experts for questioning and can demand information from the government. Select committees publish their findings in a report and the government is expected to respond to any recommendations that are made.

Speaker's House

Speaker's House, the official residence of the Speaker, is at the northeast corner of the Palace of Westminster and is used for official functions and meetings, with private accommodation in a four-bedroom apartment upstairs.

Speaker of the House

The Speaker is an MP who has been elected by other MPs to act as Chair during debates in the House of Commons. They are responsible for ensuring that the rules are observed and order is maintained in the Chamber. When a Speaker is elected they cease to be involved in party politics and become politically impartial.

Stump

A political stump speech is a standard speech used by a politician running for office. Typically a candidate who schedules many appearances prepares a short standardised stump speech that is repeated verbatim to each audience, before opening to questions.

Tearoom

The Tearoom is where Members of Parliament go for tea and catch up with colleagues and Parliamentary affairs.

Ten Minute Rule

Ten Minute Rule Bills are a type of Private Members' Bill that are introduced in the House of Commons under Standing Order No. 23. The ten minute rule allows a backbench MP to make his or her case for a new Bill in a speech lasting up to ten minutes. An opposing speech may also be made before the House decides whether or not the Bill should be introduced. If the MP is successful the Bill is taken to have its first reading.

The Mace

The Mace in Parliament is the symbol of royal authority and without it neither House can meet or pass laws. The House of Commons Mace is a silver gilt ornamental club of about five feet in length, dating from the reign of Charles II. On each day that the House is sitting the Mace is carried to the Chamber at the head of the Speaker's procession by the Serjeant at Arms. It is placed on the table of the House, except when the House is in committee, when it rests on two brackets underneath the table. The Lords uses two Maces, one dating from the time of Charles II and another from the reign of William III. One of the Maces accompanies the Lord Speaker into the Chamber and is placed on the Woolsack whenever the House meets. The Mace is absent from the Lords during the State Opening when the Monarch is in the Chamber in person.

Three-line whip

A three-line whip is a strict instruction to attend and vote according to the party's position, breach of which would normally have serious consequences. Permission to not attend may be given by the whip, but a serious reason is needed. Breach of a three-line whip can lead to expulsion from the parliamentary political group in extreme circumstances, and even to expulsion from the party.

Two-line whip

A two-line whip, sometimes known as a double-line whip, is an instruction to attend and vote; partially binding for voting according to the party's position, attendance required unless prior permission given by the whip.

Urgent Question

If an urgent or important matter arises which an MP believes requires an immediate answer from a government minister, they may apply to ask an urgent question. Applications for urgent questions must be submitted to the Speaker to receive an oral answer on the same day. If the Speaker is satisfied that the question is urgent and of public importance it is then granted. The relevant Government Minister has to come to the Chamber to explain what the Government is doing on the issue raised. The Minister will then usually take questions on the subject from MPs.

Virtual Parliament

Virtual Parliament is the name given to the Hybrid proceedings that were put in place as a result of the Coronavirus pandemic. On 21 April 2020 the House of Commons returned from its Easter recess to the introduction of remote technology in key items of business, allowing MPs the chance to participate virtually via Zoom.

Vote of no confidence

Confidence motions are a means of testing the support of the government and for the legislature to remove the government from office. A confidence motion may take the form of either a vote of confidence, usually put forward by the government, or a vote of no confidence, usually proposed by the opposition. When such a motion is put to a vote in the legislature, if a vote of confidence is defeated, or a vote of no confidence is passed, then the incumbent government must resign, or call a general election.

Westminster Hall

Westminster Hall, built in 1097, is the oldest building on the Parliamentary estate and it has played a central role in British history. Today the Hall is used for state occasions and welcomes nearly a million visitors to the Houses of Parliament every year.

Index

9/11 133
   See also Al-Qaeda *and* Bin
     Laden, Osama *and* United
     States of America
38 Degrees 50
1922 Committee 15, 178, 195,
     222, 245

Abbott, Diane 116
Adams, Gerry 153
Afghanistan 138
Al-Marashi, Ibrahim 139
Al-Qaeda 133, 140
   See also Bin Laden, Osama
     and Islam *and* Pakistan
Altman, Lionel 6, 119
Amess, James Henry Valentine 9
Amess, Maud Ethel 9
Arbuthnot, James 60
Archer, Jeffrey 93
Aspinwall, Jack 87
Attenborough, David 241
Attewell, Ted 17

Baldwin, Stanley 84
   See also Prime Minister
Balmoral 155
Bank of England 170
Barry, Charles 28
   See also Westminster
Basildon 1–2, 7, 19, 29, 39, 55,
     58, 60, 62, 67, 69, 71, 81,
     86, 90–91, 93–95, 97–98,
     100–101, 103–108, 119,
     128, 129, 135, 165, 187–
     188, 210, 228, 232
Basildon Council 58
   See also Basildon
BBC 33, 39, 61, 69, 90, 100,
     171
BBC Radio 39
   See also BBC
Beckenham 100
Belfast 153, 248, 257
Bell, Martin 100
Bell, Ronald 161
Benn, Tony 16, 27, 52, 162
Bercow, John 39, 43–44
   See also Speaker of the House
     of Commons
Berry, Anthony 131
Betts, Leah 67
   See also Cake *and* Brass Eye
Biffen, John 153, 248
Billericay 71, 100, 103
Bills 25, 30, 32, 59, 76, 80
   Firearms Bill 70
   Rate Capping Bill 29, 58
   Warm Homes and Energy
     Conservation Bill 77
Bin Laden, Osama 133
Blackford, Ian 38, 159
Blackpool 131
Black Wednesday 164–165

Blair, Tony 30, 32, 37, 38, 42,
    80, 84, 100, 102, 104, 111,
    118, 119, 120–121, 129,
    137–140, 145, 152–153,
    175, 183, 188
    See also Prime Minister
Bloomberg speech 166
    See also Brexit
Boothroyd, Betty 39, 40, 41
    See also Speaker of the House
    of Commons
Bottomley, Peter 55
Boyson, Rhodes 87
Brady, Graham 178
Braine, Bernard 31, 91
Brass Eye 67
    See also Scandals and Cake
Brent North 87
Brexit 61, 85, 111, 153, 157,
    160, 163–164, 167, 171,
    174, 179–180, 183–184,
    189–191, 193, 196–214,
    219, 223, 224, 228–232,
    238, 240, 244
    See also Referendums
Bright, Graham 118
Brighton 131–132, 152, 258,
    261–262
    See also Brighton Bombing,
    1985 *and* IRA
Brighton Bombing, 1985 131–
    132, 152
Brittan, Leon 31, 55
Brooke, Peter 41
Broughton, Alfred 18
Brown, Gordon 102–103,
    111–112, 118–121, 156
    See also Prime Minister

Brown, Ron 39
Bullingdon Club 167
Bush, George Jr 138
    See also United States of
    America
Bush, George Snr 145, 147
    See also United States of
    America

Cabinet Room 124
Cable, Vince 122, 159
Cadbury, Jocelyn 70
Cake 67–68, 219
    See also Scandals and Brass
    Eye
California State University 139
    See also United States of
    America
Cambridge 52, 146
Cameron, David 8, 56, 63,
    109–112, 120–121, 123,
    125, 147, 155, 165–168,
    171, 173–175, 178, 180,
    184, 188
    See also Prime Minister
Campaign Against Cruel
    Sports 95
Canary Wharf 21
Carmichael, Alistair 156
Carswell, Douglas 42
Cash for questions 65, 99
Castle Point 91
Catholic University of
    America 146
    See also United States of
    America
Channel Tunnel 21
Channon, Paul 40–41, 104, 107

Charleston 140, 211
    See also United States of
        America
Chelmsford 106
Chevalier, Maurice 12
Chicken run 102
    See also Elections, General,
        1997
Chilcot Inquiry 140
    See also Iraq
Chilton, Brendan 169
Christian Solidarity 140
Churchill, Winston 84, 130
    See also Prime Minister
Circus Tavern 169
Clap for Carers 240
    See also Coronavirus and
        Covid-19
Clapham Common 72
    See also Sex Scandal
Clark, Alan 128
Clarke, Norman & Hilda 108
Clegg, Nick 14, 121, 124, 159
Clinton, Bill 138, 145
    See also United States of
        America
Clinton, Hillary 148
    See also United States of
        America
Coalition Government,
    2010 123
    See also Elections, General,
        2010
Colchester 106
Colditz Castle 131
Conference Hall 132
Conservative Party
    conference 131

Cook, Robin 139
Cooper, Henry 92
Corbyn, Jeremy 25, 103, 110,
    170, 184, 204
Cormack, Patrick 146
    See also Catholic University
        of America
Coronavirus 44, 240
    See also Covid-19
Court, Anthony 31
Covid-19 240, 259
    See also Coronavirus
Cowan, Harry 30
Cox, Jo 136, 171
Crabb, Stephen 176
Culture, Media and Sport Select
    Committee 14, 25, 84
Currie, Edwina 1, 57
    See also Major, John
Cutler, Horac 16

Dalyell, Tam 130, 160
Darling, Alistair 156
Davidson, Emily Wilding 52
Davidson, Ruth 156, 172, 176
Davies, Philip 76
Davies, Ron 72
Davis, David 175
Dean, Paul 39
Dench, Judi 241
Dickens, Geoffrey 62
Dimbleby, David 90,
    116, 173
Dines, Elizabeth 7
Dining Club 168
Douglas-Home, Alec 13
    See also Prime Minister
Downey, Gordon 99

Downing Street, Number
 10 123, 138, 221, 231
Downing Street, Number
 11 165
Doyle-Price, Jackie 113
du Cann, Edward 15
Duncan Smith, Iain 138, 167
Dunwoody, Gwyneth 40

Ecclestone, Bernie 38
Ed Stone 110
Elections 7, 8, 10–11, 16, 35,
 48, 89–90, 99, 106, 114,
 116, 118, 145, 171, 205,
 207–212, 228, 230, 232–
 233, 237, 253
 General 130, 158, 165, 180,
 199, 204, 207, 224, 226–
 227, 231, 233, 236–237,
 250, 259–260, 266
 1970 13
 1975 39, 161
 1979 1, 17–19, 86, 89–90
 1983 1, 7–8, 11, 19, 39, 54,
 57, 86, 90–92, 95, 118, 128,
 130, 162, 190, 235, 236
 1987 19, 41, 86, 91
 1992 40, 62, 86, 90–91, 93,
 96, 99, 102–103, 107, 118,
 123, 164, 165, 234, 235
 1997 1–2, 35, 42, 62, 86, 99,
 102, 113, 115, 154
 2001 36
 2010 27, 121–122, 155–156,
 179, 188, 232, 245, 248
 2015 27, 109, 111, 116, 125,
 136, 154, 158, 165, 166,
 178, 232

 2016 61, 67, 110, 136,
 160–161, 165, 253
 2017 8, 27, 44, 64, 67, 95,
 109, 111, 115, 159, 232,
 237, 246
 2019 27, 128, 164, 190–191,
 268
Greater London Council,
 1977 12
Elstree Studios 17
Enfield Southgate Conservative
 Association 62
English Votes for English
 Laws 160
Essex County Council 101
Eton 167
European Research Group 247
Exchange Rate Mechanism 103,
 164, 165

Fairbairn, Nicholas 57
Falklands War 129
Farage, Nigel 110, 169, 232
Ferrari, Nick 116
First Past the Post voting 125
Florida 145
 See also United States of
 America
Fodderwick Council 69
Foot, Michael 23, 27, 32, 53,
 162
Ford, Anna 90, 99
Forest Gate Ward Conservative
 Association Committee 12
Forth, Eric 76
Fox Hunting 95
Fox, Liam 176, 204
Frampton, Mary 36

Francois, Mark 37, 94, 136, 171, 192, 200
Fresh Start 176
Friends of the Earth 75

Garel Jones, Tristan 80
GEC Avionics 128
Good Friday Agreement 38, 153, 248
Gorbachev, Mikhail 24, 144
    See also Soviet Union
Gorman, Teresa 60, 72, 100, 163
Gould, Bryan 96
Gove, Michael 167, 176, 177, 193, 218
Gow, Ian 23
Graham, Billy 169
Grand Hotel 131
    See also ira and Brighton Bombing
Grantham 19
Grayling, Chris 167, 176
Greater London Council 12
    See also Elections
Greenway, Harry 36
Grieve, Dominic 163
Guardian, The 94
Guinness Family 104
Guy Fawkes 84

Hague, William 164
Hamilton, Neil 66, 100
Hammond, Philip 174
Hardie, Keir 19
Hargreaves, Ken 31, 193
Hawaii 164, 165
    See also United States of America

Hayman, Peter 62
Healey, Denis 16, 54, 56
Health Select Committee 1, 142
Heath, Edward 13
    See also Prime Minister
Heathrow 164
Heddle, John 70
Henry VIII 84
Heseltine, Michael 55, 56, 72, 117
Hill, Jonathan 97
Hiroshima 164
    See also World War II and Japan
HM Prison Maze 152
Hogg, Douglas 70, 79
Hogg, Sarah 97
Hollywood 140, 144
    See also United States of America
Holyrood 155, 158
Hoover, Herbert 146
    See also United States of America
Hospice St Luke's 135
Howards Road Hospital, Plaistow 9
Howe, Geoffrey 18, 56, 84, 128
Hoyle, Lindsay 39, 44
    See also Speaker of the House of Commons
Huhne, Chris 72, 121
Hurd, Douglas 92
Hussein, Saddam 121, 138, 139, 145

Independent, The 77, 196
Independent Group 164, 196

International Monetary
    Fund 249
IRA 130–132, 134–135,
    151–152
    See also Brighton Bombing
Iraq 120, 123, 133, 137–139,
    140, 146, 184
Iraq War 184
ISIS 130, 134, 140
Islam 134
Iveagh Hall 233, 239, 241
    See also Southend West
Iveagh, Lady 104

Japan 164–165
Javid, Sajid 167, 176
Jenkin, Bernard 169
Jenkin, Patrick 29
Jenkins, Roy 27
Jinping, Xi 149
Jo Cox Foundation 136
    See also Cox, Jo
Johnson, Boris 164, 167,
    176–177, 218, 223–224,
    231, 241
    See also Prime Minister
Jones, Nigel 136
Joseph, Keith 15

Kennedy, Charles 121
Kings Cross Fire 41
Kinnock, Neil 23, 96, 100, 118
Kosovo 138

Laing, Eleanor 101
Lamont, Norman 164
Lansman, Jon 103
Lawrence, Ivan 30

Lawson, Nigel 39
Leadsom, Andrea 176
Lee, Andrew 108
Lee, Gill 6
Lenin 141
    See also Soviet Union
Lennon, Paul 6, 31
Lewis, Arthur 12
Libya 140
London City Airport 21
London Electricity Board 9
Lord, Michael 43

MacGregor, Ian 20
Maclean, David (Lord
    Blencartha) 76
Macmillan, Harold 13, 89, 127,
    161, 223
    See also Prime Minister
Major, John 56–59, 61, 90–91,
    93, 96–99, 102, 117, 119,
    152, 163
    See also Prime Minister
Manchester attacks 172
Manifesto 54, 113, 115, 124,
    226, 227, 250
Marks, Dave 97
Marlow, Tony 163
Martin, John 39
May, Theresa 8, 25, 110, 112,
    149, 167, 174, 176, 179,
    201, 204, 206, 211
    See also Prime Minister
Mayor of London 149, 168, 228
McDonnell, John 103, 111
McMaster, Gordon 70
Merchant, Piers 100
Merkel, Angela 25

Middle East 138, 140
Miliband, Ed 184
Millbank Tower 119
Milligan, Stephen 71
Mills, Iain 70
Miners' Strike 155
Miss Bluebell 89
Mitchell, Andrew 72
Momentum 15, 86, 94, 118, 213, 216
Moore, John 22, 117
Morgan, Nicky 163
Morris, Chris 67
Mother Theresa 45, 263
Mottram, Buster 71, 95
Moulsham, Douglas 109
Mowlam, Mo 153
Mundell, David 156
Murdoch, Rupert 38
Murphy, Jim 156
Music Man Project 2, 210, 268

Napoleon 149
National Coal Board 20
Nazi Germany 161
Neave, Airey 15, 131
Newham 1, 16, 18–19, 86, 89, 151
Newham North West 1, 16, 19, 86
Norris, Steve 41
North Korea 24
Northern Ireland Committee 38
Northern Irish Assembly 153
Nuttall, Paul 116

Office for National Statistics 67
O'Flynn, Patrick 169

Olympics 175
Obama, Barack 147, 170
    See also United States of America
Oppenheim-Barnes, Sally 18
Osborne, George 29, 63, 173
Owen, David 27
Oxford 167

Paisley, Ian 27, 153
Pakistan 133
Palmer, PC Keith 135
    See also Westminster Bridge
Pan Am Flight 41
    See also Libya
Panorama 69
Parkinson, Cecil 22
Parris, Matthew 58
Party Political Broadcast 251
Patel, Priti 167, 220
Patten, Chris 91
Patten, John 81
Playle, Vera 101
Portillo, Michael 1, 21, 27, 39, 55, 164–165
Powell, Enoch 27, 36, 52, 71
Prescott, John 41
Prime Minister 8, 13, 19, 23, 25, 32, 56, 61, 77, 91, 94, 96, 98, 102, 109, 117, 121, 127–128, 137, 146–147, 149, 152–153, 159, 163, 165, 166–167, 174, 178, 191, 196–197, 199, 202, 220, 223, 238, 252
Prime Minister's Question Time 159
Prittlewell 91

Proctor, Harvey 71
Pugin, Augustus 28
  See also Westminster
Purfleet 169
Pursglove, Tom 168
Putin, Vladimir 25
Pym, Francis 129

Queen Elizabeth ii 185

Reagan, Ronald 24–25, 129,
  134, 144, 146
  See also United States of
  America
Rectory Road 93
Redwood, John 61, 210
Referendums 252
  European Union 21, 44,
  81, 99, 160, 164, 166,
  167–170, 173–174, 176,
  178–179, 184, 188, 190–
  192, 194, 223, 239, 240,
  247–248, 253
  1975 39, 161
  2016 61, 67, 110, 136,
  160–161, 165, 253
  Scottish Independence,
  2014 253
Right-to-Buy 81, 185
Rivers of Blood Speech 52
  See also Powell, Enoch and
  Scandals
Robertson, Angus 159
Rudd, Amber 114, 172
Rumbold, Angela 59
Ryder, Richard 59

Saatchi, Maurice 18

Salmond, Alex 156, 159
Sands, Bobby 152
  See also IRA
Scandals 27, 63–64, 73, 99
Scargill, Arthur 20
  See also Miners' Strike
Scottish independence 156–157,
  160, 253
  See also Referendums
Sex scandal 71, 73
  See also Scandals
Short, Joan 18
Sierra Leone 138
Skinner, Dennis 31, 70, 158, 238
Smith, Cyril 62
Smith, John 118–119
Soubry, Anna 163–164
Southend 1, 8, 86, 91, 99–101,
  103–108, 112, 115, 124,
  159, 168–169, 179, 190,
  194, 198, 203, 206, 208,
  210, 212, 214, 219, 223,
  228, 235–236, 239, 241, 268
Southend Rail Commuters
  Group 106
Southend West 1, 8, 86, 91,
  99–101, 103–108, 115,
  124, 159, 169, 228
Soviet Union 140, 144
Speaker of the House of
  Commons 242, 244
Special Relationship 25, 140,
  147, 149
St Anthony's Catholic Primary
  School 10
St Bonaventure 10
St John-Stevas, Norman 37
Stewart, Allan 100

Strathkelvin and Bearsden 100
Studley Road, Forest Gate 9
Sturgeon, Nicola 159
Sun, The 95, 99
Syria 140

Taylor, Teddy 109, 163
Tebbit, Norman 92, 131
Thatcher, Dennis 131
Margaret Thatcher 8–9, 12, 15,
    27, 32, 41, 54, 93, 102,
    119–120, 129, 134, 144,
    146, 159, 164, 183, 185,
    217, 222
    See also Prime Minister
Thomas, George 39
    See also Speaker of the House
    of Commons
Thorpe Bay 106
Thorpe, Jeremy 14
Thurrock 17, 100, 101, 113, 232
Thurrock Unitary Council 101
Times, The 92
Trump, Donald 25, 147, 149
    See also United States
    of America
Tuition Fees 110, 124
Twin Towers 133, 134
    See also 9/11 *and* United
    States of America

Union Jack Club 168
United States of America 129,
    140, 143, 257–261, 263,
    265
USSR 141

Vange 78, 104

Vange Working Men's Club 104
Viggers, Peter 164
Villiers, Teresa 167, 199

Wakeham, John 131–132
Wakeham, Roberta 132
Wansdyke 87
War of Independence 143
    See also United States of
    America
War on Terror 140
Washington 141
Weapons of mass
    destruction 139
Weatherill, Bernard 39, 53
    See also Speaker of the House
    of Commons
Welsh Assembly 66
Wembley 172
West Ham Clinic 10
West Lothian Question 160
    See also Scottish
    Independence
Westland 55
    See also Scandals
Westminster 3, 5, 7–8, 13, 27–
    28, 36, 39, 44, 52–53, 62,
    73, 82, 84–85, 87, 93, 97,
    112, 122–123, 126, 130,
    134–135, 146–148, 151,
    153–154, 158, 166, 172,
    175–176, 181, 183, 188,
    191–192, 194–196, 198–
    199, 201, 203, 205, 207,
    209, 210–213, 216, 218,
    220–221, 223, 225, 231,
    237, 241, 243, 246, 249,
    253, 256

1 Parliament Street 37, 67
Abbey Gardens 36
Annie's Bar 36
Committee Room 74, 122,
  139, 178, 189, 199, 202,
  206, 215, 217
Palace of Westminster 7, 82,
  84–85, 126, 181, 188, 191,
  253
Palace Yard 130–131,
  134–135
Parliament Square 37, 134,
  239
Portcullis House 36, 47, 200,
  214, 243
Restoration and
  Renewal 253
St Stephen's Crypt 134
Virtual Parliament 244
Westminster Abbey 135
Westminster Bridge 135
Westminster Hall 53, 84–85,
  135, 147–148, 158, 216,
  243, 246, 249, 256

WhatsApp 51, 73, 227, 230
White House 147, 150
  See also United States of
  America
Whittingdale, John 24, 167
Widdecombe, Ann 31, 37, 72,
  79, 176, 193, 229, 230
Wilberforce, William 84
  See also Prime Minister
William Hill 96
Williams, Shirley 27
Wilson, Harold 13, 16, 63, 161
  See also Prime Minister
Windsor Castle 149
Winter of Discontent 16
  See also Elections, General,
  1979
Wood, Leanne 116
World War ii 14, 33, 130, 143

YouTube 67

Endometriosis UK

Endometriosis UK is the UK's leading endometriosis charity and provides vital support services, reliable information and a community for those affected by endometriosis. They work to improve the lives of people affected by endometriosis and to decrease the impact it has on those with the condition and their families and friends.

Endometriosis UK provides support and guidance for those suffering from the condition through their helpline, online community and local support groups, enabling those affected to understand their disease and take control of their condition.

With the help of their volunteers, Endometriosis UK aims to raise awareness of this condition that affects one in ten women and are involved in a number of research projects.

www.endometriosis-uk.org

The Music Man Project

The Music Man Project is an award-winning, world record-breaking music education and performance service for children and adults with learning disabilities. Originally founded in Southend by Churchill Fellow and disability campaigner David Stanley, the charity supports regional teaching hubs across the UK and around the world, including South Africa, India, Nepal, the USA and the Philippines. It also gives grants for accessible music education, promotes equal access to performance, carries out research and raises awareness of the achievements of disadvantaged people in the arts.

The Music Man Project has enabled musicians with learning disabilities to tour the UK, appear in a primetime TV advert, perform at the Royal College of Music, release an Amazon chart-topping charity single, teach thousands of mainstream school children and play the world's most famous venues. In the first of two 'Sunday Night at the London Palladium' variety concerts, they performed From the Asylum to the Palladium, an original musical which revealed their journey from isolated patients in mental hospitals to stars of the West End. In the second, the students broke the Guinness World Record for the largest ever triangle ensemble, reaching 1521 triangles with the help of a capacity audience and a member of the Royal Family. In 2019, 200 Music Man Project students from across the UK performed Music is Magic at the Royal Albert Hall to an audience of 3000 people, supported by massed choirs, symphony orchestra and celebrity guests. This ground-breaking concert was the largest ever celebration of accessible music-making in the UK and the fulfilment of a promise made by David Stanley to his first ever students two decades earlier.

Acclaimed by Prime Ministers, OFSTED, music conservatoires, politicians and celebrities, the Music Man Project explores how the universal language of music can free the constraints placed on people with a learning disability across the world, joining them together through David's original music, country by country.

www.themusicmanproject.com
www.themusicmanblog.com

Prost8 UK

Prostate Cancer affects 1 in 8 men in their lifetime with around 48,000 new cases and 11,700 deaths each year. A more worrying statistic is that up to 12,000 of those men will be diagnosed with early stage treatable prostate cancer but will still receive the same invasive treatments as men with advanced cancers - such as surgery or radiotherapy. This means that 1,000s of men who could still lead normal lives after treatment will experience unnecessary and life changing side effects despite there being newer, fully NICE approved, minimally invasive alternatives. These include focal ablation which uses highly focused ultrasound waves to destroy just the tumour, leaving surrounding tissue and organs unharmed. Prost8 UK is working to generate awareness and to raise the funds to buy, donate and deploy focal therapy suites into strategic hospitals across the UK to accelerate access to these new treatments – as well as lobbying the NHS to roll them out faster than currently planned.

www.prost8.org.uk

Luath Press Limited

committed to publishing well written books worth reading

LUATH PRESS takes its name from Robert Burns, whose little collie Luath (*Gael.*, swift or nimble) tripped up Jean Armour at a wedding and gave him the chance to speak to the woman who was to be his wife and the abiding love of his life. Burns called one of the 'Twa Dogs' Luath after Cuchullin's hunting dog in Ossian's *Fingal*. Luath Press was established in 1981 in the heart of Burns country, and is now based a few steps up the road from Burns' first lodgings on Edinburgh's Royal Mile. Luath offers you distinctive writing with a hint of unexpected pleasures.

Most bookshops in the UK, the US, Canada, Australia, New Zealand and parts of Europe, either carry our books in stock or can order them for you. To order direct from us, please send a £sterling cheque, postal order, international money order or your credit card details (number, address of cardholder and expiry date) to us at the address below. Please add post and packing as follows: UK – £1.00 per delivery address; overseas surface mail – £2.50 per delivery address; overseas airmail – £3.50 for the first book to each delivery address, plus £1.00 for each additional book by airmail to the same address. If your order is a gift, we will happily enclose your card or message at no extra charge.

Luath Press Limited
543/2 Castlehill
The Royal Mile
Edinburgh EH1 2ND
Scotland
Telephone: +44 (0)131 225 4326 (24 hours)
Email: sales@luath. co.uk
Website: www.luath.co.uk